The Inner Journey
Views from the Hindu Tradition

Series Editor: Ravi Ravindra
Associate Series Editor: Priscilla Murray

Titles in *The Inner Journey* series:
Views from the Buddhist Tradition
Views from the Christian Tradition
Views from the Gurdjieff Work
Views from the Hindu Tradition
Views from the Islamic Tradition
Views from the Jewish Tradition
Myth, Psyche & Spirit
Views from Native Traditions

The Inner Journey
Views from the Hindu Tradition

Edited by Margaret H. Case

PARABOLA Anthology Series

MORNING LIGHT
PRESS

Published by Morning Light Press 2007.

Editor: Margaret H. Case
Series Editor: Ravi Ravindra
Associate Series Editor: Priscilla Murray

Morning Light Press
323 North First, Suite 203
Sandpoint, ID 83864
morninglightpress.com
info@mlpress.com

Printed on acid-free paper in Canada.

Philosophy
SAN: 255-3252

Library of Congress Cataloging-in-Publication Data

The inner journey : views from the Hindu tradition / edited by Margaret H. Case.
    p. cm. -- (Parabola anthology series) (The inner journey series)
  Articles previously published in Parabola over the last 30 years.

  ISBN-13: 978-1-59675-013-5
  ISBN-10: 1-59675-013-8

1. Spiritual life--Hinduism. I. Case, Margaret H. II. Parabola (Mt. Kisco, N.Y.)
BL1237.36.I66 2006
294.5--dc22

                    2006032110

*To the path makers
and the pilgrims on the path*

General Introduction to
The Inner Journey: A Parabola Anthology Series

When *Parabola: Myth, Tradition, and the Search for Meaning* was launched in 1976, the founder, D. M. Dooling, wrote in her first editorial:

> *Parabola* has a conviction: that human existence is significant, that life essentially makes sense in spite of our confusions, that man is not here on earth by accident but for a purpose, and that whatever that purpose may be it demands from him the discovery of his own meaning, his own totality and identity. A human being is born to set out on this quest. … Every true teaching, every genuine tradition has sought to train its disciples to act this part, to become in fact followers of the great quest for one's self.

For over thirty years, *Parabola* has honored the great wisdom traditions of every culture, turning to their past and present masters and practitioners for guidance in this quest. Recognizing that the aim of each tradition is the transformation of human life through practice supported by knowledge and understanding, *Parabola* on behalf of its readers has turned again and again to Buddhist and Christian monks, Sufi and Jewish teachers, Hindu scholars, and Native American and other indigenous peoples, evoking from each of them illumination and insight.

Over the years *Parabola*, in each of its issues, devoted to a central theme of the human condition as it is and as it might be, has gathered remarkable material. "The Call," "Awakening," "Food," "Initiation," "Dreams and Seeing," "Liberation," "The Mask," "Attention": in these and in scores of other issues, a facet of the essential search is explored, always with the aim of casting light on the way.

The purpose of the *Parabola Anthology Series* is to gather the material published in *Parabola* during its first thirty years in order to focus this light and to reflect the inner dimensions of each of these traditions. While every religious tradition has both external and inner aspects, the aim of each is the transformation of the whole being. The insights and understandings that ring true and carry the vibration of an inner meaning can provide guidance and support for our quest, but a mere mechanical repetition of forms which were once charged with great energy can take us away from the heart of the teaching. Every tradition must change and evolve; it has to be reinterpreted and reunderstood by successive generations in order to maintain its relevance and application.

Search carries a connotation of journey; we set out with the hope for new insight and experience. The aim of the spiritual or inner journey is transformation, to become more responsible and more compassionate as understanding and being grow. This demands an active undertaking, and insights from those who have traveled the path can provide a call, bring inspiration, and serve as a reminder of the need to search.

For this series, selections have been made from the material published in *Parabola* relating to each of the major traditions and teachings. Subtle truths are expressed in myths, poetry, stories, parables, and above all in the lives, actions, and expressions of those people who have been immersed in the teaching, have wrestled with it and have been informed and transformed by it. Some of these insights have been elicited through interviews with current practitioners of various teachings. Each of the great traditions is very large, and within each tradition there are distinct schools of thought, as well as many practices, rituals, and ceremonies. None of the volumes in the present series claims to be exhaustive of the whole tradition or to give a complete account of it.

In addition to the material that has been selected from the library of *Parabola* issues, the editor of each volume in the series provides an introduction to the teaching, a reminder of the heart of the tradition in the section, "The Call of the Tradition," as well as a list of books suggested for further study and reflection. It is the hope of the publishers and editors that this new series will surprise, challenge, and support those new to *Parabola* as well as its many readers.

—*Ravi Ravindra*

Contents

The Call of the Tradition

To many it is not given to hear of the Atman.
Many though they hear of it do not understand it.
Wonderful is one who speaks of it. Intelligent is one who learns of it.
Blessed is one who, taught by a good teacher, is able to understand it.
The truth of the Atman cannot be fully understood
when taught by an ignorant person, for opinions
regarding it not founded in knowledge, vary one from another.
Subtler than the subtlest is this Atman, and beyond all logic.
Taught by a teacher who knows the Atman and Brahman as one,
a person leaves vain theory behind and attains the truth. ...
The Atman is not known through study of the scriptures,
nor through subtlety of the intellect nor through much learning;
but by one who longs for it. It is to be attained only by the one whom the
Atman chooses. To such a one the Atman reveals its own nature. ...
Like the sharp edge of a razor, the sages say, is the path.
Narrow it is, and difficult to tread.[1]

—Katha Upanishad

That is fullness, this is fullness. Fullness comes from fullness.
If fullness is taken from fullness, fullness remains.[2]

—Yajurveda

Once, when Balarāma and the other cowherd boys were playing, they
complained to mother Yaśodā: "Kṛṣṇa has eaten mud."
Yaśodā was concerned for his welfare, and scolded Kṛṣṇa, whose eyes seemed
to be full of fear. Grasping him in her hands, she said to him: "Why have you
secretly eaten mud, you unruly boy? These young friends of yours are saying
so, and so is your elder brother."

"Mother, I didn't eat any mud. They are all spreading false accusations.
If you think they are speaking the truth, then you look into my mouth yourself."

"If that is the case, then open wide," she said.
Lord Hari [Kṛṣṇa] whose supremacy cannot be constrained,
but who is God assuming the form of a human boy for play, opened wide.
Yaśodā saw there the universe of moving and non-moving things;
space; the cardinal directions; the sphere of the earth with its oceans,
islands and mountains; air and fire; and the moon and the stars.
She saw the circle of the constellations,
water, light, the wind, the sky, the evolved senses,
the mind, the elements, and the three guṇa qualities.
She saw this universe with all its variety differentiated
into bodies, which are the repositories of souls.
She saw the time factor, nature and karma.
Seeing Vraj as well as herself in the gaping mouth in the body
of her son, she was struck with bewilderment:

"Is this actually a dream? Is it a supernatural illusion, or is it just the
confusion of my own intelligence? Or is it, in fact, some inherent divine
power of this child of mine?

"Therefore, I offer homage to his feet, which are the support of this world.
From them, and through their agency, this world manifests.
Their true nature cannot be known by the senses, nor by reason.
They are very difficult to perceive by thought, words, deeds, or intellect.

"He is my refuge. Through his illusory power arise ignorant notions such as:
'I am me; he over there is my husband, and this is my son;
I am the virtuous wife, protectress of all the
wealth of the ruler of Vraj; and all the gopīs and gopas,
along with the wealth derived from the cattle are mine.'"

Then the omnipotent supreme Lord cast his yogamāyā
[divine power of illusion] in the form of maternal affection
over the gopī, who had come to understand the truth.
Immediately, the gopī's memory was erased.

She sat her son on her lap and returned to her previous
state of mind, with her heart full of intense love.
She considered Hari [Kṛṣṇa], whose glories are sung by the three Vedas,
the Upaniṣads, Sāṇkhya yoga and the Sātvata sages, to be her very own son.[3]

—Bhagavata Purana

Thus the knowledge which is more mysterious than mystery has been
explained to you by Me. Reflect upon this without leaving anything out.
Then do what you wish.[4]

—Bhagavad Gita

When the awakening takes place, scripture ceases to be authoritative.[5]

—Shankara

Water in the pail, pail in the water
Water outside, water inside.
Breaking the pail, water merges into water.
This truth is all that the wise say.[6]

—Kabir

I came out alone on my way to my tryst.
But who is this that follows me in the silent dark?
I move aside to avoid his presence but I escape him not.
He makes the dust rise from the earth with his swagger;
he adds his loud voice to every word that I utter.
He is my own little self, my lord, he knows no shame;
but I am ashamed to come to thy door in his company.[7]

—Rabindranath Tagore

I have escaped and the small self is dead;
I am immortal, alone, ineffable;
I have gone out from the universe I made,
And have grown nameless and immeasurable;
I am the one Being's sole immobile Bliss;
No one I am, I who am all that is.[8]

—Sri Aurobindo

The Inner Journey: Introduction

The subtitle of this volume, "Views from the Hindu Tradition," suggests that the articles and stories here look out from inside the tradition, seeing and shedding light on "the inner journey" of the reader. But in the Hindu tradition, viewing within a spiritual context, called *darshan*, is a two-way process. The seeker gazes at the deity, and the large eyes of the deity gaze back (unlike the eyes of a Buddha or bodhisattva, which are inner-directed). There is a subject and an object, and both parties play both roles. The premise of this volume is, in fact, that the articles and stories will shed light on the inner journey. But as in darshan, this is a two-way process—the seeker also needs to see and understand something of the Hindu tradition. Before we begin, therefore, it is appropriate that we, travelers on our own inner journeys, catch at least a glimpse into that tradition.

Hinduism, it has been said, is defined not by its beliefs but by its practices. The individual is amazingly free to hold whatever beliefs he or she chooses—which deity to worship (if any), which teacher to follow, and so on. The practices through which people express these beliefs include stories and songs, rituals and festivals, respect and support for holy men and women, patronage of temples—the practices that define the religious culture. People of many different beliefs share freely in each others' festivals, and show reverence to holy men and women who profess many varieties of belief. Hindus go on a pilgrimage or fast to fulfill a vow as a matter of course, though the exact form of pilgrimage or vow and the deity whose aid is sought is entirely up to the individual.

Complementing this freedom of belief, there is considerable constraint in approved behavior in daily life. As each individual aims to find meaning in life, although he or she may believe just about anything, the field of action—what is considered appropriate or virtuous living—is quite closely defined by such basic aspects of identity as gender, age, and one's family's place in the world. The hand of cards one is dealt in life is accepted as providing the conditions of the journey.

In Hinduism, it is accepted as part of the world that people manipulate one another, try to get ahead, try to survive by whatever means. Stories of wily counselors to kings and cunning merchants are part of the mental equipment of all Indian children. But it is also accepted that other levels of reality exist and are important to one's spiritual well-being. Hindu tradition accepts that unseen powers pervade the affairs of this world. These unseen powers are elaborated on in the stories told everywhere: they are part of the lives of children, the basis of all forms of art, and they underlie the daily habits of worship for most of the population. The diversity of the ways these powers are visualized is beyond grasp. The thousands of gods and demons, many of them in the shape of animals, or with multiple arms or heads, vividly embody the unseen and unforeseeable, the parts of experience not subject to ordinary, reasonable, control.

Consciousness of these other levels can be cultivated—again through stories, but also by practice. This consciousness is an awareness—fed by narrative tradition—that things and people may be both ordinary and divine. "Divinity is a continuum," writes Wendy Doniger in "A Wake-up Call" in this volume. "Some creatures are more divine than others, and some gods are more divine in certain texts than in others." Things and people are not either one or the other—they are both. Some strands of Hinduism hold that divinity can most readily be glimpsed when one is performing dedicated service to family or others to whom service is due. However achieved, awareness of one's relationship with the unseen powers may be glimpsed, but doesn't last. It is usually forgotten—as Yashoda forgot her son Krishna's awesome nature in the story in "The Call of the Tradition." But as that same story indicates, a relationship of love, however understood, is the basis for retaining a consciousness appropriate to the continuing reality of divine influence.

There are three broad avenues of approach to a parallel consciousness: knowledge (*jñana*), ritual (*yajña*), and devotion (*bhakti*). Most Hindus follow one or more of these paths to greater or lesser extent.

Knowledge is traditionally embodied and cultivated among brahmin scholars. For centuries in antiquity they learned by heart the sacred Sanskrit scriptures, before these were committed to writing. Even after the texts were written, those who knew by heart the texts and commentaries on them remained highly respected. Their knowledge was traditionally considered the highest authority on sacred matters. There is no single organization or hierarchy of authority that structures Hinduism, but the recognized and respected authority of those masters of the sacred texts provides the framework of orthodoxy.

The path of knowledge has attracted many great minds. There are traditionally six major schools of Hindu philosophy, and many lines of teaching within these schools. Logic and grammar as approaches to understanding the world and the human condition have been developed to a degree perhaps unsurpassed in any other culture. The logic, it should be said in passing, is not Aristotelian: the fundamental tendency of thought is to posit the approach to truth not in either/or syllogisms, but in both/and formulations. But for our purposes, the salient development in philosophy was Advaita ("non-dual") Vedanta, a school of thought founded by the great ninth-century teacher Shankaracarya. This formulation held that Brahman—the Absolute, Infinite Self, the ultimately unknowable—is the only true reality, that all else is contingent or illusory, and that salvation lies in the realization that one's innermost being (atman) is identical with Brahman. This line of teaching was highly influential in Indian thought, even when it was held simultaneously with a devotion to one of the innumerable forms of the deity's manifestations—which Shankara admitted as a lesser form of knowledge. And to Western eyes and hearts, whereas the multitude of gods and demons seemed alien, even appalling, Advaita Vedanta was very attractive. It was the most exportable form of Hinduism.

The *Bhagavad Gita*, claimed by Vedanta as one of its source texts, is often considered the quintessential text of the Hindu tradition. Its popularity, however, is relatively recent and is strongest among the educated elite. Part of the very long epic the *Mahabharata*, it is widely known in the West (it was first translated into English in 1785), and is quoted frequently in this volume—with good reason. Krishna's instruction to Arjuna on the battlefield of Kurukshetra contains some of the most inspiring visions of a higher order of being that have ever been composed:

> *Men without understanding think that I am*
> *unmanifest nature become manifest;*
> *they are ignorant of my higher existence,*
> *my pure, unchanging absolute being.*
>
> *Veiled in the magic of my discipline,*
> *I elude most men;*
> *this deluded world is not aware*
> *that I am unborn and immutable. . . .*

Trusting me, men strive
for freedom from old age and death;
they know the infinite spirit,
its inner self and all its action.

Men who know me as its inner being,
inner divinity, and inner sacrifice
have disciplined their reason;
they know me at the time of death.[1]

Knowledge of divinity has also been composed and transmitted in languages understood by the vast majority of the population who do not know Sanskrit. The great Sanskrit epic, the *Ramayana*, for example, is the basis of a wealth of material in popular religion and culture. It is most widely known not in its Sanskrit form but in the numerous retellings of the story of Rama and Sita in vernacular languages—and the stories are often changed, the point of view altered, in these retellings. And there are innumerable other stories—a veritable ocean of story. Each village, each temple, each region has its tales—variations on pan-Indic themes or stories particular to the locality. The tales shape and populate the landscape—stones and trees, hills and shrines are the homes of deities and demons; forests and river banks are where kings, heroes, and villains have lived and died—and live still. Their feats, the lessons they learned, their tragic fates create a moral landscape for those raised from childhood with these stories.

The path of ritual, similarly, is traditionally cultivated among brahmin priests who conduct the rites in Sanskrit. The requirements of ritual are strict—the worshiper must reproduce the prescribed hand gestures, offerings, and words spoken, with full attention, in the right order, and accurately so as to activate the power they hold. The rituals create, maintain, and perpetuate the relationship between the practitioner and divine presence. They may be public or private. Public rituals are, for all the rigor required, not set pieces, rehearsed and performed in an environment from which contingent influences have been removed. These contingencies—relationships and external conditions—are, rather, enfolded within the rituals. The priests who participate in them interact with one another on the basis of their knowledge and experience, to enact the words and actions that create the relationship with the divine. The priests must observe strict rules of personal ritual purity from pollution, but they may argue with one another, comment, or instruct one another in the course of a ritual, without destroying its efficacy.

On the personal and domestic level, *puja*—worship with offerings to a personal or family deity—is usually a daily event. A clerk in the railway station may open a drawer of his desk, light a stick of incense, and conduct a brief puja while his customers are waiting, before beginning work. At home, each member of a family may conduct private devotions in a small shrine in the corner of a room; in each family someone will be responsible for looking after the family's shrine. Children are encouraged to participate from a very early age. Many people will visit a temple on the way to or from work, to practice a personal ritual or observe a ritual conducted by the temple's priests before the image of the deity. In private worship, the devotion in one's heart is generally considered more important than the strict forms of worship.

This devotion is reinforced by knowledge of its reciprocity—the deity's love for his or her devotees, and is the backbone of bhakti, emotional love for a personal deity. This is a theme hardly touched on in the articles in this book, but it underlies the consciousness of everyone raised in the Hindu tradition. The consciousness of the deity and the narrative traditions that accompany it shape a view of the inner journey that, though it cannot be exported in its full emotional richness, can be a source of delight and inspiration to those who learn about it and enjoy its artistic expressions.

A note about transliterations in this volume: in the interest of minimizing the reader's difficulties with unfamiliar names and terms, spelling of all material written for *Parabola* has been edited to be phonetic for the English speaker. Articles reprinted from other sources have been left as originally printed. In these cases, ś and ṣ may be pronounced sh, c pronounced ch, and ṛ pronounced ri. Other diacritical marks can be ignored.

Notes:

1   From Seventh Teaching, verses 24–25, 29–30, *The Bhagavad Gita: Krishna's Council in Time of War*, translated by Barbara Stoler Miller (New York: Bantam Books, 1986).

Hindu Imagery

How many ways can we experience the search for truth? The images of Hinduism tell us that we can start anywhere and that the search can take innumerable forms. In many forms of practice, individuals follow the threads of the knowable toward the unknown. Temples, crowded with images, invite us to enter and catch a glimpse of the single, unifying presence within. Each of the many deities presents an aspect and a vision of the truth which cannot be contained by any representation.

For captions regarding these images see pages 340–41

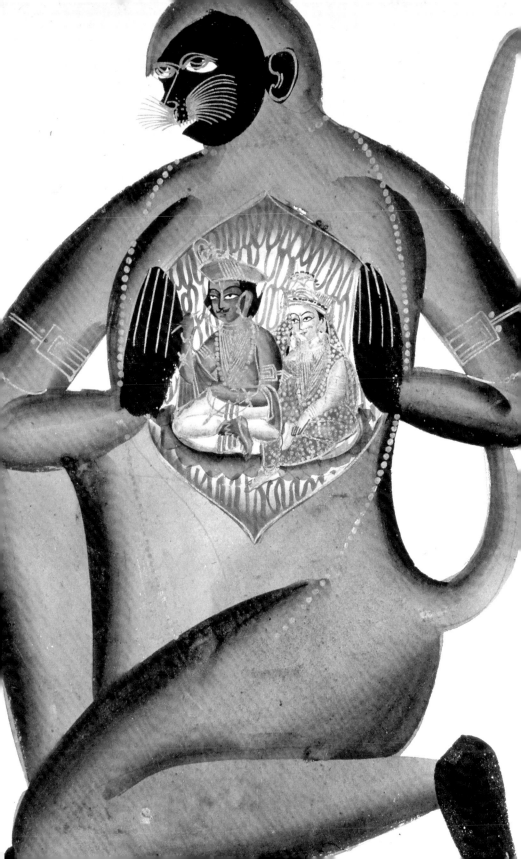

•

The Macrocosm

*It is important to keep in mind
a central idea of the Indian tradition,
namely that of levels.
There is a hierarchy of levels within a person,
in the society, and in the cosmos.
The lower levels in all these are lower precisely
because their insight and understanding
is not as subtle nor as comprehensive
as it is at the higher levels.*

*For example, those parts which are at a lower
level in a person or in humanity
wish to live by their own likes and dislikes and not by what is good
or right for the whole person or the whole society.
Those parts of us, or those among us, which understand the needs
and requirements of the whole, need to control,
persuade, or coerce the lower parts to obey the higher vision.
Otherwise, there will be chaos internally,
in the society, and in the cosmos,
leading to a violation of right order (*dharma*) and of wholeness.*

—Ravi Ravindra

Much of the wisdom of Hinduism lies in the vast treasure house of
stories that are a fundamental wealth of the Hindu tradition. What is
perhaps most distinctive about these stories is, as the epigraph states,
the "hierarchy of levels" illustrated or at least implicit in each one. Some
stories are of follies and achievements on a human scale, though the

actors may be epic heroes or divinities. But some stories are much larger in scale. As Ravi Ravindra writes, "Great myths are human beings writ large, and such myths are always true, now as much as in the beginning." Such stories tell of the universe, how it evolves and devolves in cosmic cycles of unimaginable duration.

Chapter One addresses questions of cosmic scale: gods and mortals each living out their destiny. The first two selections place humankind in the cosmos that encompasses deities who, like people, are born, live, and die to be reborn, but in much longer cycles. "The Breath of Brahma" introduces the four *yugas*, the great eras, infinitesimal in the life of Brahma, which are each thousands of human years long. Ravi Ravindra's "Worlds Living and Dying" explores how a framework that dissolves human time in the vastness of cyclic Time can free the searcher from the limitations of conditioned existence.

Another great myth, "Blue Throat," is the story of how the god Shiva saved the world from the poison released when gods and demons worked together to churn the cosmic ocean, each seeking the elixir of immortality. In "The Sleeping Dragon and the Waters," Stuart Smithers tells how another god, Indra, released the energies of the universe by slaying the "serpent or dragon who is responsible for holding back 'the waters'." He suggests how this cosmic struggle parallels that of the *yogin*, "an extraordinary hero whose questioning and inner struggle leads to the creation of a world between two chaoses."

The *Rig Veda's* "Hymn of Man" again places mankind in a cosmic scale: "Man alone is all this [world]." The gods, the poem says, sacrificed this cosmic man, and from his parts came all creatures, the sun and moon, and the gods themselves. The sacrifice of this Man of cosmic proportion, "born in the beginning," lays down "the first rules, and these powers reached the sky." The mysteries of this interpenetrating cosmic order are explored by A. K. Coomaraswamy in "An Indian Temple," where he draws on the work of the art historian Stella Kramrisch to describe how the structure of a Hindu temple maps the nature of the universe, of the deities, and of human consciousness.

Thus Chapter One explores the human experience with a telescope, as it were, mapping the human drama on an unimaginably large scale. The following chapters consider questions of how the individual can conduct a life in this world, but consciousness of the cosmic order is never very far from the surface. The final chapter will come full circle from the macrocosm to the microcosm, considering the mystery of the inmost self, consciousness—which, we will find, can perhaps only be understood on a cosmic scale.

Parabola
Volume: 2.3
Cosmology

The Breath of Brahma

Retold by Paul Jordan-Smith

"And does Brahma live as mortals live?" the ragamuffin asked the Old Man as he scurried beside him along the forest trail.

"No, child: it is we mortals whose lives are like Brahma's, only much reduced. Let us stop by this tree, and I will teach thee." With not a trace of weariness, though he had walked fourteen miles since the morning, the Old Man sat beneath the tree, his bowl beside him, and adjusted the folds of his rags. The child also sat down, scratched a little, fidgeted, played with a stick with a beetle—under the Old Man's careful scrutiny, lest he harm it—and heard every word spoken.

"You must know, first of all, the Brahma too has a beginning and an end to life: but one hundred years does he live. And yet, those hundred years are so long they are beyond count. Consider: each year as we reckon it is equal to a single day in the Divine Year. Thus a Divine Year is equal to 360 of our own. Now, a million Divine Years are allotted to each hour of the Day-and-Night of Brahma, of which there are 360 in a Brahma Year. If Brahma lives a hundred years, reckon if you will, the years of man contained in one of Brahma's lifetimes!"

The child made a few marks in the dirt with his stick as he had seen the merchants do in the marketplace, but soon returned to teasing the beetle.

"Every day in the life of Brahma, he breathes one thousand times, and his eyes open and shut one thousand times: each time they open, a universe appears and each time they close, the universe dissolves. Now, there are four stages in the opening and closing of the eyes of Brahma, and these are called *yugas*.

"In the first, or Krita Yuga, the Cow of Virtue stands on four legs: men are perfectly virtuous and the laws of the caste are kept.

"In the Treta Yuga, the Cow stands on three legs.

"In the Dvapara Yuga, she stands on two legs.

"And in the Kali Yuga—"

"I know!" said the urchin. "The Cow stands on one leg!" He giggled and tried to flip the beetle over on its back, but the Old Man moved his foot ever so slightly and the stick broke.

"In that age—which is the one we are living in now—men have forgotten virtue almost entirely. The castes are mixed, their meaning is lost. That age is the shortest—

"When will it end?" the child asked, squinting up at the Old Man through interlaced fingers. The other smiled and said nothing.

"And when it ends—then what?"

"Then Brahma opens his eyes again, and a new universe begins."

"And after Brahma dies?"

"At the close of his life, it is said, Brahma and all will dissolve into the body of Vishnu as he lies sleeping in the cosmic ocean. Then he will sleep for a space of time equal to a lifetime of Brahma, until the lotus dream flowers and all begins again."

Then there was silence under the tree. The Old Man seemed absorbed in dreams beyond proportion and measure. The child scratched himself, yawned, then lay down and fell asleep.

Parabola
Volume: 23.1
Millennium

Worlds Living and Dying

Ravi Ravindra

There is a marvelous story in the *Brahmavaivarta Purana* (*Krishna-janma Khanda*, 47.50.161) that dramatically illustrates the stupendous scale of Indian cosmology, and the distinctiveness of the Indian attitude to time:

> *Indra, king of gods, had become too self-important. Vishnu, the Supreme Being, visited him disguised as a small boy and said, "Ah, who will count the universes that have passed away, or the creations that have risen afresh, again and again, from the formless abyss of the vast waters? Who will number the passing ages of the world, as they follow each other endlessly? And who will search throughout the wide infinities of space to count the universes side by side, each containing its Brahma, its Vishnu, and its Shiva? Who will count the Indras in them all—those Indras side by side, who reign at once in all the innumerable worlds; those others who passed away before them, or even the Indras who succeed each other in any given line, ascending to godly kingship, one by one, and one by one, passing away? King of Gods, there are among your servants certain who maintain that it may be possible to number the grains of sand on earth and the drops of rain that fall from the sky, but no one will ever number all those Indras. This is what the*

Knowers know. … Beyond the farthest vision, crowding outer space, the universes come and go, an innumerable host. Like delicate boats they float on the fathomless, pure waters that form the body of Vishnu. Out of every hair-pore of that body a universe bubbles and breaks. Will you presume to count them? Will you number the gods in all these worlds—the worlds present and the worlds past?"

A procession of ants had made its appearance in the hall during the discourse of the boy. In military array, in a column four yards wide, the tribe paraded across the floor. The boy noted them, paused, and started, then suddenly laughed with an astonishing peal, but immediately subsided into a profoundly indrawn and thoughtful silence. When Indra appealed to him with humility to explain, the boy disclosed the "secret that smites with an axe the tree of worldly vanity, hews away its roots and scatters its crown," and said, "I saw the ants, O Indra, filing in long parade. Each was once an Indra. Like you, each by virtue of pious deeds once ascended to the rank of a king of gods. But now, through many rebirths, each has become again an ant. This army is an army of former Indras.

"Life in the cycle of the countless rebirths is like a vision in a dream. The gods on high, the mute trees and the stones, are alike apparitions in this fantasy. But Death administers the laws of time. Ordained by time, Death is the master of all. Perishable as bubbles are the good and the evil of the beings of the dream. In unending cycles the good and evil alternate. Hence, the wise are attached to neither, neither the evil nor the good. The wise are not attached to anything at all."[1]

According to ancient Hindu cosmology, a cosmic unit of time is *kalpa*, a day of the creator, Brahma (literally, the Great Being). Creation unfolds during the day of Brahma, and the three worlds—heaven, earth, and the nether world—enter into a period of chaos during the night when Brahma sleeps. But all beings retain their essential karmas, which take form in the morning when Brahma wakes up. After a hundred years of Brahma, there is a great collapse, a *mahapralaya*, in which not only the three worlds, but all essences, beings, *daityas, devas*, matter, and Brahma himself enter into a great sleep. After a hundred years, another Brahma is born and the cycle begins again. Universes unfold and collapse endlessly.

Each kalpa is 4,320,000,000 earth-years. A kalpa is divided into a thousand *mahayugas* of equal length, and each *mahayuga* consists of four *yugas* of uneven duration and quality. The first one is called Satyuga or Kritayuga. In this yuga, which lasts for 1,728,000 years, dharma is stable and is supported on four legs, the fourfold virtues of truthfulness, kindness, love, and charity. In Tretayuga, which lasts 1,296,000 years, dharma is three-legged. Next is Dwaparayuga, which lasts 864,000 years and during which dharma is supported only on two legs.

The last is Kaliyuga, the present age, which is calculated to have begun at midnight between February 17 and 18, 3102 BCE (the traditional date of the war recounted in the *Mahabharata*); this will last 432,000 years. Thus we are living in the sixth millennium of the Kaliyuga of the present Mahayuga. And the current kalpa is computed to be the first day of the fifty-first year of the hundred-year life span of our Brahma. His total life is 311,040 billion human years. After him, there will be other Brahmas for other cycles of the universe.

In Kaliyuga, dharma is very unstable, supported by only one leg. In this age, according to the *Bhagavata Purana*, "most people are always subject to temptation; they are wicked, unkind, quarrelsome, unlucky and beggar-like. Deception, idleness, sloth, malice, dullness, distress, fear and poverty are foremost among people and darkness prevails upon them. They highly prize what is low and degraded. They are ever attended by misfortunes. They eat voraciously." The moral and social degradation of the Kaliyuga is also described in a passage of the *Vishnu Purana*: "When society reaches a stage, where property confers rank, wealth becomes the only source of virtue, passion the sole bond of union between husband and wife, false-hood the source of success in life, sex the only means of enjoyment, and when outer trappings are confused with inner religion. …"

In addition to the vastness of time scale, what is striking is the cyclical nature of time.[2] Universes arise and dissolve with their own Brahmas, Indras, and other gods. Evil and good increase and decrease in never-ending cycles as the world drama is repeated again and again. The cosmic dance of Shiva goes on, different steps heralding the creation and destruction of the worlds. The wheel of time will keep on revolving—without pause, without mercy, forever. According to Hinduism, the world is not progressing towards perfection under the direction of God. In contrast, the Judeo-Christian evaluation of time is teleological. Yahweh made his covenant with Abraham at a particular historical time, and the hopes of Jews were bound up with the fulfillment of this covenant in the future. A well-known Christian hymn succinctly characterizes this perspective: "God is working His purpose out, as year succeeds to year."

The Hebrew view of history contains the whole course of time, from the very moment of the world's creation to its final apocalyptic end, and the whole vast panorama of events is seen as a gradual unfolding of Yahweh's purpose toward the final triumph of his chosen people, Israel. Perhaps the most important single legacy passed on by Judaism to Christianity was this conviction that the course of historical events has a profound significance. Here time is viewed with complete linearity, as temporal events move toward their completion in eternity. We find a classic expression of this view in Tennyson's words:

> One God, one law, one element,
> And one far-off divine event,
> To which the whole creation moves.[3]

That history would soon come to an end, with the Second Coming of Christ,[4] was a very definite conviction with the early Christians: "For the hour of fulfillment is near," reads Revelation, and, "I am coming soon." Similar notions about the imminence of the end of the world continued for a long time. Thus Luther declared, "The world will perish shortly. The last day is at the door, and I believe the world will not endure a hundred years."[5] This impatient waiting for the end of the world was used as an exhortation to repent, and even today we find this exhortation on revivalist placards.

In the Judeo-Christian view of time, the world was created at a definite moment; Jesus was born, crucified, and resurrected on specific, unique, and momentous days. The belief of the uniqueness of these events—particularly of the Incarnation—depends upon a belief that history is a straight linear sequence guided by God. Pagan belief in purposeless temporal undulation was entirely unacceptable to early Christians: the idea of repetitive cosmic cycles was the worst of blasphemies. Origen argued that from such a theory it would follow that "Adam and Eve will do once more exactly what they have already done;

the same deluge will be repeated; the same Moses will bring the same six hundred thousand people out of Egypt; Judas will again betray his Lord; and Paul a second time will hold the coats of those who stone Stephen." "God forbid," cried St. Augustine, "that we should believe this. For Christ died once for our sins, and, rising again, dies no more."[6] Thus, with the rise of Christianity, the prevalent doctrines of undulation and recurrent cycles vanished from the Mediterranean world. According to Lynn White, Jr., "No more radical revolution has ever taken place in the world-outlook of a large area."[7]

Along with the uniqueness of key events and the linearity of time, the Judeo-Christian world-view is permeated with the thought that history is going somewhere. The idea of progress is also intimately connected with this. God rules over history and works his plan out in time; both in the history of the Church and in the life of an individual, the divine purpose is still being worked out. Ultimately, it is expected that this Divine purpose will reach its culmination. Christ will return, the dead will be raised, and the Final Judgment will be enacted, with beatitude for the saved and eternal punishment for the damned.

What is of profound psychological significance here is that there is only one chance for the individual, and each person's death is a moment of crucial importance. This adds a sense of urgency and anxiety to a person's life, as well as a sense of personal responsibility. When this anxiety is coupled with the idea of the selection of a chosen few who will be saved, competitiveness and exclusivism result.

In the Indic traditions, to hold onto a separate individuality in any ultimate sense is a mark of ignorance, whereas in the Biblical traditions a lack of individuality—even in the presence of God—marks a lack of responsibility. In one case, the general emphasis is very much on the *oneness* of all that is, whereas in the other case the emphasis is on the *uniqueness* of human beings from all other creatures and from each other. The words *oneness* and *uniqueness* are derived from the same root, but their meanings diverge radically. The traditions which hold the ideal of oneness are insight-oriented. They have developed wisdom relating to the various levels of consciousness: the degrees of steadiness of attention, and the gradations of clear perception. The traditions extolling uniqueness are faith- and obedience-oriented, and have a great deal to say about individual responsibility and moral conscience: the quality of virtuous conduct, or the degrees and the gravity of sinfulness. Whereas levels of consciousness are emphasized in one case, levels of conscience are stressed in the other. These differing views are illustrated in two well-known texts, *The Tibetan Book of the Dead* and Dante's *Divine Comedy*, both of which deal with the journey of the soul after death and are concerned with the cultivation of the right quality of life.[8]

It is possible, but neither generous (and generosity is said to be the specific saving virtue of Kaliyuga) nor insightful, to convince oneself that half the sages in the world have simply misunderstood the matter and only the other half have found the truth. All the great teachers have said that experiences of approaching God or Truth or Nirvana or Brahman or the Ultimate cannot be expressed in the language of the lower levels, and that a radical transformation of conscience/consciousness—a spiritual rebirth—is needed in order to experience the Real. Apart from selflessness and the natural feelings of compassion and love which are characteristic of all the sages, there is one feature they possess which needs to be underscored, and which is rarely remarked upon: a sage simultaneously sees the *oneness* of all there is and the *uniqueness* of everything. The sages are aware that each human being is a manifestation of one Divine Energy, but that at the same time each person presents a unique potential. The One is unique in each manifestation: each person is seen by the sage as both one with the Source and singularly oneself.

Krishna says in the *Bhagavad Gita* (4: 6–8):

> *Unborn, imperishable in my own being,*
> *Lord of creatures, I take as my basis*
> *material existence*
> *and appear through my own power.*
>
> *Whenever dharma declines*
> *and adharma prevails*
> *I manifest myself.*
>
> *To protect the good, and to destroy those who*
> *do evil*
> *to establish dharma, I appear yuga after yuga.*

Great myths are human beings writ large, and such myths are always true, now as much as in the beginning. There is a constant battle between the *daityas* and the *adityas*, externally in the universe and internally in our psyche. Often translated respectively as "demons" and "gods," the doers of evil and good, daityas and adityas have a very suggestive etymology. First of all, they both have a common father, Kashyap, but different mothers, Diti and Aditi. They are stepbrothers, closely related to each other. Now *kashyap* means "vision," while *diti* means "limited." Daityas thus are products of limited vision, while in contrast adityas are products of a vaster vision. Within ourselves and in our society, as well as in the cosmos, there is a continual struggle between limited vision, which is self-occupied and is driven by fear, and a higher and freer vision.

Right order, dharma, is always fragile and is constantly threatened, for the simple reason that the daityas are more in number and stronger than the adityas, although less wise. Dharma can be protected and established only by the Highest (called Krishna in the *Bhagavad Gita*), who naturally resides in our deepest self. The establishment of dharma—or its reestablishment—is possible at any time and at any place when the need is felt deeply enough that a person is willing to engage in *yajña*, sacrifice and the exchange of substances between levels of being.[9] Yajña, however, cannot be undertaken without *yoga*, a spiritual discipline.

Yoga and yajña can be practiced at any age and in any yuga, always corresponding to what is suitable to the time and place. From a mythological point of view, both the end and the beginning are always and now.

Notes:

1   For the full story, see Heinrich Zimmer, *Myths and Symbols in Indian Art and Civilization*, edited by J. Campbell (New York: Harper Torch Books, 1962), chapter 1.

2   For a fuller discussion, please see the chapter "Time in Christian and Indian Traditions" in Ravi Ravindra, *Yoga and the Teaching of Krishna* (Adyar, India: Theosophical Publishing House, 1997).

3   *In Memoriam*, Conclusion, stanza 36.

4   It is relevant to remark that *second coming* is mentioned only once in the New Testament—in Hebrews 9:28. Otherwise, there is no sense of the presence of living Christ among the people. Thus, there could be no awareness of the *second* coming. It's only the imminent coming of the Lord which is stressed.

5   Quoted in S. Toulmin and J. Goodfield, *The Discovery of Time* (London: Penguin Books, 1967), p. 92.

6   Quoted by Lynn White, Jr., "Christian Myth and Christian History," *Journal of History of Ideas* 3 (1942): 147–58.

7   *Ibid.*

8   For a further discussion, see Ravi Ravindra, "Gurdjieff Work and the Teaching of Krishna," in *Gurdjieff: Essays and Reflections on the Man and his Teaching*, edited by J. Needleman and G. Baker (New York, Continuum, 1996), pp. 214–24 and republished in Ravindra, *The Spiritual Roots of Yoga: Royal Path to Freedom* (Sandpoint Id.: Morning Light Press, 2006).

9   For a further discussion of *yajña*, see the article "Teaching of Krishna, Master of Yoga" in *The Spiritual Roots of Yoga: Royal Path to Freedom.*

Parabola
Volume: 6.4
Demons

Blue Throat

Retold by Paul Jordan-Smith

It was during the many transformations of Shiva and the other gods that the strife arose between the gods and the demons. Only the highest of the gods—Indra, Brahma and Shiva—remained aloof from the conflict. Indeed, it was through Shiva's assistance that the demons acquired the power of resuscitation, thus maintaining a balance between the two forces. Now the demons were able to revive themselves with the magical spell which Shiva had given their priest, and after this, the battle did not go well for the gods.

Worried about the outcome of the struggle, the gods approached Brahma, who interrupted his meditations long enough to tell them to cooperate with the demons, and together to churn the cosmic ocean and produce *amrita*, the elixir of immortality. The demons were agreeable to this, since by drinking the nectar, they would no longer need the spells of resuscitation. So, for a time, the struggle was suspended, and the churning of the Great Sea was undertaken.

The method of the churning was this: the cosmic serpent Ananta uprooted the mountain Mandara, with all its trees, and Indra fastened its tip on the back of the King of Tortoises. The great serpent Vasuki was chosen for the rope to turn the mountain, with the demons placed at his head, and the gods holding his tail. The demons were at first quite proud of their position, but in fact they were all scorched by the flames that shot from Vasuki's throat. Now the serpent wrapped his long body around the mountain, and alternately pulling on the head and tail, the demons and gods turned the mountain now this way, now that. Vigorously they churned the cosmic ocean, and from the mouth of Vasuki billowed smoke and flames, which rose into the air as clouds and lightning. A deep and terrible roar came from the deep, as a maelstrom arose and sucked into itself all the trees that grew on the mountain slopes. All living things were crushed by the churning, and their vitality oozed into the ocean and mingled with its waters.

The churning lasted a long time and many marvelous things issued from the ocean: the sun and moon, the goddess Luck, the gem of Vishnu, and countless other treasures. When the gods and demons became tired, Vishnu gave them strength, and they continued their labors, avid for the nectar that should sustain them forever. But alas, from the churning of their agony and greed came not nectar but a black poisonous mass, the terrible Kalakuta. This venom rose to the surface and its fumes asphyxiated the triple world. Flames shot from its surface, and it threatened to consume the universe. In shame and despair, the gods approached Lord Shiva. "We alone are to blame," they said, "for it was greed that drove us to seek amrita. The demons strove also with greed, but that is to be expected of them. We lust after immortality, but we have found only death."

When Shiva heard the confessions of the gods, he took compassion upon them, and upon the world. Bending his head down to the poisonous sea, he drank in all the venom, holding it in his throat at the Center of Purity. So virulent was the concoction of agony and greed that as it descended, it turned Lord Shiva's throat a deep blue, which is why, among his many names, he bears that of Nilakanthus—Blue Throat. By that name he is called, who is also the Destroyer, in recognition of his role as liberator from death and destruction.

With the poison sucked up from the deep, the churning was resumed, and at last the amrita arose, milky-white, from the cosmic sea. It was contained in a white vessel, held by the physician of the gods, to save gods and demons alike from death. But no happiness came from it. Once more deception, strife and war arose between the gods and demons, ending in a tumultuous battle. The gods won the divine nectar, and it was given to Vishnu for safekeeping. With Lord Vishnu resides the elixir of life; and in the throat of Nilakanthus resides still the poison whose name means "the puzzle of Time."

Parabola
Volume: 17.4
Power and Energy

THE SLEEPING DRAGON AND THE WATERS

Stuart Smithers

*Swift Swift from Chaos to chaos from void to void a
road immense…*

—*William Blake*, The Four Zoas

*If a man wants to become a hero the serpent must first
become a dragon: otherwise he will lack his proper enemy.*

—*Friedrich Nietzsche,*

Human, All Too Human

Among the most important Hindu cosmogonies is the
cycle of myths relating the story of the battle between
Indra and Vritra.[1] Indra is the Vedic hero whose ancient
and sacred path charges him "to fight" and "to question"
(*Rig Veda* 4.18.2). His most important act is the slaying
of Vritra, the serpent or dragon who is responsible for
holding back "the waters." The symbols of the Indra-Vritra myths are enigmatic and protean, and although "the
waters" are variously celestial, terrestrial, and oceanic, the
nature and function of Vritra's action is explicitly revealed
in his name which is derived from the Sanskrit verbal
root meaning to enclose, envelop, obstruct, or hold back.
Thus the literal meaning of *vritra* is "obstacle," an adver-

sarial and hostile force, or, as suggested by the late Sanskritist Jan Gonda, "the power or force of resistance."

In his struggle to free the waters, Indra fights the dragon with magic, supernatural powers, and weapons. The most famous account of the battle (RV 1.32) describes how Indra killed Vritra and overcame the "magic of the magicians with his own magic." Indra destroyed the dragon with his thunder-bolt and split open the bellies of the mountains, allowing the waters to flow down. In the same moment, his colossal victory brought forth the sun, the sky, and the dawn. After the battle, Vritra's smashed and lifeless body is described as a "broken reed," shattered and in pieces, with the rising waters flowing over him until finally his body is hidden and "sunk into long darkness." The episode results in the release of "the seven streams" (RV 1.32.12; 4.19.3) which originate on a mountain top—a region that symbolizes the meeting of the terrestrial and the celestial realms—and rush down to the ocean. Until this time, life was threatened because the waters that "flow for man" had been obstructed. Indra's triumph allows the waters to flow again and transforms an "inhabitable chaotic universe into a cosmos."[2]

A passage in the *Śatapatha-Brahmana* tells us that the cosmos was already extant, but that Vritra lay covering all of it, including the space between heaven and earth. After he was destroyed, the waters flowed, becoming both mixed and pure (*ŚB* 1.1.3.4). In opening up the space between heaven and earth, Indra has literally "made room" for light and rain (i.e., water). In another version (*ŚB* 1.6.3.17), when Indra is about to finish him off, Vritra suggests that the two have exchanged roles, so they make a deal: instead of "killing" him, Indra cuts Vritra in two, fashioning the moon from one half, and the bellies of all creatures from the remaining "demonic" portion. In this way, "... whenever these creatures crave for food, they pay tribute to this Vritra, the belly where previously he had been a 'consumer of food.'"[3]

This version of the story includes a unique spin, the intention of which could not be clearer: Vritra, as the power of resistance, continues to exist both cosmically as the moon and microcosmically in human beings as "hunger." For Philo and Plutarch the "serpent" is the lower, irrational, physical aspect of the soul, that aspect of the soul which is known by its appetites, desires, and hunger. Philo comments that the idea of the "snakefighter" is a

*symbolic representation of self-control, waging a fight that never ends
and a truceless war against incontinence. ... For if serpentlike pleasure
is a thing unnourishing and injurious, sanity, the nature that is at war
with pleasure, must be most nutritious and a saving power.*[4]

In addition to his primary role as obstacle or force of resistance, Vritra,
as a dragon, is undivided (*aparvan*), unawakened (*abudhyam*), sleeping
(*abudhyamânam*), and fast asleep (*sushupanam*) (RV IV.19.3). His undivided nature symbolizes the undifferentiated and formless primordial
chaos which existed before the separation of energies, or in this instance,
heaven and earth: a condition which seems to equate "sleep" with chaos
and the lack of space.

But the mythology of the "sleeping dragon" is ambiguous and enigmatic. Vedic stories generally reflect the negative character of the dragon
as the dark power which controls and holds back the waters. Other passages, however, indicate that this view is one-sided, missing the more
sophisticated aspects of the Indra-Vritra cycle. As the "undivided" serpent, Vritra is known as the *ananta*, the "endless" or infinite world-ser-
pent who encircles and encloses the world, and in whom all possibilities
of cosmic manifestation rest latent. In one of the most famous images of
Vishnu, he is found resting on the coils of the cosmic serpent, *Ananta*,
who floats upon the primordial waters forming a bed for the god. In a
different light, the *Rig Veda* suggests (1.103.7) that Indra's great feat was
not killing Vritra, but awakening him:

> *You, Indra, have performed the heroic*
> *deed, you aroused the sleeping serpent*
> *with your vajra (lightning-bolt).*

Furthermore, Indra's victory over Vritra, like Gilgamesh's victory over
Humbaba, is followed, not by celebration, but by fear, flight, and the
threat of chaos. In several later account Indra must be purified for the
transgression of "Brahmanicide."

The fear that follows Vritra's death is an especially difficult paradox.
There is an implication that Vritra's existence is necessary, an idea which
is consistent with accounts of his continued existence in new forms.
It is also true that Indra's fame actually depends upon a worthy and

formidable opponent or obstacle: once awakened, the sleeping serpent becomes the Dragon that Indra needs in order to fulfill his heroic destiny. In this light we must consider the serpent, or the dragon, as not only the possessor, but also as the protector, of "the waters"—*ahi-gopa*. In the myths and legends of the Buddha's "great awakening," the serpent was not destroyed, but was transformed, to serve as the Buddha's protector: Immediately after the Buddha's enlightenment, a "great storm" appeared which threatened his meditation. According to the story, Muchalinda the Serpent King emerged from the darkness and coiled his body around the Buddha seven times, spreading his giant cobra-like hood above the Buddha. When the storm finally subsided on the seventh day, the Serpent King unwound himself from the Buddha, transformed himself into a young man, and bowed respectfully. As Heinrich Zimmer wrote, the image of Muchalinda's protection and support of the Buddha's effort is the representation of the "perfect reconciliation of antagonistic principles."[5]

The hero's struggle requires an ever greater opponent. The serpent or dragon must be awakened and engaged in combat, not because the serpent is evil and must be destroyed, but because all possibilities of growth and transformation depend upon the life-energy he represents: if the serpent is killed and the struggle ends, then the growth of the hero likewise ends. But Buddhist legend also maintains that humankind was not prepared to accept this deeper understanding of our serpent-nature and the path of transformation, and consequently the Buddha entrusted his deep teaching to an audience of serpents (*nagas*), until men and women were ready for this more subtle instruction. Here too the serpents reemerge as "protectors."

In Vedic mythology, the symbolism of serpents and dragons as well as that of "the waters" describes the undifferentiated, formless, and latent potential of chaos. A well-known hymn in the *Rig Veda* suggests that "in the beginning" there was neither death nor immortality, neither night nor day: without distinction, everything was *water* (10.129). What then, are "the waters"? What is it that is unorganized, indistinct, and chaotic? What is the water of the alchemists, "that does not make the hands wet"?

Jung, Eliade, Guénon, and Coomaraswamy are in general agreement that in all traditions "the waters" stand for "universal possibility" or "the universal sum of virtualities"; they are the origin and the reservoir of all realms of existence; they are the ground of every form, precede all forms, and *support* all forms.[6] Water very nearly approaches the Vedic concept of *brahman*, the mysterious and most fundamental power or energy (*viryam*) of the universe (*Śatapatha-Brahmana* 1.2.1.7). The Upanishads state that everything in *this* world, in our visible and manifest universe, "is woven, warp and woof, on water…" And when the great sage Yajnavalkya is asked by Gargi, on what then is the "water woven, warp and woof?" He tells her, "on the world of *brahman*."

The symbolism of water occupies a similar role in Western cosmogony, representing chaos as the source from which all of manifest creation springs. In the beginning, we are told, the earth was without form and void, and the Spirit of God moved over the face of the waters. Dark and formless, this watery depth is known as *chaos*: the primordial stuff of creation in a condition of mixture, disorder, and confusion—a state in which accident and chance rule the day. In the Genesis account the order and harmony of the cosmos appears, as in many cosmogonies, as a result of the paradigmatic creative act: separation. The alchemists discerned this riddle in Genesis, leading Paracelsus to claim that separation is

> … *the greatest wonder of the philosophies.* … *When the* mysterium magnum *in its essence and divinity was full of the highest eternity,* separatio *started at the beginning of all creation.*[7]

In the first four "days" of creation the light was separated [divided] from the darkness, the waters were separated from the waters, the earth was separated from "the waters under the heavens," and the day was separated from the night. The first four days of creation provide an extraordinary metaphysical map which moves from higher, invisible light and space, to the lower manifestations of visible space (Earth and oceans) and light (the appearance of visible lights—sun, moon, and stars—and day and night); or more accurately, as a movement from Light and Energy to less subtle forms of energy and light.

The prevailing view of chaos is mostly reductionistic, overlooking the idea of double chaoses symbolized by the separation of the waters: the waters above the heavens from the waters under the heavens. Commenting on the Vedic "Realm of Water," René Guénon notes: "The reference here is to the higher or celestial Waters, representing the totality of formless possibilities, as opposed to the lower Waters, which represent the totality of formal possibilities…"[8] In other words, the celestial waters are symbolic of the higher energies, while the "lower waters" correspond to the energies in the disorderly, chaotic, unharmonious world of humankind, a world which acknowledges the potentiality of real form or individuality; energies which exist in order to be given form and expression. The yogin who wishes for transformation must first occupy himself or herself with giving form and order to the "lower waters," to the energies of the human constitution. This idea is indicated in Genesis by the "gathering together" of the "waters under the heavens" and the appearance of firm ground. Once this has occurred, the formless and unnameable celestial waters, or higher energies, can be known—an experience which tradition tells us can be something of a shock for the unprepared ego and its sense of "individuality."[9]

Eliade suggests that one can "divine" in yogins the wish to transform the chaos of a human life into a cosmos; and furthermore, that this process of "creating" a cosmos is a necessary intermediate stage: the yogin cannot pass directly from chaos to freedom.[10] The process is one of creating the world through *form*ation: giving form to the lower energies, the yogin creates a condition in which the higher energies of the "waters above" can *in*-form him or her. In this process the totality of the cosmos is increasingly *embodied* and humankind's *raison d'être* is honored as an intermediary being between the two chaoses, partaking of both the lower and higher energies.

The Vedic Sanskrit word that most closely approaches the idea of cosmos is *loka*. Jan Gonda, in his influential study of loka, reminds us that Indra rescued "the waters" by creating "free room" or space when the waters were previously obstructed. Gonda emphatically concludes that the Sanskrit term for world or cosmos, loka, means "free, unoccupied, adequate space to flow in and over."[11] The cosmos, then, is the space created by the separation of the waters. Macrocosmically this corresponds to the separation of the celestial and the terrestrial waters, the higher and the lower energies, while microcosmically the idea suggests the differentiation between the lower energies and the creation of an "adequate" container, receptacle, or vessel for the higher energies to "flow in and over."

The sources of these higher energies, the *Rig Veda* cautions, do not "belong" to us: the gods have reserved the "power-to-do" (*kratum*) for themselves. But when this power flows down from the gods, it can inform us, it can be gathered "back again into bodies" (RV 10.56).

Like the exemplary Vedic warrior, Indra, the yogin is an extraordinary hero whose questioning and inner struggle leads to the creation of a world between the two chaoses, and in the process honors humankind's *raison d'être:* struggling with the sleep and chaos of ordinary existence while at the same time resisting the temptation to "kill" the lower energies in pursuit of "higher energies." In between the lower and the higher energies, the yogin creates a condition in which our chaotic but inhabitable world becomes increasingly ordered and harmonized as it is informed by higher energies. This is an extraordinarily non-violent approach in which transformation takes place without destroying anything; chaos is both transformed and transformative. The necessity of not only struggling with the dragon, but keeping him alive, may be a key to understanding the fearful, confusing, and tragic tone that sometimes follows the death of dragons in mythology.

Notes:

1   Wendy Doniger O'Flaherty's anthologies, translations, and studies are the most successfully accessible works dealing with Vedic and Hindu myths of Indra and Vritra. See *Hindu Myths* (Baltimore: Penguin, 1975) and *The Origins of Evil in Hindu Mythology* (Berkeley: University of California Press, 1976).

2   Jan Gonda, *Aspects of Early Visnuism* ([1954] reprint Delhi: Motilal Barnarsidass, 1969), p. 30.

3   Julius Eggling, tr., *The Śatapatha-Brāhmana* ([1882] reprint Delhi: Motilal Barnarsidass, 1963), part 1, pp. 167f.

4   See A. K. Coomaraswamy, "Ātmayajña: Self-sacrifice," in *Coomaraswamy*, Volume 2, *Selected Papers: Metaphysics*, edited by Roger Lipsey (Princeton: Princeton University Press, 1977), p. 146.

5   Heinrich Zimmer, *Myths and Symbols in Indian Art and Civilization*, edited by Joseph Campbell (Princeton: Princeton University Press, 1946), p. 67.

6   See A. K. Coomaraswamy, "The Nature of Buddhist Art," reprinted in *Coomaraswamy*,

Volume 1, *Selected Papers: Traditional Art and Symbolism*, edited by Roger Lipsey (Princeton: Princeton University Press, 1977), p. 171; René Guénon, *Man and His Becoming According to the Vedánta*, translated by Richard C. Nicholson (London: Luzac: 1945), pp. 56f.; Mircea Eliade, *The Sacred and the Profane*, translated by Willard R. Trask (New York: Oxford University Press, 1959), pp. 130ff.

7　*Paracelsus: Selected Writings*, edited by Jolande Jacobi, translated by Norbert Guterman, second edition (New York: Pantheon, 1958), p. 15.

8　René Guénon, *L'Homme et son devenir selon le Vedánta* (Paris, 1925), translated by Richard C. Nicholson as *Man and His Becoming According to the Vedanta* (London: Luzac: 1945), p. 152. See too, p. 56, note 3.

9　That, at least, seems to be a possible and plausible explanation of Indra's "fear" (RV I.32.14) after the "release of the waters." This also partially explains the expression, "Fear not," which is attributed to the angels of the Old Testament, Christ, and Buddha.

10　Mircea Eliade, *Le Yoga. Immortalité et Liberté* (Paris, 1954) translated by Willard R. Trask as *Yoga: Immortality and Freedom*, second edition (Princeton: Princeton University Press, 1969), p. 97.

11　Jan Gonda, *Loka—World and Heaven in the Veda* (Amsterdam: N. V. Noord-Hollandsche Uitgevers Maatschappij, 1966), p. 18.

Parabola
Volume: 3.1
Sacred Space

The Hymn of Man

Translated by Barbara Stoler Miller

The Purusha-sukta *is one of the later poems of the* Rig Veda. *The hymn is central in the conception of the building of the Hindu temple, which is constructed in the likeness of* Purusha *or Universal Man, as an echo of the cosmic creation. This hymn was translated for* Parabola *by Barbara Stoler Miller.*

Thousand-headed is Man,
thousand-eyed, thousand-footed;
having covered the earth on all sides,
he extended beyond it by ten-fingers' length.

Man alone is all this [world]—
past and future;
he is also lord of immortality
when he grows even beyond his food.

Great is the greatness of all this,
yet greater than this is Man;
a fourth of him is all beings,
three-fourths of him is immortality in heaven.

With three-fourths Man rose up,
A fourth of him came into being again here—
from that he moved out in all directions
to what eats and what does not eat.

From him the great expanse was born,
From the great expanse Man came;
when born he surpassed the earth
in the West and also in the East.

When, with Man as the oblation,
the gods stretched out the web of the sacrifice,
spring was the melted butter of it,
summer was the kindling, autumn the oblation.

That Man, born in the beginning,
they sprinkled as sacrifice on the straw—
with him the gods sacrificed,
and perfected beings and seers too.

From that fully offered sacrifice
the clotted butter was collected—
it made the animals of air,
forest, and village.

From that fully offered sacrifice
hymns and chants were born;
the meters were born from it,
the sacrificial formula arose from it.

From that horses were born
and whatever else has teeth on both jaws;
cows were born from that,
from that goats and sheep were born.

When they divided Man,
into how many parts did they distribute him?
What is his mouth, what are his two arms,
what are his thighs, his two feet called?

His mouth was a Brāhman priest,
his two arms were made into a Rājanya warrior,

and his thighs became a Vaishya peasant—
from his two feet a Shudra servant was born.

From his mind the moon was born,
from his eye Sūrya the sun was born,
from his mouth Indra and Agni,
from his breath Vāyu the wind was born.

From his navel was the atmosphere,
from his head the sky was turned,
from his feet the earth, from his ear the directions—
thus they constructed the worlds.

Seven were the sticks which enclosed it,
three times seven were the faggots they made
when the gods, spreading out the sacrifice,
bound Man as the sacrificial animal.

Through the sacrifice the gods sacrificed to the sacrifice—
these were the first rules
and these powers reached the sky,
where the ancient perfected beings are—gods.

Parabola
Volume: 3.1
Sacred Space

An Indian Temple

The Kandarya Mahadeo

Ananda K. Coomaraswamy

My subject in the present short article is really that of
the Hindu temple, irrespective of period and relative
complexity or simplicity. The choice of this subject is
one that is made especially appropriate by the recent
[1946] publication of Dr. Stella Kramrisch's magnificent work, *The Hindu Temple*. It may be remarked, in
the first place, that the most essential part of the concept of a temple is that of an altar on which, or a hearth
in which, offerings can be made to an invisible presence
that may or may not be represented iconographically.
The types of the oldest shrines are those of the "stone
tables" of megalithic cults and those of the stone altars
of tree or pillar cults; or the shrine may be a hearth,
the burnt offering being conveyed to the gods with
the smoke of the fire, Agni thus functioning as missal
priest. In all these cases the shrine, even when walled
or fenced about, remains open to the sky. On the other
hand, the oldest Indian type of sacred architecture both
enclosed and roofed is that of the *sadas* ("seat," the sacrificial operation being itself a *sattra*, "session") of the
Vedic Sacrifice or Mass. Made only for temporary use,
this enclosure is a place "apart" to which the gods resort
and in which the Sacrificer, having put on the "garment
of initiation and ardor," sleeps, becoming "as it were one

of themselves" for the time being; he becomes, indeed, an embryo, and is reborn from the sacred enclosure as from a womb. This hut or hall is a microcosm, of which the corners, for example, are called the "four quarters." At the same time, it must be recognized that no fundamental distinction can be made between the god-house as such and the dwellings of men, whether huts or palaces, as is evident in the case of those cultures, notably the Indian, in which the paterfamilias himself officiates as household priest, daily performing the Agnihotra in the domestic circle.

In addition to this, it must be realized that in India, as elsewhere, not only are temples made with hands, the universe in a likeness, but man himself is likewise a microcosm and a "holy temple" or City of God (*brahmapura*). The body, the temple, and the universe being thus analogous, it follows that whatever worship is outwardly and visibly performed can also be celebrated inwardly and invisibly, the "gross" ritual being, in fact, no more than a tool or support of contemplation, the external means having (just as had been the case in Greece) for its "end and aim the knowledge of Him who is the First, the Lord, and the Intelligible"—as distinguished from the visible. It is recognized also, of course, that the "whole earth is divine," i.e. potentially an altar, but that a place is necessarily selected and prepared for an actual Sacrifice, the validity of such a site depending not upon the site itself but on that of the sacerdotal art; and such a site is always theoretically both on a high place and at the center or navel of the earth, with an eastward orientation, since it is "from the east westwards that the gods come unto men."

It is constantly emphasized, accordingly, that the Sacrifice is essentially a mental operation, to be performed both outwardly and inwardly, or in any case inwardly. It is prepared by the Sacrificer's "whole mind and whole self." The Sacrificer is, as it were, emptied out of himself, and is himself the real victim. The true end of the cult is one of reintegration and resurrection, attainable not by a merely mechanical performance of the service, but by a full realization of its significance, or even by this comprehension alone. The Agnihotra, or burnt offering, for example, may be—and is for the comprehensor—an interior self-sacrifice, in which the heart is the altar, the outer man the offering, and the flame the dompted self.

The human frame, the constructed temple, and the universe being analogical equivalents, the parts of the temple correspond to those of the human body no less than to those of the universe itself. All these dimensioned (*nirmita, vimita*) forms are explicitly "houses," indwelt and filled by an invisible Presence and representing its possibilities of manifestation in time and space; their *raison d'être* is that it may be known. For this unifying and constructive Principle, the Spirit or Self of all beings, is only apparently confined by its habitations which, like other images, serve as supports of contemplation, none being ends in themselves but more or less indispensable means to liberation from every sort of enclosure.

Each of the "houses" we are considering is dimensioned and limited in six directions, nadir, quarters, and zenith—the feet, floor, or earth; bulk, interior space, or atmospheric space; and cranium, roof, or sky—defining the extent of this man, this church, and this world respectively. Here we can consider only one or two particular aspects of these and other analogies. The temple has, for example, windows and doors from which the indweller can look out and go forth, or conversely return to himself, and these correspond in the body to the "doors of the senses" through which one can look out in times of activity, or from which one can return to the "heart" of one's being when the senses are withdrawn from their objects, i.e., in concentration. There is, however, in theory, another door or window accessible only by a "ladder" or the "rope" by which our being is suspended from above, and through which one can emerge from the dimensional structure so as to be no longer on a level with its ground, or within it, but altogether above it. In man, this exit is represented by the cranial foramen, which is still unclosed at birth, and is opened up again at death when the skull is ritually broken, though as regards its significance it may be kept open throughout one's life by appropriate spiritual exercises, for this God-aperture (*brahma-randhra*) corresponds to the "point" or "eye of the heart," the microcosmic City of God (*brahma-pura*) within us, from which the Spirit departs at death. Architecturally, the *brahma-randhra* or foramen of the human cranium or man-made temple corresponds to the luffer, smoke hole, or skylight (*Lichtloch*) of the traditional house; and in some ancient and even relatively modern Western temples, this oculus of the dome still remains an open circular window, and the structure therefore remains open to the sky. In the early Indian timbered domes, the opening above is apparently closed by the circular roof-plate (*kaṇṇikā*) on which the rafters rest like the spokes of a wheel or the ribs of an umbrella, but this plate is perforated, and in any case functions as a doorway or place of exit through which the Perfected (Arahants) movers-at-will and "skyfarers" are repeatedly described as making their departure; it is an "upper door" (*aggadvārā*). It is through the cosmic opening that the Man, the Son of God, looks down, and descends. And just as the kaṇṇikā is a symbol of *samādhi*, "synthesis," so is this Greek capstone a "harmony," as Pausanias says, "of the whole edifice." In later Indian lithic structures, in the same way the summit of the spire is apparently closed by a circular stone slab (*āmalaka*), but this, too, is perforated for the reception of the tenon of the finial that prolongs the central axis of the whole structure; and the term brahma-randhra remains in use. Finally, in the world of which the sky is the roof, the Sun himself is the Janua Coeli, the "gateway of liberation" (*mokṣadvāra*), the only way by which to break out of the dimensioned universe, and so "escape altogether."

We have considered so far the altar (always in some sense a sacrificial hearth, analogous to the heart) and the oculus of the dome (always in some sense a symbol of the Sun) as the proximate and ultimate goals of the worshipper who comes to visit the deity, whose man-made "house" is the temple, there to devote himself. The altar, like the sacred hearth, is always theoretically at the center of the ceiling or *coelum* immediately above it; and these two are connected in principle, as in some early structures they were in fact, by an axial pillar at once uniting and separating floor and roof, and supporting the latter; as it was in the beginning, when heaven and earth, that had been one, were "pillared apart" by the Creator. The primordial separation of heaven and earth is common to the creation myths of the whole world. It is by this pillar—regarded as a bridge or ladder, or because of its immateriality, as a bird on wings, and regarded in any case from its base, for "there is no side path here in the world"—that the "hard ascent after Agni" (*dūrohaṇa, agner anvārohaḥ*) must be made from below to the Sundoor above, an ascent that is also imitated in countless climbing rites, and notably in that of the ascent of the sacrificial post (*yūpa*) by the Sacrificer who, when he reaches its summit and raises his head above its capital, says on behalf of himself and his wife: "We have reached the heaven, reached the gods, we have become immortals, become children of Prajapati." For them the distance that separates heaven from earth is temporarily annihilated; the bridge lies behind them.

The nature and full significance of the cosmic pillar (*skambha*), the Axis Mundi referred to above, can best be grasped from its description in *Atharva Veda* x.7 and 8, or understood in terms of the Islamic doctrine of the Qutb, with which the Perfect Man is identified, and on which all things turn. In the Vedic *Sadas* it is represented by the king-post that the Sacrificer himself erects, and that stands for the Median Breath, in the same way as within man, as the axial principle of one's own life and being. In the Vedic (Fire-) altar, a constructed image of the universe, this is also the axial principle that passes through the three "self-perforated bricks," of which the uppermost corresponds to the Sundoor of the later texts; it is an axis that—like Jacob's ladder—is the "way up and down these worlds." In visiting the deity whose image or symbol has been set up in the womb of the temple, the worshiper is returning to the heart and center of his own being to perform a devotion that prefigures his ultimate resurrection and regeneration from the funeral pyre in which the last Sacrifice is made.

We are thus brought back again to the concept of the three analogous—bodily, architectural, and cosmic—"houses" that the Spirit of Life inhabits and fills; and we recognize at the same time that the values of the oldest architectural symbolism are preserved in the latest buildings and serve to explain their use. I shall only emphasize, in conclusion, what has already been implied, that the Indian architectural symbolism briefly outlined above is by no means peculiarly or exclusively Indian, but rather worldwide. For example, that the sacred structure is a microcosm, the world in a likeness, is explicit among the American Indians; as remarked by Sartori, "Among the Huichol Indians … the temple is considered as an image of the world, the roof as heaven, and the ceremonies which are enacted during the construction, almost all relate to this meaning," and as related by Speck in his description of the Delaware Big-House, "the Big-House stands for the universe; its floor, the earth; its four walls, the four quarters; its vault, the sky-dome atop, where resides the Creator in his indefinable supremacy … the centrepost is the staff of the Great Spirit with its foot upon the earth, with is pinnacle reaching to the hand of the Supreme Being sitting on his throne."

In the same way, from the Indian point of view, it is said with respect to the way up and down that "within these two movements the Hindu temple has its being; its central pillar is erected from the heart of the Vāstupurusa in the Brahmasthāna, from the center and heart of existence on earth, and supports the Prasāda Purusa in the Golden Jar in the splendor of the Empyrean."[1]

Finally, inasmuch as the temple is the universe in a likeness, its dark interior is occupied only by a single image or symbol of the informing Spirit, while externally its walls are covered with representations of the Divine Powers in all their manifested multiplicity. In visiting the shrine, one proceeds inwards from multiplicity to unity, just as in contemplation; and on returning again to the outer world, one sees that one has been surrounded by all the innumerable forms that the Sole Seer and Agent within assumes in his playful activity. And this distinction between the outer world and the inner shrine of an Indian temple, into which one enters, "so as to be born again from its dark womb,"[2] is the same distinction Plotinus makes when he observes that the seer of the Supreme, being one with his vision, "is like one who, having penetrated the inner sanctuary, leaves the temple images behind him—though these become once more first objects of regard when he leaves the holies; for There his converse was not with image, not with trace, but with the very Truth."[3]

The deity who assumes innumerable forms, and has no form, is one and the same Purusa, and to worship in either way leads to the same liberation: "however men approach Me, even so do I welcome them." In the last analysis, the ritual, like that of the old Vedic Sacrifice, is an interior procedure, of which the outward forms are only a support, indispensable for those who—being still on their way—have not yet reached its end, but that can be dispensed with by those who have already found the end, and who, though they may be still in the world, are not of it. In the meantime, there can be no greater danger or hindrance than that of the premature iconoclasm of those who still confuse their own existence with their own being, and have not yet "known the Self"; these are the vast majority, and for the them the temple and all its figurations are signposts on their way.

Notes:

1   Stella Kramrisch, *The Hindu Temple*, II (Calcutta, 1946), p. 361.

2   *Ibid.* p. 358.

3   Plotinus, *Enneads* VI.9.II.

Adapted from Roger Lipsey, ed., *Coomaraswamy*, Volume 1, *Selected Papers: Traditional Art and Symbolism* (Princeton: Princeton University Press, 1977), pp. 3–10.

•

CHAPTER TWO

MAINTAINING SOCIAL ORDER:
RITUAL AND SACRIFICE

There are five great sacrifices,
namely, the great ritual services:
the sacrifices to all beings,
sacrifice to men,
sacrifice to the ancestors,
sacrifice to the Gods,
sacrifice to Brahman.

Day by day a man offers sustenance to creatures:
that is the sacrifice to beings.
Day by day a man gives hospitality to the guests,
including a glass of water; that is the sacrifice to men.
Day by day man makes funerary offerings,
including a glass of water; that is the sacrifice to the ancestors.
Day by day a man makes offerings to the Gods,
including wood for burning; that is the sacrifice to the Gods.

And the sacrifice to Brahman?
The sacrifice to Brahman consists of sacred study.

—The Vedas

If it is difficult for us to understand the
primitive belief in the efficacy of symbolic rites,
it is largely because of our limited knowledge
of the prolongations of the personality,
which forces us to think in terms of a purely physical causality.
We overlook that while we may believe that the anticipatory rite

has no physical effect in the desired direction,
the rite itself is the formal expression of a will directed to this end,
and that this will, released by the performance of the rite,
is also an effective force, by which the environment in its totality
must be to some extent affected.

—A. K. Coomaraswamy

Just as order is established in the cosmos by the powers created in sacrifice of the cosmic man, so order in society is created and maintained by the power of individuals' and priests' sacrifice and ritual. This takes many forms, as said in the first epigraph. The power of ritual is more than the projection of individual will (*pace* Coomaraswamy in the second epigraph). It is a vehicle of communication between the levels—human, divine, and cosmic. Chapter Two begins with a story that explores this theme. "Agni, God of Fire" is interesting for the relationships among demon, sage, god, and Brahma, the great God of Creation. Agni, whose power is limited in a way that humans can relate to, is bound by his vow of truth to reveal to the demon the identity of the beautiful woman the demon desires. The result is disaster. Agni—a god!—is cursed by the woman's father, a great sage, for his indiscriminate adherence to truth. The blessing by which the great god Brahma redeems him transposes his lack of discrimination to the indiscriminate power of fire to purify everything he—it—touches. The result is that ordinary life can resume for humankind and sacrifices can be made to the gods. Order is restored.

In "Threshold of Chastity," Devdutt Pattanaik explores the role of ritual in maintaining the social boundaries of the household through retelling the story from the epic *Ramayana* of Sita, the long-suffering wife of Rama, that paragon of virtue. It suggests the ways that ritual boundaries are believed to shape and reinforce good character.

The discipline of ritual is also a basic element in the creative process, as will be seen in selections in Chapter Four, "Teachers," and Chapter Seven, "Meditation and Yogic Discipline." Here Stella Kramrisch introduces this theme briefly in "Craftsman."

How ritual and story come together in the creation of sacred space and time is narrated in "The Birth of a Shrine" by Shrivatsa Goswami and Margaret Case. The god Krishna is believed to have manifested very recently—in a form made appropriate by story—in Vrindaban, a major pilgrimage center, in the context of a week-long ritual. As a result, a shrine was built, and it became a new focus of devotion.

The rituals of death in the holy city of Banaras are described by Diana Eck in "The Last Sacrifice." Here again sacrifice marks a boundary between ordinary, ordered life and the unknown or uncontrolled—in this case death, or the beginning of a new life.

Parabola
Volume: 20.1
Earth, Air, Fire, Water

Agni, God of Fire

Retold by D. K. M. Kartha

Puloma, beloved wife of the great sage Bhrighu, once became pregnant. Beautiful to begin with, Puloma grew even more so through the sacred and mysterious transformations of pregnancy.

One day, when Bhrighu was away, an unannounced visitor arrived. His name was Puloman, and he was a Rakshasa, a powerful demonic being. A guest, though, is still a guest, whatever his nature, and so Puloma welcomed him, giving him a seat of honor near the ever-burning fire in the sacrificial pit. One after another, she performed the prescribed rites of hospitality. But when Puloma was at the back of the hermitage, the demon addressed Agni, the god of fire eternally present in the pit.

"Agni, isn't my hostess Puloma?" he asked. "Isn't she the wife of the renowned sage Bhrighu? Curiosity is consuming me—tell me! I was once about to take her as my wife, but she was married off to Bhrighu. I am still enamored of her; she still kindles my desire. Isn't she Puloma? Tell me the truth!"

Agni, who witnesses every event in the world through his triple eyes—sun, moon, and lighted fires and lamps— was bound by the vow of truth. How can the truest of witnesses lie, even if the question is posed by a demon with evil intent? So Agni disclosed to Puloman who his hostess was.

Fires of lust erupting inside him, Puloman grabbed the pregnant Puloma and in the form of a wild boar began to carry her away. Hearing his mother's terrified screams, the spiritually potent baby inside her pushed himself out and was suddenly born. With righteous anger blazing in his heart, the newborn opened his eyes and cast a burning glance at the fleeing demon. Puloman was instantly turned into a heap of ashes.

Puloma limped back to the hermitage crying and carrying her miraculously born son. When Bhrighu returned, she told him how Agni had identified her to the Rakshasa, and a flame of rage leaped up into Bhrighu's voice as he cursed the god of fire: "In your blind allegiance to truth, you indiscriminately told truth to a demon. In retaliation, I curse you to become indiscriminate in your consumption. May you consume everything, even the rotting or rotten, the tasteless or revolting, the polluted or long dead!"

The curse was hurtful, and Agni said, "Your curse is unjust, great Bhrighu, because you fault me for telling the truth. Out of respect for your spiritual status, I will not curse you in return. But remember that I am the mouth of the gods, because it is into me that their devotees pour sacrificial objects. Remember that I am present in all beings—I support life through digestion and other indispensable processes. I will disappear now, and refrain from my functions until I am redeemed from your curse."

When Agni disappeared, his sorrow shrouded the created world in freezing darkness. Sacrifices could not be performed. Lamps remained full of oil and wick, but incapable of burning, and hearths choked with fuel yearned for life-giving flames. The worlds were beginning to die, and the divinities became weak. In terror, the gods evoked Brahma, the great God of Creation, and asked for his help. Moved by compassion for his creatures, Brahma summoned Agni.

"O Agni!" he said. "I redeem you from Bhrighu's curse by giving you a blessing. Though you will still be indiscriminately all-consuming, you will always remain pure, and your very touch will purify everything that you consume, however polluted it may be. May you burn all impurities in the world into ashes, the purest substance imaginable! May you become the greatest purifier of all! Now go back into creatures and light the fires within them. Go back into the sacrificial pit and receive gifts meant for the gods. Go back redeemed!"

Agni bowed his head in respectful obedience to Brahma. His heart gladdened by his redemption, he reappeared in all the worlds as the all-consuming, all-purifying element of Fire.

Parabola
Volume: 25.1
Threshold

Threshold of Chastity

Devdutt Pattanaik

She was told not to cross the threshold of her husband's house. She stepped out, nevertheless, and ended up being rejected by society. The story of Sita's rejection forms the controversial conclusion of the much-revered Hindu epic *Ramayana* (so much so that a few versions of the narrative edit out the episode altogether). At the heart of the plot is the concept of *Laxmana-rekha*, the line that must not be crossed, the line that circumscribes Hindu ideas of duty, decorum, chastity, and civilization.

The *Ramayana* is an extremely popular epic that encapsulates values most Hindus hold dear. First written in Sanskrit almost two thousand years ago, it has since been adapted and translated into over three hundred languages and dialects by bards and minstrels who have taken the tale to every hamlet in India, allowing it to inspire beliefs, customs, rituals, art, music, theater, and dance.

Rama, the protagonist, is the noble prince of Ayodhya who sacrifices personal happiness to perform deeds that are expected of him as a son, husband, and king. His selfless deference to social obligations transforms him into a manifestation of the divine. He attains the status of *maryada purushottam*, exemplar of rectitude, an incarnation of Vishnu, the god who establishes and maintains cosmic order.

On the eve of Rama's coronation, his father Dasharatha—who plans to retire into the forest—is summoned into the chambers of his junior queen Kaikeyi. She demands the two boons he had promised her long ago, on the day she had saved his life in battle: "Tell Rama to live in the forest as a hermit for fourteen years and crown my son Bharata king in his place." Bound by his word, Dasharatha orders Rama to abandon his crown, wear clothes of bark, and leave Ayodhya. Rama obeys without remorse or resentment. Neither the arguments of ministers nor the pleas of his people make him question his father's decision.

Rama's wife Sita follows him into the forest because as a wife she is duty-bound to share her husband's fate. Rama's younger brother Laxmana also joins him, as the two have never parted company. For years, the trio endures the harsh wilderness—the unrelenting weather, the hostile tribes.

In the fourteenth year of their exile, Sita sees a golden antelope and asks her husband to catch it. Rama runs after the antelope, leaving Laxmana behind to watch over the hermitage. Hours pass. There is no sign of Rama or the antelope. Afraid that a mishap might have befallen her husband, Sita forces Laxmana to go and look for him. Before setting out, Laxmana traces a line—the *Laxmana-rekha*—around the hermitage with an arrowhead. He warns Sita never to cross the line or let anyone in.

No sooner does Laxmana leave than a mendicant comes to the hermitage and asks Sita for food. Sita does not invite him in. Instead, she stretches out her hand and offers him some fruits, taking care not to cross the line traced by her brother-in-law. Her behavior angers the mendicant and he chides her for her rudeness. Ashamed, Sita crosses Laxmana's line and places the fruits in the mendicant's hand. To her horror, she discovers that the mendicant is no holy man; he is Ravana, king of the Rakshasas. Ravana grabs hold of Sita and carries her off to his island kingdom of Lanka, determined to make her his queen.

The narrative proceeds to describe how Rama raises an army of monkeys, launches an attack on Lanka, kills Ravana, and rescues Sita. The story, however, does not end here. Before accepting Sita, Rama orders that she prove her chastity. Sita goes through a trial by fire. The flames do not touch her. She is deemed pure. Still, when Rama returns to Ayodhya, his subjects refuse to accept her as their queen. How can a woman who has lived under another man's roof sit beside him, they ask Rama. It stains his family name, they tell him. To uphold family honor, Rama is obliged to abandon Sita. He sends her back to the lawless wilderness that lies across the threshold of his kingdom.

Had Sita not crossed Laxmana's line, she would not have been abducted by Ravana and her reputation as a chaste wife would have remained intact. This message is driven home every time the *Ramayana* is narrated in Hindu households. All girls are warned never to cross the Laxmana-rekha that has come to represent the threshold of social propriety for women in Hindu society. Stepping out brings dishonor, shame, and ultimately leads to social ostracization.

Laxmana's line circumscribes all that is culturally acceptable. It keeps out that aspect of Nature that is undesirable within society. It is the line of *dharma*, the law that ensures social stability. In a patriarchal world, the law upholds what men, not women, consider proper. Dharma is different from *ritu*, natural law of seasons. Dharma changes with time and space. Ritu does not. Social law discriminates between man, woman, and animal; natural law does not.

Seen symbolically, the *Ramayana* is a conflict between Nature and culture. Laxmana's line separates civilization from the wilderness. Within the line, there is society. Without, there is the jungle. Within, the rule of man tames the animal urges. Without, the beast is unbridled. Within, the strong have duties and the weak have rights. Without, there is no right or duty; only the fit survive. Within, the dignity of marriage is upheld. Without, fidelity holds no meaning. Within, earth is domesticated. Without, the earth is wild. Within, Sita is Rama's wife. Without, she is a woman for the taking.

Ravana—a learned man well-versed in the ways of culture—does not cross the threshold. He chooses to stay out of Rama's hermitage for he knows that within the island of civilization marked by Laxmana's line he is bound by ethics and morality. He tempts Sita to come out. Outside, she is at the mercy of the elements. Rama's rules hold no meaning, and Ravana can claim what he wants by force.

Earlier in the narrative, Ravana's sister Surpanakha solicits Rama and Laxmana. Both reject her amorous advances. Enraged, she behaves like a creature of the forest and tries to take what she wants by force. She tries to kill Sita hoping that with her out of the picture the brothers will look upon her more favorably. Laxmana stops her by cutting off her ears and nose (and the tips of her breasts, in some versions). Ravana decides to avenge his sister's humiliation by abducting Rama's wife. He uses guile, not force, to get what he wants. He sends a golden antelope to lure Rama and Laxmana away. But he is taken by surprise when Laxmana traces the perimeter of the hermitage and declares the space within as Rama's realm. Suddenly, the rules change. Ravana cannot force his way into the hermitage without breaking the code of civilized conduct. So he disguises himself as a mendicant and compels Sita into shedding the mantle of protection granted by Laxmana's line.

Thus, the narrative holds Sita responsible for her miserable fate. Yet, unlike the Biblical Eve, Sita has no choice. As the wife of a prince and the daughter-in-law of a royal and respected household, she is bound to feed every hungry person who comes to her doorstep. The rules of hospitality form part of the laws of civilization. She does not want to taint her husband's reputation or insult a guest. As the mendicant cannot enter her hermitage, on grounds that it is improper for him to enter her house while her husband is away, she is obliged to cross the line.

The main doorway of a Hindu house is the physical manifestation of Laxmana-rekha. In an orthodox setup, a woman is expected to remain within the doorway at all times. She may "cross the threshold" only twice in her life: once as a bride on the way to her husband's house and the second time as a corpse on her way to the crematorium. If she has to leave the house to visit relatives or to go to the village well, she has to be chaperoned. "Stepping out" for any other reason brings disgrace to the household. It indicates that the woman is of loose character and that the men of the household are incapable of taking care of her needs. It is even considered bad luck for a woman to stand on the threshold with a foot out. "Stepping out of the house" has over time become an inauspicious phrase. It is a phrase that until recently led to the internment of women in the inner courtyard, restricting their social growth and movement.

When a woman crosses the threshold and enters the house as a bride, conches are blown. The bride's feet are decorated with anklets and lined with red dye. In Maharasthra, a state in Western India, a jar of rice is placed on the threshold and the bride is told to kick it in. As the rice spills into the house, it is hoped that the incoming bride will usher in prosperity and fertility. "Stepping into the house" is an auspicious phrase that is pregnant with hope. Events that occur following the entry of the bride into the house decide her *pigoon* or "quality of her feet." If good things happen after her entry, she is seen as the harbinger of good fortune. If bad things happen, she is seen as the harbinger of bad fortune.

For centuries, the Hindu woman has been seen as a double of Laxmi, goddess of wealth and fortune. Her entry into the household is a much-desired event. It marks a turning point in the life of a man and his household. He ceases to be a *brahmachari*, a celibate student preparing to be a member of society. He transforms into a *grihasthi*, a householder who has to shoulder family and social responsibilities. With his bride by his side, he is allowed to perform sacred rituals. With her support, he can bring children to the world and keep the cosmic wheel of rebirth rotating, thereby fulfilling his obligation to his ancestors. The doorway of the house is the entrance into sacred space. Through it, with the bride, come the benevolent forces of the cosmos. The bride therefore is expected to stay within the house and make it fruitful. Should she leave, the benevolent cosmic forces leave with her and the household faces ruin.

Having entered the domestic sacred space, it is the duty of the Hindu bride to perform rituals that help harness benevolent energy from the environment. Special attention is paid to the doorway of the house. It is bedecked with charms, talismans, and sacred symbols to ward off negative energies and to attract positive ones.

The goddess Laxmi, dressed in red and seated on a lotus, represents Nature's positive energies. Wreaths of marigold flowers and mango leaves are tied to the doorsill, and colorful diagrams are painted in the front yard during festivals to attract her into the house. Her footprint, the *Laxmi-pada*, is commonly painted on the threshold using rice-flour paste. Care is taken to make sure that the footprint is painted pointing inward, for her entry brings good luck, while her departure heralds misfortune.

According to one story, a merchant had turned his house into a den of vices. The merchant's wife, Srimati, was a pious woman. One day, at dusk, Srimati noticed a strange but beautiful woman dressed in a red sari and holding a pot leaving the house. On inquiry, the stranger identified herself as Laxmi and said that she was leaving the house as the man of the house did not value her. Srimati tried hard but failed to make Laxmi change her mind. Finally, she said, "Please don't cross the threshold until I make you an offering of flowers." The goddess agreed and waited in the house while Srimati went into the garden to fetch flowers. In the garden was a well. The merchant's wife jumped into the well and killed herself. The goddess, who had promised not to leave until she had received Srimati's offering of flowers, was thus forced to stay in the house for all eternity.

In another story, Laxmi, the goddess of fortune, and her sister, Alaxmi, the goddess of misfortune, visited a shopkeeper and asked him who was more beautiful of the two. Knowing the consequences of angering either goddess, the shopkeeper said, "Laxmi is beautiful when she enters the shop and Alaxmi is beautiful when she leaves the shop." By this wise judgment, the shopkeeper ensured his prosperity.

To keep Alaxmi out, shopkeepers in the city of Mumbai tie lemons and green chilies to the doorsills of their shops. It is said that the goddess of misfortune likes sour and pungent food. When she finds it at the threshold, she turns around satiated without bothering to cast her malevolent eye into the shop.

In a traditional Hindu household, since women are confined to the house, the men have to cross the threshold repeatedly to bring home the abundance of Nature. Stepping out results in pollution; stepping in necessitates purification. Hence, every time a man is about to cross the threshold, either to enter or leave the house, the women of the household wave lamps around him. This ritual, the *aarti*, purges negative influences before a man enters the house and creates a protective shield around a man before he leaves the house.

The perimeter of a house, a temple, a village, a town, or a city has traditionally been seen as the fence between the sacred and the profane, the auspicious and the inauspicious, the wild and the tame. Beyond the picket fence of society lurk wild forces and dark spirits. In villages, idols of *viras*, or ancestral heroes, riding horses and brandishing swords, are placed on the edge of fields facing the forests to screen out hostile forces of Nature that cause disease and drought. In temples, idols of fanged and armed doorkeepers scare away the undesirable.

In the *Ramayana*, when Kaikeyi forces her husband to banish Rama, she sends him into the wild, profane, inauspicious, and inhospitable wilderness hoping that he will succumb to the malevolent forces there. What she does not realize is that while she can drive a man out of civilization, she cannot drive civilization out of a man. Wherever Rama goes he takes the law of man with him. The jungle does not make a savage out of him; he tames the wild.

When Rama comes upon Sugriva, a monkey driven out of orchards and deprived of his mate by the alpha male Vali, he raises his bow and becomes Sugriva's champion, refusing to accept the law of the jungle. He kills Vali, makes Sugriva king, and earns his friendship. Friendship—a relationship that forms the foundation of civilization—commits Sugriva to help Rama find his wife. In Sugriva's minister, the monkey-god Hanuman, who though animal adopts the greatest human discipline of celibacy, Hinduism finds its mightiest doorkeeper.

And yet this man who personifies civilization abandons his wife because his subjects consider her impure, unworthy of queenship. How does one reconcile Rama, rectitude personified, with Rama, the man who abandons his wife? This is and has been a contentious issue among Hindu intellectuals and feminists.

By abandoning Sita, Rama does what his patriarchal society expects of him. Is that just? That's a difficult question to answer, since justice is a social term and society with all its constituents is a cultural construction, not a natural phenomenon. What is just at one time and in one place may not be just at another time, in another place. The civilization-generating law of man, upheld by Rama, is based on discriminating between what a particular society deems to be fit and unfit, good and bad, right and wrong. Nature does not make such arbitrary distinctions—everything always has a place in the grand web of life. Rama's society is undoubtedly patriarchal, demanding fidelity to the point where even a woman who has casual contact with another man is deemed "unchaste." While no such demands are made of Rama, he insists on remaining "chaste." This is a significant point.

Even after abandoning Sita, Rama never remarries. In a polygynous society, his behavior is highly unusual, so unusual that Rama is the only character in sacred Hindu lore to have the distinction of being identified as *ekam-patni-vrata*, he-who-was-faithful-to-one-wife. Rama's father Dasharatha has three queens. But Rama chooses to be with only one. While he agrees to abandon the woman his people do not accept as their queen, he never rejects the woman who is his wife. To testify to his eternal fidelity, he performs his religious and stately duties by placing an effigy of Sita beside him. He uses gold, the metal of purity, to mold the image of the woman his subjects have declared unchaste. Years later, when Sita disappears into the earth, he refuses to carry on alone. He walks into a river and abandons his mortal body.

While there were laws preventing Rama from disobeying his father and from rejecting the will of his people, there was no law preventing Rama from taking another wife. By remarrying, Rama would have crossed no Laxmana-rekha. Rama's fidelity therefore goes beyond the call of dharma. It overcomes biological urges, withstands social pressures, and towers over patriarchal whims. It takes the threshold to its limit. In a society that thought less of women, this display of self-imposed chastity has made Rama, in the opinion of ancient and modern Hindu bards, the acme of civilization, worthy of worship.

Parabola
Volume: 16.3
Craft

Traditions of the Indian Craftsman

Stella Kramrisch

In many parts of India to this day, the craftsmen worship their tools at the Daśhahara festival on the day of Viśvakarmā Pūjā. From the day of the Sūtras, both the materials and the tools of a craft are known to be sacred, for they are the seat of particular powers. The tree which is to be felled by the carpenter or sculptor is propitiated with offerings; he lays his hand on it with a mantra, asking pardon of the spirits residing in the tree. The axe which is to fell the tree is anointed with honey and butter so that the tree is not hurt when the transformation is begun by the craftsman by which a shape of nature becomes a work of art.

Before a craftsman takes up his tools for any particular assignment, the axe, the line, the hammer, and all the other instruments are worshiped with incense, flowers and unhusked rice, for they are that extension of the craftsman's hand through which he reaches beyond the ranges of his limited human person. All the work is done in a secluded place, with self-control and concentration. The bricks being invoked as goddesses, the material itself is deified prior to the consecration of the building.

This is a short extract from "Traditions of the Indian Craftsman," in *Traditional India: Structure and Change*, edited by Milton Singer (Philadelphia: American Folklore Society, 1959), p. 20.

Parabola
Volume: 18.2
Place and Space

THE BIRTH OF A SHRINE

Shrivatsa Goswami and Margaret H. Case

Some seventy-five miles south of Delhi, as the Yamuna River flows south from the foothills of the Himalayas and just before it passes the ancient and holy city of Mathura, it makes a loop to the east. This loop encircles the temple town of Vrindaban, where residents and pilgrims alike believe the god Krishna lived and played as a boy.

On the north side of Vrindaban, there is a stretch of the riverbank that is particularly rich with stories about Krishna. Here, in November 1992, a gathering of his devotees witnessed his appearance in the form of a *bhramara*—a large insect resembling a bumblebee—on three separate evenings. The event was unanticipated, and yet painstakingly prepared for. It occurred at a conjunction of time and space in the spiral of remembered history; and it appeared as an opening to a different dimension made possible by the attentive efforts of the devotees.

There were many layers to the event that contributed to the richness of its meaning: the feelings evoked by remembering the life of Krishna, said to have lived here some 5,000 years ago—and to be living here still; the places associated with the sixteenth-century saint, Sri Caitanya Mahaprabhu; the buildings erected here in the early eighteenth-century by the chief lieutenant of the last great Mughal emperor; and the preparations made by the present generation to express their devotion to Krishna.

This god, with skin the color of blue-gray storm clouds, had spent his childhood and adolescence in Vrindaban, on the pastoral shores of the Yamuna River. There he faced and defeated demons, played pranks on the women of the countryside, and, when he was older, enjoyed all the moods of love with the beautiful Radha. One of his most famous pranks was to tease a group of cowherd women who had left their clothes on the bank of the Yamuna while they bathed. While they were in the water, Krishna stole their clothes and hung them in the branches of a *kadamba* tree on the riverbank. The young women pleaded with Krishna to give them back their clothes, but he refused to do so until they came out of the river and faced him in their nakedness. Once they had dropped their veils before the divine presence, it is said, Krishna promised them that for the first time they could join him in the great circle dance of union.

In time Krishna had to leave the scenes of his happy youth, and assume his rightful place in the royal house of Mathura. He left behind Radha and her friends, who were inconsolable. One day as the women were sitting on the banks of the Yamuna, at the spot where Krishna had come ashore for his nocturnal trysts with Radha, Krishna's trusted friend Uddhava arrived from Mathura to comfort them. He told them that Krishna, the fundamental essence of everything in the world, could in no way be separated from them, so why should they grieve?

In reply, the women spoke eloquently of their love for Krishna, of their delight in caring for him, serving him, and embracing him. So great was their feeling that Uddhava was convinced that devotion like theirs was a more direct path to realization of Krishna than all the knowledge and ritual practice he had assiduously cultivated. Overcome, he was about to prostrate himself before them and touch Radha's feet in devotion. Just then, a bhramara landed on the ground near Radha's feet. But Radha pulled back saying, "Go away! You are like the fraud and cheat who has left us—you are dark, like him, and draped in yellow. You are fickle, like him, and flirt with one flower after another. Your moustaches, like his clothes, are yellow with the pollen of garlands pressed to the breasts of the women at the court of Mathura. Go away!" Some say that the bhramara was the embodiment of Uddhava's new-found devotion, others that it was Krishna himself, who could not bear the separation from his beloved Radha.

The places where these events occurred are known to the followers of Krishna. The kadamba tree, the landings where Radha and Krishna met for their nightly trysts, and the riverbank where Uddhava came to comfort Radha and the cowherd women are all within a few hundred feet of each other. In 1515 CE, when the area around what is today Vrindaban was still an uninhabited forest, the Bengali saint Caitanya came here to identify the sites. He used to sit in meditation near the same long-lived kadamba tree under which the cowherd women had emerged without their clothes, and pray that he, too, would lose the veils before his eyes. In a state of ecstasy, he became aware of the location of many of the sacred sites, and other holy men associated with him identified additional ones.

When Caitanya left Vrindaban, he charged his most able follows, the Six Goswamis, to establish Vrindaban as a pilgrimage center where reenactments of the pastimes of Radha, Krishna, and their companions could by enjoyed by devotees.

About two hundred years later, Raja Sawai Jai Singh of Amber, the most powerful minister of the Mughal emperor Aurangzeb and a devout worshipper of Radha and Krishna, established a retreat for himself in Vrindaban. The two-and-a-half acre site he chose was a stretch of riverbank just downstream from the kadamba tree, which included Radha's and Krishna's landing places and the place where Caitanya used to sit. There he constructed a house for himself; a pavilion on the riverfront, marking the place where Caitanya had sat; behind it, a shrine to Caitanya and two of his close companions: *ghats* or steps leading down to the river at Krishna's and Radha's landing places; and a temple for his personal deity. Jai Singh also built a large platform next to his house, for the performance of *rasa lilas*, musical dance dramas depicting the pastimes of Krishna and his companions.

This compound came to be known as Jaisingh Ghera, and today the kadamba tree and all the buildings are still standing. It was here that Jai Singh drew up the plans for the pink city of Jaipur. After his death, Jaisingh Ghera remained in the hands of the rajas of Amber and Jaipur, and after Independence it passed under the control of the state government of Rajasthan.

In 1962 Jaisingh Ghera was purchased by the foremost leader of the

Caitanyite branch of Krishna worship, Parampujya Jagadguru Sri Purushottam Goswami ji Maharaj, known to his followers as Maharaj-ji. He
is a direct descendent of one of the followers of the Six Goswamis. An
energetic leader, he, his family, and followers have established a thriv-
ing spiritual and cultural center at Jaisingh Ghera. The center patronizes
music and the arts, scholarship on Vrindaban as well as on the spiritual
traditions of those who worship Krishna, and supports the rasa lilas
with their associated arts. A building to house these activities was built,
encompassing Jai Singh's residence, as well as a performance hall on the
site of the old rasa lila platform.

Part of the property along the river had been leased to a small school
by the Rajasthani government, and for thirty years this area could not
be used by the Goswamis. In the late summer of 1992, the school was
vacated, and Jaisingh Ghera was once again nearly complete, lacking only
the temple in the center of the compound. This remained in the hands of
the Rajasthan government, which is not permitted to sell temples.

At this time, Maharaj-ji decided to organize an *astayama* lila—the
eternal lila—eight successive daily performances depicting the twenty-
four hours in the life of Radha and Krishna, three hours at a time.
Throughout the summer both the site and the event were prepared. Work
was begun to excavate the ghats and restore the existing structures. Mean-
while Maharaj-ji wrote scripts and devotional songs for the lila, based
on the sixteenth-century Sanskrit text of the *Govindalilamrtam*, which
in twenty-three chapters describes the divine day in detail. Maharaj-ji's
family and followers created sumptuous costumes in brilliantly colored
silks and gold cloth, stage hangings of rich velvets, settings of forest groves
and bowers, thrones of red, peacock blue, and gold fabrics, and lighting to
highlight the dramas being enacted on the stage. In September, rehearsals
began for the troupe of boys and men who play all the parts.

His devotees believe that Krishna still lives in Vrindaban and the land
around it, and that he and Radha play there still. Before the lila could
begin, it was necessary to invoke these eternal performers, to bring the
space and the time to life. Beginning on the morning of October 31, for
twenty-four hours, a relay team of sadhus recited the *mahamantra*: "Hare
Krishna, Hare Krishna, Krishna, Krishna, Hare, Hare, Hare Rama, Hare
Rama, Rama, Rama, Hare, Hare," marking out time and space with the

name of the divinity.[1] In addition, the 350 chapters of the *Bhagavata Purana*—the basic sacred text for devotees of Krishna—were read in one day by fourteen scholars, each one reading twenty-five chapters. The sound of the chanting transformed time and place. Within this setting, Maharaj-ji performed *puja* (worship) at Krishna's ghat, which was also the place where the bhramara had appeared to Uddhava and Radha. Then he led the way to Radha's ghat, a place of particularly intense feeling for Maharaj-ji, since he had twice had a vision of Radha there. There he performed a puja a second time. That evening, Krishna was evoked again in the performance hall by the great dancer Birju Maharaj, whose choreography for the occasion was based on the text of the *Govindalilamrtam*.

The next day was devoted to intense preparation, particularly blessings by the various groups of the brahmins of Vrindaban. During the morning and afternoon, five groups of thirty-one brahmins came to be honored by Maharaj-ji: ritual priests, scholars of the *Bhagavata Purana*, secular scholars and teachers, pilgrim guides, and the men and boys who would be performing the rasa lila. Each spoke briefly about the place and its significance.

These ceremonies all took place under a large tent which covered the site of Radha's and Krishna's trysts, right behind Krishna's ghat. On the rear wall of the tent was a large painted hanging that had been created especially for the occasion. It depicted Radha and her companions under a tree, looking at a large bhramara at Radha's feet.

After all the brahmins had spoken, Maharaj-ji asked one of his followers to speak. Just as she finished her invocation, a large black insect, about two inches long and looking very much like the bhramara in the painting, flew into the tent from the direction of the river, and landed on the ground in front of her. Astounded, those devotees who were close enough to see rose to their feet, exclaiming "Jai ho!" and "Jai Sri Radhe!" The visitor danced on the ground and flew up to dance in the air, alighting two or three more times. After less than a minute, it flew off again in the direction from which it had first come. Maharaji-ji spoke, saying that the divine spirit can take any form, and for those who could see with devotion and love, it was Krishna's presence that had become visible. He declared that a beautiful bower should be created to commemorate this manifestation.

Among the devotees who had gathered in Jaisingh Ghera for the astayama lila, the general reaction that evening and the next day was happiness (but not complete acceptance) that a real miracle had occurred. A wonderful, unusual event, yes—the appearance of this bhramara with such perfect timing—but to fully absorb and accept that this was a manifestation of divinity was difficult. Trying to help his followers absorb what had happened, Maharaj-ji told the devotees that four factors contributed to this miracle: first, this was the site of the original bhramara's appearance; second, that the deity was summoned by the devotion of the people gathered there; third, this was the site of the eternal astayama lila; and fourth, the day of the bhramara's appearance had been spent in concentrated spiritual activity by the one hundred fifty-five brahmins, which had compelled it to appear.

At 3:36 AM on November 2, the astayama lila began in the great hall, watched by a packed house of about 1,500 enthusiastic devotees of Krishna. At 6:00 AM on November 3, the second lila began. Since this was a day in the lunar ritual calendar which is considered to be a time when any action taken would not decay, Maharaj-ji decided to consecrate the site of the bower that evening. An octagonal platform was prepared from the sand of the Yamuna River and decorated with small statues of Radha's companions, as well as flowers, banana wood carvings, and auspicious patterns drawn with colored powders. In the center was an eight-petaled lotus made of banana wood. To dedicate a shrine to a deity, an image is needed, so a photograph of the bhramara taken at its first appearance was placed in a silver frame, and kept to one side until needed by the priest. During the first part of the ritual, all went as planned. But then, just at the moment when the priest asked for the photograph of the bhramara to be placed on the platform, the bhramara itself was sighted. It flew in again from the north and landed on the ground next to the octagonal platform, opposite the priests. A devotee picked it up carefully on a leaf and placed it on the platform, where it walked directly to the central lotus and installed itself underneath the flower. There it stayed quietly throughout the rest of the ceremony.

Pandemonium broke out. This time everyone saw the bhramara and began shouting and pushing to come closer. Transforming the bedlam into celebration, Maharaj-ji led the chanting devotees in several circumambulations of the platform. Throughout all this, a brahmin sat quietly a few yards from the platform, continuing to read the chapters of the *Bhagavata Purana*. After things had quieted down, the consecration ceremony continued, and throughout that evening and the next day there grew among the devotees an appreciation of the significance of the bhramara's perfectly timed appearance and precisely appropriate behavior. Maharaj-ji announced that he was now determined to restore the riverfront to its original glory, as described in the *Govindalilamrtam* and planned and built by Raja Jai Singh. He also vowed never again to go outside the boundaries of Vrindaban, and that the reading of the *Bhagavata Purana* would continue for perpetuity.

The bhramara made a third appearance two nights later. This was the night in the ritual calendar when the gods are awakened from a four-month sleep, and the auspicious season begins for marriages and other rituals. Evening pujas were held in the temple and the Goswami household, and for the first time since its consecration, the new shrine was used as a ritual site. This time there was no image on the platform—the site itself was the sacred object of worship. Puja was performed: oblations of milk, honey, yogurt, *ghee*, and sugar were poured into the sand of the platform during the chanting of mantras. Then as devotional songs were being sung, the bhramara flew in. This time it stayed behind the small gathering, landing on the rug and rising repeatedly to dance and swoop in the air, with every appearance of pure happiness. There was little commotion this time—the miracle had been accepted, the manifestation of divinity was acknowledged.

A sacred space is a place where two worlds intersect. At Jaisingh Ghera, time measured in centuries (Krishna's boyhood, Caitanya's ecstatic discoveries, Jaisingh's building) came together under Maharaj-ji's direction with time measured in hours and minutes (depictions of the daily activities of Krishna, regular recitation of sacred text, and the offerings of music and song that defined and filled the space). In the moment when these two came together, the concentrated devotion of a holy man and those who looked to him for teaching had evoked the manifestation of divinity. Time and space had danced together like the flight of the bhramara. What had been and what eternally is came together to create a new beginning.

Note:

1   Hare is the vocative of Hara, which means "one who steals the heart" of Krishna—that is to say, Radha. "Hare Krishna" thus means "Radha Krishna." Rama comes from the Sanskrit root meaning "to dally, go around with, keep company with" Radha, so "Hare Rama" again invokes the names of Radha and Krishna.

Parabola
Volume: 20.1
Earth, Air, Fire, Water

THE LAST SACRIFICE

Diana L. Eck

At Manikarnika cremation ground, there is a sacred fire which is said to have burned constantly for as long as anyone can remember. It is kept by the Doms, the untouchable caste that cares for the cremation ground and tends the pyres. With the flame of this sacred fire, the cremation pyres are lighted, although some groups of mourners may bring embers from home.

The cremation rite is called the "last sacrifice"—*antye-shti*. The rite is, indeed, a sacrifice, having a certain structural continuity with all fire sacrifices in India, from the most complex to the most simple. What is prepared, ornamented, and offered into the fire is, in this case, the deceased. When the body arrives at the cremation ground, after the chanting procession through the lanes of Banaras, it is given a final dip in the River Ganges. It is sprinkled with the oil of sandalwood and decked with garlands of flowers. The deceased is honored as would befit a god.

The word for a dead body is *shava*, and Hindus have often underlined the phonetic relation between shava and Shiva. The identification of the dead with Shiva is suggested by the brahmins in their *mahatmyas* of Kashi. In the great cremation ground, they say, the dead receive the form and emblems of Shiva. They become three-eyed, wearing the crescent moon in their hair, carrying the trident. Little cares Shiva for the pollution usually associated with death, and here in Kashi he takes up his post on the cremation ground and transforms the dead into his very likeness. In the fire of the "last sacrifice," the shava is a holy offering indeed.

It is the chief mourner, usually the eldest son, who takes the twigs of holy *kusha* grass, flaming, from the Doms' eternal fire to the pyre upon which the dead has been laid. He circumambulates the pyre counterclockwise—for everything is backward at the time of death. As he walks round the pyre, his sacred thread, which usually hangs from the left shoulder, has been reversed to hang from the right. He lights the pyre. The dead, now, is an offering to Agni, the fire. Here, as in the most ancient Vedic times, the fire conveys the offering to heaven.

After the corpse is almost completely burned, the chief mourner performs a rite called *kapalakriya*, the "rite of the skull," cracking the skull with a long bamboo stick, thus releasing the soul from entrapment in the body. Now, truly, nothing but ash remains. The chief mourner takes a large clay pot of Ganges water, throws it backward over his left shoulder upon the dying embers, and walks away without looking back. "These living have turned back, separated from the dead," they say; "this day our invocation of the gods became auspicious. We then went forward for dancing, for laughter, firmly establishing our long life." The members of the funeral party do not grieve openly, for it is said that many tears pain the dead.

The rites for the dead that follow the cremation last for eleven days and consist of daily offerings of rice balls, called *pindas*, which provide a symbolic, transitional body for the dead. During these days, the dead person makes the journey to the heavens, or the world of the ancestors, or the "far shore." As a whole, these rites are called *shraddha*, or *pindadana*, the "offering of pindas." The rites also include the providing of feasts for a group of brahmins, who take nourishment on behalf of the dead. On the twelfth day, the departed soul is said to reach its destination and be joined with its ancestors, a fact expressed symbolically by joining a small pinda with a much larger one.

Death is dangerous because it is a time of transition. It is a liminal or marginal time, a space between life and life. In this transitional period, the soul is called a *preta*, literally one who has "gone forth" from the body but has not yet arrived at its new destination. The rites following the cremation enable the preta to become a *pitri*, an ancestor, or more precisely, a "father." Without such rites, one might remain a homeless preta for a long time. For those who are very great sinners or who have died hideous deaths, this transition from life to new life might be obstructed by becoming a *pishacha*.

But death is not only a time of danger, for it is also held to be a time of great illumination. At death, they say, the light is very intense, and what separates this shore from the far shore is almost transparent. The time of death, therefore, is a time of clear seeing, of vision, of insight. One's thoughts are to be on God at such a time, for what one thinks and sees at the time of death directs one's first steps toward the next life. Those close to the dying should whisper the name of God in that person's ear. While death may be the final event in one life, it is also, in a sense, the first event in the life beyond. For Hindus, death is not the opposite of life; it is, rather, the opposite of birth. The great transition which death occasions is not from life to death, but from life to life.

•

CHAPTER THREE

THE DISRUPTION OF ORDER: MAYA AND PLAY

Maya's the super swindler.
Trailing the noose of three qualities,
she wanders, whispering
honeyed words.
For Vishnu she's Lakshmi,
for Shiva she's Shakti,
for priests an idol,
for pilgrims a river.
To a monk she's a nun,
to a king she's a queen
in one house a jewel,
in one a shell.
For devotees she's a pious lady,
for Brahma, Mrs. Brahma.
Kabir says, seekers,
listen well:
this is a story
no one can tell.

—Kabir

The snake itself is not affected by the poison in its fangs,
but when it bites, the poison kills the creature bitten.
Likewise Maya is in the Lord but does not affect Him,
while the same Maya deludes the whole world.

—Sri Ramakrishna

Two aspects of the disruption of order—evil and creativity—are addressed in this chapter. Evil clearly disrupts order. But so do playfulness and creativity.

One strand of Hindu thought that is well known in the West is the perception that the ordinary world as we know it is illusory, hidden behind the veil of maya. Maya is the trickster function in Hindu thought—the power of the gods to create the world and to hide the truth behind its phenomena.

One important strand of Hindu thinking emphasizes that multiplicity (not to mention duality) is a delusion, the result of ignorance, and that to perceive the singular reality behind all the forms one must become detached from one's ordinary experiences. These themes are elaborated in Eknath Easwaran's "Three in One: Spirit, Matter, and Maya," where he remarks that maya "denotes the central mystery of life: how each of us, pure, eternal spirit in our essence, has come to think of himself or herself as a puny, limited, physical creature." The implication is that the limitations of human consciousness and the operations of the deities' maya are codependent causes of a miserable world. In "What Is Evil?" Christopher Isherwood and Swami Prabhavananda also take this point of view, though they claim that there is both a good and a bad kind of maya, one leading to evil actions, one to good actions that can bring one to a higher consciousness.

There is a vast body of Hindu lore, however, that does not consider the world a place of misery, but exuberantly embraces the multifarious connections between various levels of experience—not claiming that all experience is of equal value to the seeker after truth, but not denying the reality or importance of any of it for mankind as we are. Similarly, on the cosmic level maya is seen positively, as the creative power of the deity (which one depends on one's choice). This is the power that permits the gods to play and to create the conditions under which individuals, including sages and lesser gods, can come to understand reality. In "Magical Wars and Spirited Debates: Divine Play in Ancient India," Stuart Smithers opens up a view of maya as the life force itself, saying that the popular understanding of it as illusion is partial and misleading. Maya, the impulse of play, "is at the heart of the transformation of energies and forces. Play subverts boundaries and opens us … to a wider field of experience and phenomena." But the secret of maya itself, says the god

Vishnu in "The Fabric of Life," remains mysterious—"inscrutable and not to be known." And Vishnu is not the only god whose maya creates the world as we know it. "Indra Gets Caught" has Brahma teaching the god Indra about the power of his maya.

The gods' power of play may create our world, but play, as suggested by Lee Siegel in "The Laughter of the Weaver," may also be a surer path for individuals to holy knowledge than the ways of "the more sensible, judicious, or certain." Uncertainty, not security, leads to wisdom.

Parabola
Volume: 14.4
Triad

Three in One:
Spirit, Matter, and Maya

Eknath Easwaran

India's ancient scriptures tell of a king's son kidnapped by a gang of highwaymen when still quite small. The boy grows up among this rough crew as he might have in Sherwood Forest. He forgets about the lap of luxury, about palaces and culture, even about his mother and father. Instead of kingship, he learns the arts of banditry: how to master the bow and arrow, to travel through the forest without a sound, to pounce on passersby and disappear without being caught. By the time he is twenty, he commands a band of robbers of his own. Yet he remains a loner, different from the rest. In his heart, he senses that the forest is not where he belongs. But he knows nowhere else to go.

This story illustrates our human predicament. From birth, we too feel isolated and out of place in a world we don't quite fit. In "Animula," T. S. Eliot takes a cue from Augustine to evoke the soul's first encounter with this baffling realm of duality:

> *"Issues from the hand of God, the simple soul"*
> *To a flat world of changing lights and noise,*
> *To light, dark, dry or damp, chilly or warm.*

We look out and contemplate the endless sky, the stars; we sense the vastness of the universe outside us; and we become aware that we too are a kind of island universe, with a world inside us which no one really knows. As we grow up, we see that no one ever can know this secret self; it eludes our own understanding. So we feel doubly alone; and in this isolation from the rest of life, buffeted by forces within and without that we can neither fathom nor control, even the most sophisticated of us may sometimes feel like exclaiming, as Tennyson does in "In Memoriam":

> *But what am I?*
> *An infant crying in the night:*
> *An infant crying for the light:*
> *And with no language but a cry.*

In Indian philosophy, this primal sense of separateness—of a self set apart from everything else that is not-self—of a self set apart from everything else that is not-self—is the root of all the dualities that life holds out for us. It is by being able to make this distinction that we make the other distinctions which give order to sensory experience: light and dark, pleasant and unpleasant, winning and losing, life and death.

But as we go on making distinctions, they become finer—and paradoxically, less clear. Black and white become shades of gray until life becomes an oppressive tangle. So Eliot continues:

> *The heavy burden of the growing soul*
> *Perplexes and offends more, day by day;*
> *Week by week, offends and perplexes more*
> *With the imperatives of 'is' and 'seems'*
> *And may and may not, desire and control.*

Nowhere is this tension more pervasive than in the stubborn experiment that characterizes our species: to isolate happiness from life's rough mixture of pleasure and pain. In history and literature we read of those who tried and failed. And in religion and philosophy we are told consistently that they had to fail, because pain is woven together with pleasure into the very fabric of life. To ask for joy without sorrow is like wanting fire that cannot burn.

Yet we still try. Despite the unanimity of human experience, something in us insists that we dedicate our lives to this quixotic experiment. We know that no one has ever isolated pleasure, but perhaps we will be the first. We know that all who live must die, but in our hearts we believe it won't really happen to us. Like the prince who grows up a highwayman, we keep feeling that something at the core of our lives is radically wrong. In the midst of change, we yearn for something permanent and whole. The tighter the world of duality binds us, the more we struggle to break free.

Are we wrong in this stubborn refusal to face life as it is? Yes, the mystics tell us unanimously: yes, and no. Duality is the nature of life; to deny it is absurd. But our yearning for oneness is rooted in an even deeper reality. As human beings, we have access to a realm of awareness in which life is undivided and whole—and not some other life, but this one here and now.

How can this be? Because, the world's sacred traditions explain, the division we feel as "self" versus "not-self" is a misreading of experience. Life *is* trying to tell us something, but we don't understand the language. The real duality is not "I" as opposed to the rest of the universe, but spirit as distinct from matter.

In Hindu mysticism, these two are called *prakriti* and *purusha*. Prakriti is the phenomenal world, everything that is subject to change—not only material objects but energy too, as well as the fabric of space and time. And purusha is spirit, pure consciousness: *atman*, our real Self. But this Self is an entirely different order of being from any of our emotions or mental states. Everything that changes, even the mind, is part of the created world, part of prakriti. So what we call mind in English is not really conscious—not really our self. It is an instrument of consciousness, a field of forces used by the Self very much the way the body is used as an instrument of action.

Unconscious matter and Conscious spirit, body and Self: two utterly unlike levels of reality. These are the poles of human experience, felt in every moment of our lives.

Many philosophies, of course, oppose spirit and matter. But Hindu mysticism is unique in insisting that these two elements are not enough to explain the baffling tension between spirit and matter in our lives. The human drama needs a third member in the cast: and that third is the confusion of the other two, the mix-up of their roles.

This element is called *maya*, and it denotes the central mystery of life: how each of us, pure, eternal spirit in our essence, has come to think of himself or herself as a puny, limited, physical creature "that struts and frets his hour upon the stage and then is heard no more."

Maya is often translated as "illusion," but that is misleading. Maya is the illusion of separateness, the hallucination that I am separate from the rest of life and that the source of meaning and fulfillment lies "out there." Like trick glasses that we cannot take off, maya stands between knower and known, so that when we look at the seamless whole that is life, we see it fractured into countless separate things.

Why can we not ordinarily take these glasses off? Because they are the very structure of perception: in fact, they are the structure of the mind. Once that first division between "I" and "not-I" is made, we see duality everywhere we look. Only when the mind is stilled in meditation does the illusion of separateness fall away, and we see that life is one.

At first, calling spirit, matter, and their relationship a triad seems a categorical mistake, like lumping together an orange, an apple, and roundness. But maya is as real as matter. Like a scientist's theory, the concept of maya explains an experiential observation, the central paradox of mystical experience. In the unitive state, life is seen to be one; outside that state, it is infinitely diverse. How can the same world be both? Because of this third element, the structure of the perceiving mind. It is the distorting lens of maya that makes us see the One as many.

What we call the world, then, is really maya. Modern physics would support this assertion. After all, when we talk about an apple or an orange, "things" with certain shapes and colors and so on, we are really talking about constructs of the mind, made from the data of sense-impressions. This does not mean that apples and oranges are unreal. But it is the mind which gives them names and forms, stamping as separate objects what is, to the best of our knowledge, pure energy. Similarly, maya is not a passive but an active, creative, interpreting force: *shakti*, the creative power of consciousness. Personified, Maya is the cosmic magician, who spreads a veil of infinite diversity over the unity of life.

If you know a little magic, you know that the secret lies in attention. If you can hold your audience's eyes on your right hand, you can do anything you like with your left and no one will notice. Maya works her magic through a similar trick. With one hand, concealment, she draws a curtain of ignorance over the Self. And with the other hand, distraction, she turns our attention outside to the world of the senses, away from our spiritual core. "Look," she says. "Everything you want is out there!" And we watch avidly, spellbound in darkness. What a show! It is so absorbing that only one person in a million ever suspects a deeper reality, let alone thinks to look deep within consciousness where the senses, mind, and intellect cannot reach.

Why is this magic so potent? No matter how many times we try to complete ourselves in the world outside us and come up empty-handed, we go on trying again in the same old places. What gives maya such a hold on us? The answer is simple: our desires. Pleasure beckons, and we do not want to look away. "Charmer who will be believed," Emerson says in his poem "Maia," "by man who wants to be deceived." In the end, we see life as we want to see it. So we confuse blind matter and pure spirit. We impose the qualities of the sense-world—transience, separateness, change, and death—on the eternal, changeless Self, and believe we are petty, short-lived fragments of life adrift in an alien world. And we attribute the qualities of spirit—joy, fulfillment, compassion, love—to the passing play of the world outside us, and spend out lives trying to get that world to give us what it does not have.

What does maya mean in practice? Precisely this bewildering, frustrating confusion of what is real and what is passing. Because we think we are separate, our primal need is in relation to ourselves. We have to look out for "number one." All the pursuit of things outside us, the mystics say—money, prestige, power—is merely to bolster an ego that feels isolated from the rest of life. Sure that we are no more than this body, we feel incomplete, so we consume ourselves in trying to get more, hold more, own more, be more.

For the same reason we are constantly on the defensive in our relationships, so we can't help manipulating those around us. This sense of incompleteness makes us try to fulfill ourselves in our partner and children, and infatuates us with qualities we want to see in others that they do not have. When such relationships break down, we feel even more isolated and alone.

In all these ways, the more we grasp for what we want, the more it eludes us. And the more it eludes, the more desperately we grasp. That is the devastating effect this illusion of separateness has on daily living.

A few years ago, some friends and I had an opportunity to see the Russian film version of *War and Peace*. It is a majestic rendering, fully seven hours long—long enough to involve the viewer in the rich detail of individual lives and still catch the sweep of history. For those seven hours I forgot myself. I was Pierre, struggling to master himself, trying to find some meaning in life; yet I was also Tolstoy, standing behind the scenes, watching the way these small lives so like yours and mine played themselves out in the impersonal tide of war and suffering.

Only after I came out of the theater did I remember who I was and where. No one had suffered, though we suffered, watching them. No one had died, though we wept to see them die. Nothing had happened, though I was changed by what I had seen. The experience was real, but it was not reality. The projection of light on a blank screen through a series of photographs created the illusion of real life.

Very roughly speaking, maya is like that. The light is consciousness; the blank screen, the backdrop of matter. And the refracting power that makes the pure light seem full of discrete objects and events is maya. Shelley suggests a similar idea in famous lines from "Adonais":

> *The One remains, the many change and pass;*
> *Heaven's light forever shines, earth's shadows fly;*
> *Life, like a dome of many-colored glass,*
> *Stains the white radiance of Eternity ...*

This word "projection" is suggestive. The reality of a movie is created only partly by the projection of light. It becomes real only when we project ourselves into the action, when we identify with the characters on the screen. Otherwise it has no meaning; it is just separate stills and a mechanical process.

Now, you can find mystics in every tradition who say there is no relationship between spirit and matter at all. We are not the body, they tell us; we are not the ceaseless play of thoughts and feelings and so on that we call the mind. We are the Self, pure spirit, and once the veil of maya falls, the illusion of being involved with this world and its creatures falls away. In this view, we are never really part of life at all, and the human drama has no more significance than an absorbing film.

There is truth in this perspective, and we have to remember that when the mystics speak like this, they are not weaving theories out of thin air. They are trying to express, in the inadequate language of duality, their own experience of unity. But to me—as, I expect, to most of us who live in the world and love it—this explanation leaves out what gives life meaning.

Some of the greatest mystics in India must have felt the same, for this tradition offers another view—also based on experience—which represents the loftiest expression of Hindu mysticism. In this view, spirit, matter, and maya are not three but one. Magic and show may be dependent on the Magician, but they are nonetheless real. So the *Shvetashvatara Upanishad*, one of the most lyrical of India's ancient scriptures, sings:

> *Conscious spirit and unconscious matter*
> *Both have existed since the dawn of time.*
> *With maya appearing to connect them,*
> *Misrepresenting joy as outside us*
> *When all these three are seen as one, the Self*
> *Reveals its universal form and serves*
> *As an instrument of the divine will.*[1]

"When these three are seen as one, the Self reveals its universal form." What is the universal form of this Self of ours, the very core of our being? Nothing less than the whole of life: the vast magic show of diversity, made of the power of the Godhead itself. This is the cosmic aspect of maya, worshipped all over India as the Divine Mother. It is the feminine face of the Godhead, ever creating, sustaining, destroying, and recreating the endless web of life.

Images like these make for fascinating philosophy and mythology, but the mystics are talking neither. They are telling us what life *is* when we see it whole. For them, talk of "mother earth" is not mere poetry. The whole of creation is *Jaganmata*, "Mother Universe," alive with the power of God.

This, of course, is not merely a Hindu idea. It is the experience of mystics everywhere. In this transcendent state, the Blessed Angela of Foligno confides in her *Book of Visions*,

> *the eyes of my soul were opened and I beheld the fullness of God, in which were comprehended the whole world, both here and beyond the sea, and the abyss and ocean and all things. In all this I saw nothing but the divine power, in a way beyond the power of words to explain; so that my soul, through excess of marveling, cried out with a loud voice,* This whole world is full of God!

What does this vision mean in practical terms? When we cease to think of ourselves as separate creatures, we live not just for ourselves but for all. We "serve as an instrument of the divine will." We see, we know, that the power of life which moves our hands and hearts and minds is not really ours. It is a trust, given us for the service of life; we are only trustees. And when creation is seen as made of God, caring for the environment becomes not just sound ecology but living worship. Earth, air, water, creatures, all are treated with reverence. Standing in the land of maya we see them as separate things, but to the man or woman established in the unitive vision, they are nothing but God. "Names and forms are like gold bangles," our mystics say, "the Lord is like the gold."

Now I have to confess that I did not finish the story with which I began.

One day, as it happens, a party of the king's retinue passes through the forest where the young robber lives in hiding. He and his men take the party by surprise and overpower them. But the royal family's spiritual teacher is among them, and something about the chief of this rough band catches his eye. Behind the young man's fierce features he recognizes the king's high forehead and aquiline nose, the queen's soft eyes, the royal bearing that these violent thieves instinctively obey. He looks the prince in the eye and says, "You're not a highwayman, your highness. I know who you are."

The prince is outraged. "What do you mean? I'm not 'your highness' or anybody else's. I'm a robber, and everybody in this kingdom is afraid of me."

But the teacher's faith is unshaken. Instead of being repelled by this young man's violent manners, he puts his arm around him and begins to tell him stories about his childhood: how his father used to carry him on his shoulders, how his mother used to sing him to sleep, the games he used to play in the palace.

And gradually the prince begins to remember. He draws himself up straight, his eyes clear and steady, altogether a different man. "I understand," he says slowly. "I'm not really a bandit; I'm not really violent. I simply forgot who I was." And truly a prince now, he goes home to his father, the king.

Here the mystics ask a penetrating question. After that instant of insight, between the man who thinks he is a highwayman and the man who knows he is a prince, what is different? His body is the same; his personality has not changed. No facts are altered: the king, for example, has always been his father. Both the prince and the world are what they always have been. Yet the veil of ignorance has fallen, and because of that, everything is changed forever.

It is the same when the veil of maya falls. Then, as Meister Eckhart says, where there stood a pauper now stands a prince. One man has ceased to be, and a new man is born: "not the same person," the Buddha says, "and yet not different."

Similarly, the world is the same and yet utterly different, because the observer is new. What was fragmented is now whole, both within and without at once. In that instant of insight, the great Flemish mystic Ruysbroeck says in *The Sparkling Stone*, "We behold what we are, and we are what we behold ... in this simple gazing we are one life and one spirit with God."

How simple it sounds! Why is it that, as the *Katha Upanishad* says, only one in a million even hears about this vision, let alone actually strives for it; and of a million who strive, only one attains the goal? Eckhart, with that wonderful lofty earthiness of his, answers point-blank: "Because he who would be what he wants to be must cease to be what he is." The whole of consciousness must be transformed, down into the depths of the unconscious. And the unconscious mind is a world of its own, vast beyond limits, seething with race—old urges and instincts almost impossible to control. In one of his "Dark Sonnets," Gerard Manley Hopkins hints at its dangers:

O the mind, mind has mountains; cliffs of fall
Frightful, sheer, no-man-fathomed. Hold them cheap
May who ne'er clung there …

No wonder the mystics of all traditions echo the haunting words of the *Katha Upanishad*: "Sharp like a razor's edge, the wise say, is the path, difficult to traverse."

Yet when the summit is reached, the travail of our climb falls away like the memory of a dream—the long, lurid dream of separateness we used to call life. Such simple words for an experience that transfigures personality! Yet that is the image the Buddha chose, and I think no one can improve on it. After he attained nirvana, the Anguttara Nikaya says, men awed by his shining presence went up to him and asked: "Are you a god? Are you a *gandharva*, an angel?" "No," the Buddha replied. "None of these. I am awake"—the literal meaning of the word *buddha*, from the Sanskrit word for waking up.

And once awake, the mystics assure us, we never fall under the spell of maya's dream again. We live in the same world as before, but behind its appearance of separateness we never lose awareness of unity. Where we needed to get, we want only to give. And where we felt isolated we now live free, at home in a compassionate universe.

Note:

1   The Upanishads, translated by Eknath Easwaran (Petaluma, Calif.: Nilgiri Press, 1987).

Parabola
Volume: 24.4
Evil

What Is Evil?

Christopher Isherwood and Swami Prabhavananda

Every religion or system of philosophy has to deal with the problem of evil—and unfortunately it is a problem which is usually explained away rather than explained. "Why," it is asked, "does God permit evil, when He Himself is all goodness?"

One of two answers is usually given to this question by Western religious thought. Sometimes we are told that evil is educational and penal. God punishes us for our sins by visiting us with war, famine, earthquake, disaster, and disease. He employs temptation (either directly or through the agency of the Devil) to test and strengthen the virtue of the good. This is the answer given by the Old Testament. It repels many people today and has become unfashionable—although, as we shall see in a moment, it contains a certain degree of truth, according to the philosophy of Vedanta.

The other answer—now more generally accepted—is that evil does not exist at all. If we view Life *sub specie aeternitatis* we shall know that evil has no reality; that it is simply a misreading of good.

Vedanta philosophy disagrees with both these answers—with the second even more radically than with the first.

How, it asks, can evil be changed into good, merely by viewing it in a special manner? Pain and misfortune may be borne more easily if we fix our minds upon God—but they are very real experiences nevertheless, even though their duration is limited. Vedanta agrees that evil, in the absolute sense, is unreal. But it reminds us that, from this standpoint, good is unreal also. The absolute Reality is beyond good and evil, pleasure and pain, success and disaster. Both good and evil are aspects of *Maya*. As long as Maya exists, they exist. Within Maya they are real enough.

The question, "Why does God permit evil?" is, in fact, most misleadingly phrased. It is as absurd as if one were to ask, "Why does God permit good?" Nobody today would ask why rain "permitted" a catastrophic flood; nobody would blame or praise fire because it burns one man's house and cooks another man's dinner. Nor can it be properly said that Brahman is "good" in any personal sense of the word. Brahman is not "good" in the sense that Christ was "good"—for Christ's goodness was within Maya; his life expressed the light of Reality reflected upon the relative world. The Reality itself is beyond all phenomena; even the noblest. It is beyond purity, beauty, happiness, glory, or success. It can be described as "good" only if we mean that absolute consciousness is absolute knowledge, and that absolute knowledge is absolute joy.

But perhaps the question does not refer to Brahman at all. Perhaps, in this connection, "God" means Iswara, the Ruler of Maya. If this is granted, can Vedanta philosophy agree with the Old Testament that God is a law-giver, a stern and somewhat unpredictable father, whose ways are not ours, whose punishments and rewards often seem unmerited, who permits us to fall into temptation?

The answer is yes and no. The Vedantic doctrine of Karma is a doctrine of absolute, automatic justice. The circumstances of our lives, our pains and our pleasures are all the results of our past actions in this and countless previous existences, from a beginningless time. Viewed from a relative standpoint, Maya is quite pitiless. We get exactly what we earn, no more, no less. If we cry out against some apparent injustice, it is only because the act that brought it upon us is buried deep in the past, out of reach of our memory. To be born a beggar, a king, an athlete, or a helpless cripple is simply the composite consequence of the deeds of other lives. We have no one to thank but ourselves. It is no use trying to bargain with Iswara, or propitiate Him, or hold Him responsible for our troubles. It is no use inventing a Devil as an alibi for our weakness.

Maya is what we make of it—and Iswara simply represents that stern and solemn fact.

Looked at from a relative standpoint, this world of appearance is a bleak place, and as such it often drives us to despair. The seers, with their larger knowledge, tell us otherwise. Once we become conscious, even dimly, of the *Atman*, the Reality within us, the world takes on a very different aspect. It is no longer a court of justice, but a kind of gymnasium. Good and evil, pain and pleasure, still exist, but they seem more like the ropes and vaulting-horses and parallel bars which can be used to make our bodies strong. Maya is no longer an endlessly revolving wheel of pain and pleasure, but a ladder which can be climbed to consciousness of the Reality. From this standpoint, fortune and misfortune are both "mercies"—that is to say, opportunities. Every experience offers us the chance of making a constructive reaction to it—a reaction which helps to break some chain of our bondage to Maya and bring us that much nearer to spiritual freedom.

Shankara, therefore, distinguishes between two kinds of Maya—*avidya* (evil or ignorance) and *vidya* (good). Avidya is that which causes us to move further away from the real Self, and veils our knowledge of the Truth. Vidya is that which enables us to come nearer to the real Self by removing the veil of ignorance. Both vidya and avidya are transcended when we pass beyond Maya into consciousness of the absolute Reality.

The principle of Maya is the superimposition of the ego-idea upon the Atman, the real Self. The ego-idea represents a false claim to individuality, to being different from our neighbors. It follows, therefore, that any act which contradicts this claim will bring us one step back towards right knowledge, to consciousness of the inner Reality.

If we recognize our brotherhood with our fellow-men; if we try to deal honestly, truthfully, charitably with them; if, politically and economically, we work for equal rights, equal justice, and the abolition of barriers of race and class and creed, then we are in fact giving lie to the ego-idea and moving towards awareness of the universal, non-individual Existence. All such actions and motives belong to what is known as ethical goodness—just as all selfish motives and actions belong to ethical evil. In this sense, and in this sense only, goodness may be said to be more "real," or more valid, than evil—since evil actions and thoughts involve us more deeply in Maya, while good thoughts and actions lead us beyond Maya, to consciousness of the Reality.

The words "sin" and "virtue" are somewhat alien to the spirit of Vedanta philosophy, because they necessarily foster a sense of possessiveness with regard to thought and action. If we say, "I am good," or "I am bad," we are only talking with the language of Maya. "I am Brahman" is the only true statement any of us can make.

St. François de Sales wrote that "even our repentance must be peaceful"—meaning that exaggerated remorse, just as much as excessive self-congratulation, simply binds us more firmly to the ego-idea, the lie of Maya. We must never forget that ethical conduct is a means, not an end in itself. Knowledge of the impersonal Reality is the only valid knowledge. Apart from that, our deepest wisdom is black ignorance and our strictest righteousness is all in vain.

From *Shankara's Crest-Jewel of Discrimination* ([1947] Hollywood: Vedanta Press, 1978), pp. 21–26. Reprinted by permission of Vedanta Press.

Parabola
Volume: 21.4
Play and Work

Magical Wars and Spirited Debates

Divine Play in Ancient India

Stuart Smithers

The life-force of all traditions and teachings is somehow reflected in play. Play appears for the first time in Sanskrit literature under the guise of *maya*, a term now common to Western readers. The popular understanding of maya as an "illusion" that distorts reality or covers the true world is too limiting (although it reminds us that in Greek "truth" was indeed thought to be covered or concealed; as pointed out by Heidegger, the Greek term *aletheia* is derived from *aletheuein*, "to uncover"). Nevertheless, Schopenhauer and the philosophers he influenced were attracted to the idea of maya as illusion in the sense that the world is only a mental construction, a projection of consciousness, and therefore the "world" has no reality because it depends on the consciousness or being that projects it.

This sense does correspond to one aspect of maya in the Vedic period—to the notion that, as "illusion," it is literally *in*-play (according to the etymology of "illusion"), and that which is projected is the *dis*-play. The great Sanskrit scholar Gonda laments that maya as the "power of illusion" is universally understood as an unreality, a trick, a deception or fraud.[1] Maya stems from the Sanskrit root *ma*, "to measure, to mete out, to mark off," and in the *Rig Veda* it is clear that maya suggests a power in gods and extraordinary human beings to do extraordinary things: a power of being, *Daseinmacht*, that is in this case a convergence of art and wisdom. This power connects with the traditional meaning of "craft" (a skill in planning and making or doing) as well as with the secondary association of "crafty" (being guileful, skillful in achieving one's goals). The pioneer Sanskritist A. A. Macdonell observed that maya "has an almost exact parallel in the English word 'craft,' which in its old signification meant 'occult power, magic,' then 'skillfulness, art' on the one hand and 'deceitful skill, wile' on the other."[2] The rendering of maya as "magic" discloses the extraordinary power of play, of illusion. But the question of how best to understand magic and maya remains—are we thinking of the "mere" magic of a Las Vegas illusionist, or the more suggestive and enigmatic image of a sorcerer like Merlin?

The mythological contests in the *Rig Veda* are contests of maya, displays of power and being in-play. In a famous passage from the Indra-Vritra cycle of cosmogonic myths (*RV.* 1.32.4), when Indra killed the dragon Vritra, he defeated the maya of the "maya-possessors" with his own maya. Or, as Wendy Doniger has translated, "When you [Indra] killed the first-born of the dragons and overcame by your own magic the magic of the magicians. ..."[3] Thus, Gonda suggests that the meaning of the term might be more accurately understood as an "incomprehensible wisdom and power enabling its possessor, or being able itself, to create, devise, contrive, effect, or do something," a creative wisdom-power or the display of a wondrous ability to create.[4] The Vedic texts presume that the "doings" of the gods are no ordinary "doing," that the gods have reserved the "power to do" (*kratum*) for the gods, but this power which issues from them can be gathered back into extraordinary human beings.[5] The divine play of the gods is the power to manifest, to act, to create, and to do in the world.

The shifting, enigmatic cosmic wars of the *devas* and the *asuras* ("gods" and "demons") suggests a world which can be viewed as a battleground of forces, a realm in which the play of powers is tested and revealed. Many deities display a fickle allegiance, so that we read of waxing and waning maya. In a hymn in which Indra attempts to lure Agni back to the side of the gods/devas, Indra declares: "Varuna, these Asuras have lost their magic powers [maya], since you love me" (*RV.* 10.124.5). Varuna, originally an asura, is the Vedic deity most often associated with the possession of maya, and frequent reference is made to his feats of creation and ordering of the universe: "I will proclaim the great magic [maya] of Varuna, the famous Asura, who stood up in the middle realm of space and measured apart the earth with the sun as with a measuring-stick" (*RV.* 5.85.5).[6]

The display of maya, in hostile or beneficent circumstances, reflects the measure of one's wisdom-power. In the Vedic world of power and action, it is not enough to be the uncontested possessor of being-power, Daseinmacht; it must be tested. To emerge victorious is to occupy an intermediate space of expanding influence and power: "Clothing himself in those that move toward the same center but spread apart, he rolls on and on inside the worlds" (*RV.* 10.177.3). Likewise, the Vedic son of heaven and earth is a clever charioteer and a *kavi* (poet-seer), who possesses the "power to make things clear" and purifies the universe by maya (*RV.* 1.160.3). Like Varuna who stands between earth and heaven, the kavi reflects the intermediate principle suggestive of play, for play occurs in space, a neutral field in which forces engage and compete, displaying their power and skill. In Vedic mythology, the play-space is the mid-space created between heaven and earth, where forces not only engage, but can be reconciled and transformed. Heaven and earth give birth to the "poet of space" (*RV.* 1.160.1), who symbolizes and embraces the essential characteristics of play: free, voluntary, creative, risky activity.

Dumézil's study of the ancient Indo-European "sorcerer" (the kavi) shows an extraordinary being who stands between the gods and demons, a third type of powerful being who exhibits remarkable independence and stature.[7] Although gods are often described as kavis, this occupation is not solely divine. The composers of the Vedic hymns are "kavis," and the term is often translated as "poet." But the kavis are not "mere" poets, but rather creators, fashioners, doers, who have among other activities composed the hymns. In this capacity, the kavi's activity is not so different from that of maya.[8] Above all, the kavi is "the performer of ritual, by deed and word," who possesses the "know-how" (*kavya*)—once again, a "wisdom-power" which takes charge of the ritual. This "know-how" does not refer to a technique or knowledge of ordinary technical operations, but to a knowledge from a higher level which "directs" by allowing for the play of higher forces and energies. Kavis are most often portrayed as questioning and being questioned—the kavi must speak, proving by his speech that he is a kavi (*RV.* 1.164.18). The kavi is a priest, poet, seer, and sorcerer all at once—a free magician.

In the fantastically complicated and ambiguous battle of the devas and asuras in the *Mahabharata*, the ultimate fortunes of the competing factions depend on the figure of the kavi, whose independence and know-how can play with and balance the forces. In this cosmic war there is no ground for moral superiority on either side. The demons, or asuras, are powerful, but not particularly evil. One does not have the impression that a victory by either gods or demons would change the existing moral and social customs. In early stages of the competition, the demons solicit Kavya Ushanas, a super-magician, to serve as their *purohita*—literally "the one who is placed first." The devas have their own counselor and purohita, Brihaspati, who is himself a god. One might assume that Brihaspati had a distinct advantage over the super-kavi Kavya Ushanas, but they are virtual equals in function and competition. Ironically, the one great advantage is found with Kavya Ushanas, who possesses a secret knowledge:

> *The gods killed off the Danavas [asuras, demons] who had gathered for battle, but Ushanas drew from the power of his knowledge and returned them to life. They stood up again and warred on the gods. The asuras in turn cut down the gods in the thick of the battle, but the wise Brihaspati could not revive them; for he did not have the knowledge of revivification, and so the gods became utterly desperate.*[9]

Kavya Ushanas possesses the knowledge and the power to balance the forces of the cosmos and to sustain or re-create life. We can begin to see in these cosmic contests a symbolic motif that develops extraordinary resonance in the evolution of Vedic mythology and religion: the creation, destruction, and re-creation of the universe, the image of a universe which is either at play itself, or is put in play.

As the war of the devas and asuras fades from the mythological landscape, the idea of play continues in Upanishadic literature, especially in "contests" that retain the risk both of challenging and of being challenged. The Upanishadic "contests" are verbal exchanges that aim at establishing truth, but establish many other things along the way …

including "status"—that is, a pecking order of being and understanding. The contests suggest not only a *display* of being and knowledge, but also the idea that through playing the game essential knowledge can be learned.

In the *Brihadaranyaka Upanishad*, which provides the essential outline of a contest of *brahmins*, King Janaka announces his intention to perform a sacrifice at which he will give out lavish gifts. When the most eminent brahmins assemble, King Janaka has a thousand cows herded together, with ten pieces of gold tied to the horns of each, and declares, "Distinguished brahmins! Let the most learned among you drive away these cows" (3.1.2).[10] The brahmins remain frozen in silence, unable to act—all except the legendary guru Yajnavalkya who orders his pupil to drive the cows away.

The other brahmins are furious. Yajnavalkya's claim of being the most learned is first challenged by the king's *hotri*, the priest responsible for ritual recitations. When the hotri asks Yajnavalkya if he really thinks he is the most accomplished brahmin, Yajnavalkya responds by suggesting that the issue seems to be raised not so much out of an authentic concern for knowledge, but is rather about power, wealth, and prestige, which in Vedic shorthand appears as "cows": "But we are really after the cows, aren't we?" (3.1.2). The hotri is incensed at being exposed in public and determines to question Yajnavalkya in hopes of defeating him. The contest begins in earnest, and Yajnavalkya meets a series of nine challenges. After the defeat of the hotri, he is questioned by Artabhaga, who asks if Yajnavalkya truly knows what survives after death. He has pressed Yajnavalkya to the limits of public discourse, and Yajnavalkya tells him, "My friend, we cannot talk about this in public. Take my hand, Artabhaga; let's go and discuss this in private" (3.2.13). We encounter the abandonment of play in favor of the transmission of knowledge. Since Artabhaga has proven himself worthy of a more direct discussion of knowledge, play is suspended and the idea is transmitted to him simply and in private.[11]

The contest resumes, but not without apparent risk. One of Yajnavalkya's wives is among the questioners. When she presses him to the extreme (asking him about the absolute ground of existence), she does not get an answer like Artabhaga, but rather a warning: "Don't ask too many questions, Gargi, or your head will shatter apart!" (3.6.1). This warning in turn becomes part of the play as the next questioner declares that if Yajnavalkya does not give the answer to a certain question, *his* head will fall off (3.7.1). But Yajnavalkya keeps his head and survives a lengthy exchange, eventually silencing his opponent once again.

The final challenger is Shakalya, the leader of the brahmins. After a heated exchange of questioning, Yajnavalkya taunts his opponent, suggesting that the other brahmins have made Shakalya their cat's-paw (3.9.17). The contest reaches its penultimate conclusion when Yajnavalkya declares:

> *"Now, those are the eight abodes, the eight worlds, the eight gods, and the eight persons. I ask you [Shakalya] about that person providing the hidden connection (upanishad)—the one who carries off these other persons, brings them back, and rises above them? If you will not tell me that, your head will shatter apart." (3.9.26)*

Shakalya does not know the answer, and his head does shatter! A triumphant Yajnavalkya turns to his challengers and says:

> *"Distinguished Brahmins! If any one of you would like to question me, he may do so; or, if you prefer, all of you may question me together. Or else, if any one of you would like me to, I will question him; or, if you prefer, I will question all of you together." But those brahmins did not dare. (3.9.27)*

Thus the contest ends. Yajnavalkya leaves the brahmins with a series of riddles about the deepest mysteries. The head falls, and the "cows" now belong to Yajnavalkya. The triumphant guru employs his "wisdom-power," playing with the brahmins as a cat plays with mice, toying with their answers and questions, frustrating them at every opening, and refusing to let them escape until their silence signals a new humility of mind. They have been stripped of their proud possession, knowledge. They now experience that they do not know, and that another quality of knowledge has escaped them. Yajnavalkya succeeds when his challengers recognize or know that they do not know, when they give up their theological questioning and enter into *a state of questioning*, between the known and the unknown. They are *in-between* and in question.

The play-character is central to this transmission of knowledge. Like Socrates or the great Zen masters, Yajnavalkya is not interested in displaying his superiority, but craftily exercises wisdom-power to create conditions and expose the ultimate inadequacy of ordinary knowing. He stops the normal flow of thoughts, and allows everyone to learn something more about playing and knowing, and these risky exchanges. In the wars of the gods and the contests of the brahmins, the play impulse is at the heart of the transformation of energies and forces. Play subverts boundaries and opens us, sometimes painfully and against our will, to a wider field of experience and phenomena. As Huizinga writes, "To dare, to take risks, to bear uncertainty, to endure tension—these are the essence of the play spirit."[12] Play occurs in space, in a field of action and exchange. In other words, play occurs in the world, in manifestation. The measure of one's being can only be found when one is in the world, participating in ever-widening and deepening fields of forces and energies. One's measure can be found only by playing the game.

Notes:

1   Jan Gonda, "Maya," in *Change and Continuity in Indian Religion* ([1965] reprint New Delhi, 1985), p. 164.

2   A. A. Macdonell, *Vedic Mythology* (New Delhi: Motilal Banarsidass, 1981), p. 24.

3   Wendy Doniger, *The Rig Veda* (New York: Penguin, 1981), p. 149. Cf. *RV*. 1.11.7.

4   The idea of a wisdom-power is uncannily similar to the later expression in Mahayana Buddhism of the necessity of *prajna* and *upaya*, wisdom and the means or power to manifest the teaching for the benefit of others.

5   See "The Sleeping Dragon and the Waters" in *Parabola*, 17.4 (Winter 1992), pp. 26–32. Reprinted in this volume, pp. 17–24.

6   In her notes to this passage, Doniger acknowledges, "Magic here in the sense of a miracle rather than an illusion." *The Rig Veda*, p. 149.

7   George Dumézil, *The Flight of a Sorceror* (Berkeley and Los Angeles: University of California Press, 1986).

8   Louis Renou, *Journal Asiatique* 241 (1953): 180–83.

9   J. A. B. van Buitenen, tr. and ed., *The Mahābhārata* (Chicago: University of Chicago Press, 1973–), vol 1, p. 176. See also Dumézil, *Flight*, pp. 27ff.

10 I have used Patrick Olivelle's new and much-needed translation of the principal upanishads, Upanishad*s* (Oxford and New York: Oxford University Press, 1996).

11 Heesterman calls attention to this passage as an indication of the "negation of the contest ideology" in his influential essay "Brahmin, Ritual, and Renouncer" in *The Inner Conflict of Tradition* (Chicago: University of Chicago Press, 1985).

12 Johan Huizinga, *Homo Ludens* (Boston: Beacon Press, 1955), p. 51.

Parabola
Volume: 10.3
The Body

THE FABRIC OF LIFE

Heinrich Zimmer

A group of holy men had gathered around the venerable hermit, Vyāsa, in his forest-solitude. "You understand the divine eternal order," they had said to him, "therefore, unveil to us the secret of Vishnu's Māyā."

"Who can comprehend the Māyā of the Highest God, except himself? Vishnu's Māyā lays its spell on us all. Vishnu's Māyā is our collective dream. I can only recite to you a tale, coming down from the days of yore, of how this Māyā in a specific, singularly instructive instance worked its effect."

The visitors were eager to hear. Vyāsa began:

"Once upon a time, there lived a young prince, Kāmadamana, 'Tamer of Desires,' who, conducting himself in accordance with the spirit of his name, spent his life practicing the sternest of ascetic austerities. But his father, wishing him to marry, addressed him on a certain occasion in the following words: 'Kāmadamana, my son, what is the matter with you? Why do you not take yourself a wife? Marriage brings the fulfilment of all of a man's desires and the attainment of perfect happiness. Women are the very root of happiness and well-being. Therefore, go, my dear son, and marry.'

"The youth remained silent, out of respect for his father. But when the king then insisted and repeatedly urged him, Kāmadamana replied, 'Dear father, I adhere to the line of conduct designated by my name. The divine power of Vishnu, which sustains and holds enmeshed both ourselves and everything in the world, has been revealed to me.'

"The royal father paused only a moment to reconsider the case, and then adroitly shifted his argument from the appeal of personal pleasure to that of duty. A man should marry, he declared, to beget offspring—so that his ancestral spirits in the realm of the fathers should not lack the food-offerings of descendants and decline into indescribable misery and despair.

"'My dear parent,' said the youth, 'I have passed through lives by the thousand. I have suffered death and old age many hundreds of times. I have known union with wives, and bereavement. I have existed as grass and as shrubs, as creepers and as trees. I have moved among cattle and the beasts of prey. Many hundreds of times have I been a brahmin, a woman, a man. I have shared in the bliss of Shiva's celestial mansions; I have lived among the immortals. Indeed, there is no variety even of superhuman being whose form I have not more than once assumed: I have been a demon, a goblin, a guardian of the earthly treasures; I have been a spirit of the river-waters; I have been a celestial damsel; I have been also a king among the demon-serpents. Every time the cosmos dissolved to be reabsorbed in the formless essence of the Divine, I vanished too; and when the universe then evolved again, I too re-entered into existence, to live through another series of rebirths. Again and again have I fallen victim to the delusion of existence—and ever through the taking of a wife.

"'Let me recount to you,' the youth continued, 'something that occurred to me during my next to last incarnation. My name during that existence was Sutapas, "Whose Austerities Are Good"; I was an ascetic. And my fervent devotion to Vishnu, the Lord of the Universe, won for me his grace. Delighted by my fulfilment of many vows, he appeared before my bodily eyes, seated on Garuda, the celestial bird. "I grant to you a boon," he said. "Whatever you wish, it shall be yours."

"'To the Lord of the Universe I made reply: "If you are pleased with me, let me comprehend your Māyā."

"' "What should you do with a comprehension of my Māyā?" the god responded. "I will grant, rather, abundance of life, fulfilment of your social duties and tasks, all riches, health, and pleasure, and heroic sons."

" "'That," said I, "and precisely that, is what I desire to be rid of and to pass beyond."

" 'The god went on: "No one can comprehend my Māyā. No one has ever comprehended it. There will never be anyone capable of penetrating to its secret. Long, long ago, there lived a godlike holy seer, Nārada by name, and he was a direct son of the god Brahmā himself, full of fervent devotion to me. Like you, he merited my grace, and I appeared before him, just as I am appearing now to you. I granted him a boon, and he uttered the wish that you have uttered. Then, though I warned him not to inquire further into the secret of my Māyā, he insisted, just like you. And I said to Him: 'Plunge into yonder water, and you shall experience the secret of my Māyā.' Nārada dived into the pond. He emerged again—in the shape of a girl.

" ' "Nārada stepped out of the water as Sushilā, 'The Virtuous One,' the daughter of the king of Benares. And presently, when she was in the prime of her youth, her father bestowed her in marriage on the son of the neighboring king of Vidarbha. The holy seer and ascetic, in the form of a girl, fully experienced the delights of love. In due time, then, the old king of Vidarbha died, and Sushilā's husband succeeded to the throne. The beautiful queen had many sons and grandsons, and was incomparably happy.

" ' "However, in the long course of time, a feud broke out between Sushilā's husband and her father, and this developed presently into a furious war. In a single mighty battle many of her sons and grandsons, her father, and her husband all were slain. And when she learned of the holocaust she proceeded in sorrow from the capital to the battlefield, there to lift a solemn lament. And she ordered a gigantic funeral pyre and placed upon it the dead bodies of her relatives, her brothers, sons, nephews, and grandsons, and then, side by side, the bodies of her husband and her father. With her own hand she laid torch to the pyre, and when the flames were mounting cried aloud, 'My son, my son!' and when the flames were roaring, threw herself into the conflagration. The blaze became immediately cool and clear; the pyre became a pond. And amidst the waters Sushilā found herself—but again as the holy Nārada. And the god Vishnu, holding the saint by the hand, was leading him out of the crystal pool.

" ' "After the god and the saint had come to the shore, Vishnu asked with an equivocal smile: 'Who is this son whose death you are bewailing?'

Nārada stood confounded and ashamed. The god continued: 'This is the semblance of my Māyā, woeful, somber, accursed. Not the lotus-born Brahmā, nor any other of the gods, Indra, nor even Shiva, can fathom its depthless depth. Why or how should *you* know this inscrutable?'

" ' "Nārada prayed that he should be granted perfect faith and devotion, and the grace to remember this experience for all time to come. Furthermore, he asked that the pond into which he had entered, as into a source of initiation, should become a holy place of pilgrimage, its water—thanks to the everlasting secret presence therein of the god who had entered to lead forth the saint from the magic depth—endowed with the power to wash away all sin. Vishnu granted the pious wishes and forthwith, on the instant, disappeared, withdrawing to his cosmic abode in the Milky Ocean."

" ' I have told you this tale,' concluded Vishnu, before he withdrew likewise from the ascetic, Sutapas, 'in order to teach you that the secret of my Māyā is inscrutable and not to be known. If you so desire, you too may plunge into the water, and you will know why this is so.'

"Whereupon Sutapas (or Prince Kāmadamana in his next to last incarnation) dived into the water of the pond. Like Nārada he emerged as a girl, and was thus enwrapped in the fabric of another life."

From Heinrich Zimmer, *Myths and Symbols in Indian Art and Civilization*, edited by Joseph Campbell (Princeton: Princeton University Press, 1971), pp. 28–31.

Parabola
Volume: 28.4
Truth and Illusion

Indra Gets Caught

Retold by Kamla Kapur

"You called?" Brahma asked, appearing before Indra, who lay bound hand and foot in the dungeon of the Demon King, Ravana.

"Yes, I called you, you stupid old fool," Indra raged. "Can you see what Ravana has done to me?"

"I see." Brahma smiled, sitting cross-legged on the thousand-petaled lotus which hovered a little above the dirt floor of the prison cell.

"Is this the reward I get for fighting the Battle of Heaven, for confronting Ravana the Demon King?" Indra fumed, rattling the heavy chains that fettered his hands and feet.

"Lord of the Rain, let anger go," Brahma replied.

"Let anger go? Don't I have cause to be angry? When Ravana came to my gate and demanded I surrender to him, did I not draw my silver sword and brighten the darkness all around? Did I not take a sip of soma and swear not to take orders from that dark and evil Ravana? I was the only god who challenged him. I was the only one to stand up to the demon. Is this how you treat your defenders? What's the use of being a god? I have had no support from you, or from any of the other gods."

"Lord of Fertility, let bitterness go," Brahma smiled.

"Do I not have cause to be bitter? What kind of a god are you, anyway? Is there any justice in your world? All the other gods have allowed themselves to become Ravana's slaves. They have given up the fight and surrendered to the demon, this son-in-law of Maya, the deceptive Artist and Architect of the Earth who weaves illusions of power and grandeur to ensnare even the best of us. Agni, the fire god, heats the stones in Ravana's kitchen and keeps him warm; Vayu, the wind, sweeps the courtyards of Lanka; Varuna, Lord of Waters, supplies the wines for Ravana's tables; the Sun lights his halls, and the Moon his gardens. I am the only one who can see through the veil of his illusions. I alone have stood firm in truth and resisted his seductions. But for what? These shackles?"

"Defender of gods and humans, let pride go."

"Let pride go? What pride have I left here, groveling in Ravana's dungeon? Why did you allow Ravana's son, Meghananda, to capture me? Don't you have any control over your creation? All you do is sit on your lotus, three steps away from the edge of the universe, untroubled by it all. You are to blame. You are the cause of all my troubles. The only reason Ravana is so strong is because you granted him a boon. How could you say yes when Ravana asked you: *Let me be unslayable by every creature of Heaven and of the underworlds.* Are you mad? Can you truly be the Lord of Creation?"

"If I hadn't granted him the boon, he would have burnt up the worlds with his dreadful will and austerities. It was for the good of all."

"But why must I suffer now? The pain from his chains and the wounds from the battle are excruciating."

"Lord of the Thunderbolt, let pain go."

"It's easy for you to say that, isn't it? Not only do you grant boons to demons, but for capturing me in his net of illusion you have awarded Ravana's son, Meghananda, the title of Indrajit, Conqueror of Indra."

Brahma laughed a joyous laugh.

"You mock my sorrow, Brahma? If you were here, I would give you a good kick and send you flying off that lotus. You laugh at me? You stupid, ineffectual god. Be gone."

"You have to admit that Meghananda performed an admirable feat, Indra. He took the magnificent net of illusion, woven with gossamer and filaments of silk, and with his mighty, muscular arms he cast it wide, glimmering like gold dust, right above you. And your eyes, so entranced by its scintillating light, lured you toward it and your hand reached out for it … oh, Indra, how unsurpassable! Do you blame your judgment for being clouded by it? Even the illusion is Narayana's design. Even this is all His play! So? You, too, the mighty Indra, were caught. Rage against yourself, Indra, not me."

Having said this, Brahma vanished from Indra's sight in a shower of twinkling laughter. He went to Ravana's son and said, "Indrajit, mighty conqueror of Indra, free Indra now. He has had enough suffering. Free him, and take something in return from me."

"Immortality," Indrajit replied without a thought.

"Prince, I can't give you that gift. Ask for something else."

"Then give me the power of invisibility, that I may be able to attack through thoughts of despair, put out lights left unguarded, bind my enemies with strong, invisible ropes of illusion that seem real."

"Granted," said Brahma.

"Here's the key," said Indrajit, handing the key to the dungeon in which Indra sat raging.

"No, thank you, I don't touch weapons," Brahma replied.

"Weapon?" said Indrajit.

"Weapons of your illusion, Indrajit," Brahma replied, shutting his eyes as he sat on the lotus and went into meditation. Deep in trance, Brahma entered Indra's mind and removed the cobwebs of despair and fear. And then he planted in Indra's mind the thought by which he could free himself.

Weary of struggle, Indra sat down on the dirt floor and went into meditation. In the very depth of silence, the thought that Brahma had sent him floated into his mind: *I am free, I am free, I am free.*

Indra heard the sound of an elephant's trumpet. He opened his eyes and saw that his fetters had fallen from him. The prison walls had dissolved, and above him unbound blue skies bloomed. Airavata, the white elephant, hovered in the air, flapping his ears and summoning his master to mount and fly away to the celestial holy city of Amaravati, where Indra could once again rest, rejuvenate, and prepare for yet another inevitable battle.

Parabola
Volume: 12.4
The Sense of Humor

THE LAUGHTER OF THE WEAVER

Lee Siegel

One night a stray camel wandered through a field in a village and in the morning the young people asked an old weaver in that village what the strange footprints were. The old man began to weep and as he wept he began to laugh. "Why do you weep? Why do you laugh?" they asked. "Why do you laugh and weep at the same time?" The weaver explained it. "I cry because I wonder what these poor children will do for someone to explain things to them when I am dead. And I laugh because, as for these footprints, I don't know—I really don't know—what they are!"

—*Panjabi folktale*

"In order to truly understand humor, you must look back to your childhood," Gananath Sastri explained. There was a warm and honied breeze in the overgrown garden in Madras, and Mr. Sastri offered me one of his Charminars. "I'm not finished with this one yet," I held up the half-smoked cigarette. He insisted that I smoke a fresh one.

"Every time we laugh, what is it other than the little child in our heart breaking loose and jumping for joy?" With gentle delight he recollected that child within himself and I could see the boy with bright black eyes and an even more glistening, though thoroughly naughty, smile. The child was puffing on a cigarette. "I started smoking when I was six years old. I was a terrible child," he laughed. "I stole cigarettes like Krishna stole curds."

He lit a cigarette. "To hear genuine Indian laughter you must visit the villages. You won't hear real laughter in our cities. Before my father was appointed at Presidency College we lived in a village of weavers. I remember a fellow in our village called Gada. Every village has such a fellow—a 'village idiot.' You must have one, just as you must have a well. You cannot be a self-respecting village without one. Everyone always laughed at Gada. One day a man, holding out ten paise in one hand and one rupee in the other, asked him whether he wanted the ten or the one. And Gada took the ten paise. The man told the story at a meeting of the village council and everybody had quite a laugh over it. After that people would test it for themselves. Just to tease the fool, they would hold up a one-rupee note and a ten-paise coin and ask, 'Do you want the ten or this one?' And Gada always took the ten paise and people always laughed at him for that. And when they would laugh, he too would laugh. He always laughed when others laughed. Some folks postulated that he took the coin rather than the note because he was so stupid that he thought the metal was more valuable than the paper. Others assumed that he was simply fooled by the numbers, that he reasoned that ten must always be greater than one. Whenever any visitors came to our village they would inevitably be introduced to Gada and shown the prank. They would laugh at Gada. And Gada would join in and laugh with them. He was a veritable tourist attraction. Perhaps it seems cruel to you, all this laughing at Gada. But people actually liked Gada. He was quite harmless. Even after we moved from the village, I would frequently return to see my grandparents. On one of these visits I was informed that Gada was dying. Everyone was very sad. The old fool had given them such great amusement. And I think that they felt bad because they had laughed at him all the time. I went along to his place, a mere hut, and yes, he was very sick. He was weeping. 'Don't cry, please don't cry,' I begged him. And he explained the reason for his tears. 'I feel very sorry for what I have done. I have cheated these happy people who have been so kind to me. I have deceived them! Of course I know that one rupee is more than ten paise. Any fool knows that! The first time I chose the ten paise over the rupee note, it was because I didn't want to take advantage of the man's generosity. But then, when everybody started offering me that same choice, I always chose the ten paise because I knew that if I were to choose the rupee, people would stop offering me the choice at all. And so, always choosing the ten paise, I earned a great many rupees!' Realizing at that moment that Gada was the wisest man in my entire village, I could not help but laugh aloud. And when I laughed, Gada laughed. Even as he wept, he laughed. He always laughed when others laughed. The fool couldn't help himself. There is something very powerful for me about the laughter of Gada. I can hear it even now."

Mr. Sastri continued his recollections of his childhood with all the enthusiasm, irony, humor, and embellishment of a true raconteur. His eyes were the eyes of a child, extraordinarily beautiful in their setting beneath white brows. Forgetting about the cigarette burning in the ashtray, he lit another. He refused to smoke mine because "of the damned lie on the package—nothing is 'duty-free.'

I looked at the crow in the tree, turning its head from side to side as if listening to the stories, opening and closing its beak as if mocking us.

"When I began studying Sanskrit my father told me a little story about the great Kālidāsa. Imagine it—Kālidāsa was a dullard as a child, a noddy, a boob, a driveling ignoramus! He could not learn one iota of Sanskrit. He was an orphan raised by cowherds. But he was a happy boob! Why? Because he was an ardent devotee of Kālī. And the ardor of his religious conviction filled him with joy. He would go to her temple and there he would dance for her. It looked just like jumping around, but it was the best dance he could do. When he saw her hideous form he would whisper and laugh and shout, 'How beautiful you are, Mamma!' Then he would cry. Then he would sing and everyone laughed at him. 'Mamma, mamma, your baby needs you! Mamma, mamma, don't spank your little baby. Mamma, mamma, give me sweets!' Over and over again he would cry out, *Muñca mam! jāva ajjūe saāsam gamissaṃ* [(Prakrit) Release me! I shall go to my mamma].' The priests and pandits shook their heads. 'What a silly bumpkin this Kālidāsa is,' they said. He slept by the door of the temple in order to be near his mother. And one night Kālī appeared to him in his dream. 'Of all my devotees, you are the most sincere. So great and uncompromised is your devotion that you let them laugh at you for my sake. In this folly you are the wisest of all. For this devotion, I will give you the gift of eloquence and intelligence. You will be the greatest of all poets, the supreme jewel in the garland of jewels adorning the court of King Vikramaditya.' And when he awakened from that dream, he was wise and Sanskrit flowed mellifluously from his lips. He had the knowledge of all joy and of all sorrow. He had the gift of praise, and Vikramaditya gave him one lakh for each syllable that he wrote. He attained what all men aspire to—wit and wisdom, fame and fortune, the love of women and the respect of men. But with these boons came attachment to the world and the sorrow that must accompany such attainment. Kālidāsa, the wise poet, met a fate from which the foolish devotee would have been spared. In Śrī Lankā, a courtesan, jealous and designing, poisoned the bard. The poet's friend Kumaradasa found him on his deathbed. He asked him, 'Of all your works, which is the greatest, which is the most perfect?' And Kālidāsa answered, 'Only one line in all of my dramas and *mahākāvyas* is of real merit—"Release me! I shall to go my mamma."' These were Kālidāsa's last words. The line is uttered by the child of Sakuntala at the end of the *Abhijnanaśākuntalam*. Taken at face value, in the context of the play, this line is not great, certainly not the greatest line in the play, let alone in Kālidāsa's works as a whole. What then did the poet mean? This line was the only remnant of his former, foolish but holy, self. It was the simple line that he had always sung to Kālī. And because he uttered those words on his deathbed he went immediately to heaven, transported by his blessed mother, Kālī!" Gannath Sastri lit another cigarette.

I asked him if he believed that the story had any historical validity. He laughed a laugh that seemed to have been curled up in his gut, a laugh that woke up startled, leapt from the throat, through the mouth, stretching in midair to pounce with a growl and a bark, a laugh that chewed up what I had said. "What story does not have validity? History is only that which happens to have happened. These things are not any more true or untrue than those events which just happen not to have happened."

"Then anything goes?" I challenged.

"What a wonderful idea!" He laughed and continued. "After my father told me this story, he posed a question to me: 'Would it be better to be Kālidāsa, the foolish devotee and ever-happy simpleton, or Kālidāsa, the enlightened poet, prone to all of the sorrows that accompany the joys of this world?' Which would I choose? Now you must remember that he asked me this question just as I was beginning to study Sanskrit. I did not know what to say. I tried to reason it out. Since my father was a learned pandit and a poet himself, I suspected that Kālidāsa-the-poet must be the correct answer. But since the end of the story suggested that the learned bard himself would have chosen to be the happy dullard, I guessed that Kālidāsa-the-fool was the correct answer."

"Was that the right answer?"

"No. My father told me that I must aspire to be truly learned so that someday I would realize that I was truly a fool. With that realization happiness would come. Then he made me learn all the case endings for the Sanskrit nominal forms."

Mr. Sastri looked chagrined. "I'm still not happy with the question. I am still not sure about the answer. The question raises a multitude of paradoxes and problems, a myriad of confusions and conundrums. I still haven't figured it out. Who is wise? Who is a fool? Touchstone, in one of the plays which I have translated into Sanskrit, that humorous drama by the Kālidāsa of Britain, voiced the essential paradox: 'The fool doth think he is wise, but the wise man knows that he is, himself, a fool.' Here is the gist of it: if I think I am a fool, then I am wise; if I think I am wise, I am a fool. But what if I know the paradox? Then when I think I am a fool, I am actually thinking that I am wise, so I am a fool once again. On the other hand, if, still knowing the paradox, I think I am wise, I am actually thinking I am a fool, which by the previous proposition, means that I am wise. Or does it? I cannot figure my way out of it. I am a fool! I mean truly a fool. I really do think I am a fool, but I do also think it is wise to think of oneself as a fool. No! Yes! I don't know!" He laughed again. "I really can't figure it out."

"You must be too wise to figure it out!" I joked.

"You fool!" he snapped, aping anger.

"Thanks," I laughed.

"No, I meant it," he said with a gravity, real or pretended, which was almost instantly obliterated by his laughter.

While the notion of the wise fool or holy madman is an ancient one in India, that figure only became a model of religiosity and a conventional literary character with the flowering of devotionalism in the medieval period. The natural purity of the simple heart, rather than the purity of the Brahmins attained through birth, the purity of yogis attained through discipline, or the purity of sannyasis attained through renunciation, became the ideal. The gods rewarded loving faith. Vernacular stories of the medieval devotees stress their natural folly. Sur Dās, Kabīr, Tulsī Dās, Caitanya, Tukuram, and others refer to themselves as fools, as *mahā*fools in relation to god.

Caitanya once happened upon a man reading the *Bhagavadgītā* aloud in a temple. As he read everyone around the man laughed at him, for he mispronounced all of the words. The man himself was weeping and trembling, and Caitanya asked him which words had made him cry so. "I don't know the meaning of any of the words," the rube confessed, "but as I sound them out I see Kṛṣṇa in Arjuna's chariot. He is holding the reins in his hands and he is speaking to Arjuna and he looks very beautiful. The vision makes me weep with joy." Caitanya smiled at the holy fool: "You are an authority on the *Bhagavadgītā*. You know the real meaning of the text" (*Caitanyacaritāmṛta* 2.9.93.103). That fool was wiser than any pandit.

A religious irony central to devotionalism questions the relative significance of human learning and knowledge. "For the wisdom of this world is foolishness with God" (I Corinthians 3:19). Love, a natural impulse within every human being, no matter how foolish, could be transformed into the highest wisdom by the grace of its object. Knowledge, discipline, and rites were detrimental if they threatened that natural emotion. Love, the source of all folly, was suddenly the matrix of wisdom. "If any man among you seemeth to be wise in this world, let him become a fool, that he may be wise" (I Corinthians 3:18).

Needing water for his ablutions and fire for his sacrifice each morning, a fool decided to mix the fire and water together. Both were ruined and everyone laughed at him in his sadness and disappointment (*Kathāsaritsāgara* 61.9-13). But those who laughed did so with the banal wisdom that fire and water do not mix. The greater wisdom, the wisdom that the fool has but does not know he possesses, is that they do. The fool is less successful but no more foolish than Brahmā who placed the raging fire of Śiva's asceticism into the depths of the ocean where, according to the myth, it continues to burn:

> *The fire is immersed in water,*
> *the sea in which it's drenched.*
> *And yet it does not perish,*
> *for its thirst is never quenched:*

The ocean is consumed by fire,
the flames that it contains,
And yet it is so very vast
that every drop remains.
Wondrous is the fire and wondrous the sea.
Thoughts of their greatness completely dazzle me.
                    —Subhāsitaratnakosa 1198

Only fools can comprehend the great and subtle mysteries. Only fools are capable of the great faith, the act of make-believe, that all religions demand. The notion of a Christ, crucified and then resurrected, was according to Paul, utter "foolishness to the Greeks." And the Greeks were, above all else, wise.

Buddhist hagiography contains tales of a Thera named Cūlapanthaka, Brother Little Walker, who, after his initiation into the order, proved to be such a bonehead that he was unable to learn even a single stanza of the Buddha's teaching after months of study. Many of the monks laughed at the intellectual ineptitude of his efforts. The fool's brother, Big Walker, was so embarrassed by his sibling's stupidity that he urged him to leave the order. But Cūlapanthaka explained that, even though he could not memorize the Buddha's words, and even though he did not understand them, he so loved to listen to those words that he had no intention of returning to the life of a layman.

Out of shame over his younger brother's foolishness, Big Walker, whose responsibility it was to call the monks to hear the Buddha speak, refused to inform Little Walker whenever the Buddha addressed the monks. Cūlapanthaka's feelings were so deeply hurt, his sense of worthlessness became so great, that he resigned himself to leaving the order. As he was walking sadly along the road, the Buddha met him and asked where he was going. Cūlapanthaka explained to the Buddha that he was too great a fool to be a worthy disciple. The Buddha smiled and gave Cūlapanthaka a piece of cloth, instructing him to use it to wipe the sweat from his brow. Doing as he was told, Cūlapanthaka soon noticed that the cloth became dirtier and dirtier. "I have made this cloth that was clean dirty. All compounded things are impermanent!" At once he grasped the essence of the Buddha's teaching. At once the fool became wise (*Cullakasetthe Jātaka* [4] *Dhammapadatthakathā* 4.180ff).

Those who laughed at Cūlapanthaka did so on the assumption that they were superior to him, wiser than he. That was their folly. The muted, humorous laughter that the story tends to evoke is laughter at oneself over the realization that oneself is no wiser than the fool. Tradition notes that, in a previous birth, during the life of Kassapa Buddha, Cūlapanthaka had been a very learned monk, and that he had been reborn as a dolt because he had once laughed at a monk who was having trouble memorizing scripture. He needed several lifetimes of stupidity to purge himself of the arrogance that comes with knowledge.

It was Mr. Bandyopadhyaya who first interested me in Ramakrishna, "a holy man par excellence."

"I am the greatest of all fools," Ramakrishna was fond of announcing with laughter sometimes, but often with tears. The question is whether the announcement is a confession or a boast, or both, or neither. The statement is humorous if it is serious, serious if it is humorous.

The lore of the saint, at least in Mr. Bandyopadhyaya's telling of it, was familiar. "When he was a lad in school, both his teachers and his schoolmates thought he was a dullard. This was because book knowledge meant nothing to him. Life was the only book he wished to study. While his brother, Ramkumar, was mastering Sanskrit and all of the Vedas, Ramakrishna was making images of the gods. They were the toys with which he played. Unlike other children, his play was divine. His toys really were gods. Just as people thought he was a fool when he was a child, so they thought he was a drunkard or a madman when, later in life, he would worship—he would shake all over, he would fall down, jump up, fall down again. He would go silent. Then he would laugh, then cry, then laugh again. Ramakrishna was a saint par excellence."

Mr. Bandyopadhyaya kindly gave me a copy of *The Gospel of Ramakrishna*. "This will help you in all of your confusion." I was startled. "Do I seem confused?" Without any reluctance, my host, though we hardly knew each other, said that, yes, I was confused about several things: "religion, politics, women, and money. You are also very confused about India." I blushed as I laughed, "Is that all?" Premendra looked down at the floor as if out of embarrassment either for his father or for me. "No. You are also very confused about humor. I have met many people who are confused about religion and politics, about women and gold. And I have met many foreigners who are confused about

India. But you are the only person whom I have ever met who is confused about humor. You are always asking questions about that topic!"

"That's because I hope to write a book about it."

"In India we write books about topics that we understand. You want to write a book about something you don't understand. Is that not a foolish endeavor?"

I admitted my folly and promised to read *The Gospel of Ramakrishna*.

Ramakrishna, I learned, was fond of recounting a story of a boy who posted a letter to god addressed to heaven. He explained that the boy's folly was holy. "A perfect knower of God and a perfect idiot," the saint would say, "have the same outer signs." Folly was for him not something to overcome, but something to rediscover, or to attain through the grace of god. Ramakrishna stressed that he who has seen god becomes a fool. "He laughs, weeps, dances, and sings. Sometimes he behaves like a child, a child five years old—guileless, generous, without vanity, unattached to anything, not under control of any of the *gunas,* always blissful. Sometimes he behaves like a ghoul; he doesn't differentiate between things pure and things impure; he sees no difference between things clean and things unclean. And sometimes like an inert thing, staring vacantly: he cannot do any work: he cannot strive for anything." Like the fool or the child, the truly holy person, for Ramakrishna, has no sense of order, caste, hierarchy, or distinction. "He doesn't discriminate about caste. If his mother tells him that a particular man should be regarded as his elder brother, the child will eat from the same plate with him, though the man may belong to the low caste of a blacksmith. The child [like the fool, the drunkard, the madman, or the holy man] doesn't know hate, or what is holy or unholy." The *paramahaṃsa*, the greatest of all sages, according to Ramakrishna, is no different than the most foolish of all fools—"he doesn't keep track of his whereabouts. … He cannot distinguish between a stranger and a relative."

The fool has a potential for an experience of god that is denied to the more sensible, judicious, or certain. "God cannot be realized by a mind that is hypocritical, calculating, or argumentative." The fool is gullible. The truly holy person trusts the world. He is like a little child. "He becomes as quickly detached from a thing as he becomes attached to it. You can cajole him out of cloth worth five rupees with a doll worth an anna." Total trust, foolish trust, is both a symptom of, and a means to, sanctity.

Once upon a time a certain foolish herdsmen was befriended by some con men. They told him that they had arranged for him to marry the daughter of a very rich merchant in a nearby village. The fool was so happy that he gave them the money to repay them for making such a fine match for him. When the sharpers told him that the marriage ceremony had been performed, the guileless herdsman became so elated that he gave them more gifts. Soon they informed him that his wife had given birth to a son for him. In complete joy he gave them all of his wealth. The crooks left town. One day people in the village, seeing the herdsman weeping, asked the reason for his tears. He was not crying, as they had expected, over the loss of his wealth. "I am sad because I miss my son," he said, and all the villagers laughed at him (*Kathāsaritsāgara* 61.17-24). There is something holy about the man. He is wise, in a sense, than the fools who duped him. He is profoundly gullible, but gullibility is, after all, only a vulgar term for faith. Ramakrishna would certainly have done the same. He played the part of the fool. "I don't want *brahmajñāna* [knowledge of the absolute]," he would cry out, "I want to be merry. I want to play ... I don't know the Vedanta; and Mother, I don't even care to know."

•

CHAPTER FOUR

Teachers

The battle lines are drawn, the armies ready to engage, and Arjuna hesitates in order to seek counsel. How to proceed? What must he learn before taking action? Who will show the way? In his response, Krishna describes the transmission of knowledge from the beginning of time to the present:

> *I taught this undying discipline*
> *to the shining sun, first of mortals,*
> *who told it to Manu, the progenitor of man;*
> *Manu told it to the solar king Ikshvaku.*
>
> *Royal sages knew this discipline,*
> *which the traditions handed down;*
> *but over the course of time*
> *it has decayed, Arjuna.*
>
> *This is the ancient discipline*
> *that I have taught to you today;*
> *you are my devotee and my friend,*
> *and this is the deepest mystery.*
>
> —Bhagavad-Gita

"How to proceed? … Who will show the way?" asks the Focus editorial in the epigraph. The guru, the guide on the spiritual path, is the subject of this chapter. The guru is perhaps the most respected figure in traditional Hindu society. In the myths, the guru is often a great sage. In ordinary life he—or sometimes she—may be the teacher of a traditional art such as dance or music. He or she is also spiritual guide, counselor, and transmitter of traditional teachings.

In the first selection, Padma Perera poignantly recounts her relationship with "Guruji," her teacher of Manipuri dance, as he guides her through "an unimaginable stretching of [herself], within and without." Skills were taught, yes, but more important was feeling, that instrument of knowing essential to understanding the art. This account is set in a somewhat wider context in "Teacher, Student, Lineage" by Rosemary Jeanes Antze, who explores some of the customs and rituals framing the "one-to-one relationship between guru and *shishya*" by which tradition is learned.

Three short tales follow, which come from the teachings of the nineteenth-century Bengali saint Ramakrishna. The "Roar of Awakening" is a story of a teacher who led his student to knowledge of his own true nature. But students who learned wisdom from their guru sometimes failed to learn one essential element, common sense, as told humorously in "The Snake Who Lost His Hiss" and "Maya."

Next, two spiritual masters speak of the teachers who communicated to them not only a tradition of practice but also a consciousness reflected in an inner state of ecstasy or of stillness: Paramahansa Yogananda ("The Liberating Shock") and Swami Chetananda ("Stillness").

Finally, two more amusing short stories tell of students who learned more than the teachers themselves were aware of passing on. The first, "Viddhi! Kooshmāndam" is from the southern state of Kerala. "Walking on Water" is another tale from Ramakrishna's teachings.

Parabola
Volume: 9.3
Pilgrimage

GURUJI

Padma Perera

Short legs, long hair, face made up of bones and feelings, so that you never remember what he looks like, only how he is made and how he feels. How, too, he wants you to feel.

You are four-and-a-half years old when you first meet him. There at the dancing school where you have begged to go, despite your terror of strangers, because you have just witnessed your first performance of classical Manipuri dancing, and know now that this is the one thing you have to do.

Guruij teaches only an occasional group class at the school. For the privilege of including his name on their staff, the school board has provided him with a cottage at the back of the grounds. Here he trains his individual pupils. And from here he emerges to pick those envied "singles" of the babies' class. … Unobtrusively he strolls down to the classroom; unobtrusively he sits in a corner and watches; unobtrusively he makes his choice. If his actions are noted he will fly into one of his much-touted rages. Afterwards you are to realize this legendary temper has been fabricated by the school to protect him from importunate parents. "That is his way," they say, as if of an eternal verity.

His way, as far as you're concerned, is as indefinable as a leaf, the sun, the tune of a song. At four and a half, you don't even know you have been picked. "Ao," the man with the shoulder-long hair says. Come.

Astoundingly, you're not shy of him. Down you go to the cottage at the bottom of the compound, with a creeper flowering low over the front door; into a bare sunlit room containing a stringed tanpura, two drums of the tabla, and a single stick of incense burning at a shrine in the corner.

He re-ties your ankle bells more firmly and guides your feet into the first syllabic formula: *dhingte-yengta-khitta-dhenta, dhingte-yengta-khitta-dhenta.* ...

When you have learned both the steps and the matching mudras of the hands faultlessly enough so that combining them is no more difficult than walking, he kneels down, face level with yours.

"Now go home and come back to me when you are five years old." You look at him, uncertain. "That is a long time?"

"Maybe."

"I can't dance until then?"

He looks back at you in silence for a moment and then points to the starry white flowers over the door. "See that plant? It grows from the soil, *hai na?*" (Isn't that so?) "So, dancing grows from everything you do every day of your life. How you eat," he shows you. "How you bend down and pick something up from the floor. How you join palms to greet someone and say '*Namaste.*' How you move, walk, sit—" matching action to word. "You see? I am dancing. Remember that, practice your *dhingte-yenta*, and come to me when you are five years old."

Five years old.

You arrive, bearing a shiny bell-metal platter arranged with marigolds, a heap of rice grains, token silver coins, betel leaves, half a coconut and a twisted yellow bit of tumeric root. Proffer it to him, and bend down to touch his feet as a worshipful student should. He blesses you gently enough, but when you straighten up, his tone is sharper than you will ever hear it. "Never do that to me again until you have learned everything you have to learn from me, and it is time for you to leave—understand?"

The early years. Graduating slowly past the first simple syllables to more complicated measures of rhythm: *Kokilpriya, Panchamswari, Brahmatal, Vishnutal.* ...The evenings when you badger him to spice the lessons with some drama and danger. "Please, Guruji, show me the demon dance."

"No, *chal*—go—it will frighten you."

"Please, Guruji, just once. I won't be scared. I promise I won't be scared."

His one fault, everyone says, is his tenderness toward children (which of course every child knows and exploits): it breaks into the sternness and stringency required of a teacher. "*Achcha*," he gives in, and turns into a demon.

Horrible mask-face hovering over outspread talons, eyebrows flared terrifyingly over bloodthirsty eyes, mouth a snarl of fangs, it dances … crouch—leap—thud, crouch—leap—thud … nearer and nearer.

By the time you fall, panting and dusty, over the fence at the other end of the compound, the demon has disappeared. When you retrace your steps, Guruji is waiting at the window, saying resignedly: "What did I tell you?"

Seven years old. No more games. Nine years old. The stage. Which, after the initial nervousness, excitement, blinding lights, and anticlimax of Guruji picking holes in your performance afterwards, makes no difference at all. There's still milk to be gagged over at breakfast next morning, the same arithmetic to be wrestled with at school.

At twelve, a rebellion. "Guruji, it's not fair! The men can jump and leap about as much as they like. Why do *we* have to keep gliding around so gentle and passive all the time? Why should their dances have so much more life?"

"LIFE?" You've never seen him so outraged. He launches off in a spate of his incomprehensible mother-tongue before he can recollect himself enough to revert to Hindi and point to that same damn creeper over the door. "See that? Don't just look at it. Fill your eyes, fill your eyes! You think that has no life? Foolish girl! When you can dance the way it moves, you will have achieved something. Not until then. *Sancharini pallavini lata.* …" Obediently you repeat the Sanskrit quote after him but grumble in your head that you've just about had enough of being a "swaying, blossoming vine."

Shrewdly he shoots a glance at you. "Manipuri dancing must be kept absolutely pure, you hear? No jerks. No wriggles. Not even the needless flutter of a single eyelash. Go home now. I don't want you here unless you can be attentive with your whole self."

Blackmail. Pure blackmail. Semblances of docility are no use, he'll see right through them. You whip off your ankle-bells and storm home. "I'll never go there again. Never!"

When you creep back two weeks later, it is to find the lapse—both of time and manners—magnificently ignored. He never refers to the episode again; neither do you. Stalemate. On the one hand, you can't *not* dance. On the other hand, the further you progress, the subtler and more active the passivity demanded of you.

But now he speaks more about dancing than he has in all the previous years put together. A little here, a little there, explaining a gesture, a legend, a memory of the green hills of his land, he teaches you:

In Manipur, dancing is charged with faith, the devotional fervor of *bhakti*. To a Manipuri, one's whole life is a dance offering. Thus, following given dictates, the Tandava style of men's dancing is swift and vigorous, the feminine Lasya an apotheosis of grace: fluid movements merging into one another with no clearly defined beginning or end, continuous as the rhythm of birth and death. No extraneous glance or gesture should be allowed to mar the sanctity of this offering. The ignorant call it an expressionless dance. Never! The true dancer has reached a stage where the earthly audience has ceased to matter, and she is conscious only of the deity in the temple, of—another shrewd look—the gift of life itself. …

After all this, by the time you're into your teens, Guruji decides that you're perhaps disciplined enough to be allowed occasionally to choreograph your own dances in the classical mode. If your movements in the Dance of Creation are more vehement than seemly, he temporarily looks the other way. "I have to let you do this now. It's the only way you'll dance right some day. But no public performances until I say so."

If, then, you try to check your upstart originality against his standards, there's only the shrug by the window again. "That is how you do it. That is not the way it has always been done. Don't expect me to approve until you can put old and new together, and let them go, and dance as you should."

"How can I do that?"

"How? You dare to ask me HOW?"

You are silent, but it isn't a quelled-enough silence.

Grudgingly he adds: "Some things cannot be taught. They can only be learned."

Still later, he remarks in passing, "You know the difference between statement and art? *Rasa*. Simple word: juice. Complicated words: essence. Rasa, the essence and fulfillment of art. A whole world. In dancing—" he quotes again—"*eye follows hand, hand follows mind, mind follows emotions, emotions follow rasa.* Unless you achieve that mingling, you are nowhere. Enough talk now. Get back to work."

On your fifteenth birthday, in your last months at high school, Guruji starts you reading the medieval poets—Vidyapathi, Chandidas, Jnandas, Vishnudas. … "Theirs is the spirit of bhakti, child, and our dancing its body."

Squirm or rebel as you might, against the strength and pliancy of a poetry that can encompass a universe in a couplet, your own personal quirks become somehow irrelevant. Dancing changes, probably grows in you without your knowing it.

The morning after the school finals end, a hot blue April day with mangoes in the market and gul-mohur trees in masses of bloom so red that they seem to breathe (in, out … in, out …), Guruji sends for you.

"You did well in the exams? You must be tired. Rest now. Rest. Eat and sleep properly these first two weeks of the holidays. Then we will start again." He lowers his voice. "I will give you the five *parengs*."

The five parengs. Rarest and most revered of the dances; said to have been handed down by Krishna himself, so that a single misstep is tantamount to blasphemy.

Outside, a loose strand of the malati creeper, grown longer and more obdurate than ever, scrapes its starry white flowers against the door in the wind.

"It's true," Guruji says, smiling. "Shut your mouth, you don't have to say anything. Go home now. Rest. Prepare yourself."

How can you guess what you are preparing yourself for? Two years of straining yourself against limits you hadn't even known existed. An unimaginable stretching of yourself, within and without. Evenings when you weep at your sheer human inadequacy, pulverized with shame at betraying the discipline of this bare room; and Guruji says matter-of-factly: "How can you live an art until you have wept over it? When you come back from the other side of tears, you will dance as you should."

Afterwards you can never recapture the actuality, only sense in the abstract that final fusion: between how Guruji wants you to dance, and how you dance, and how (he tells you later, for you do not know) the audience "sees" you dance: completing with their eyes what you begin with your hands, so that, together, you re-create an art in the inheriting of it.

Parabola
Volume: 17.3
The Oral Tradition

Teacher, Student, Lineage

Rosemary Jeanes Antze

Knowledge in ancient India was oral in nature. The early religious texts, the Vedas and Upanishads, were passed on for many generations by word of mouth; only later were they committed to the written word. An oral tradition demanded a living representative—the *guru*—who both embodied and transmitted the traditional knowledge. In Vedic times it was customary for a father to pass on his learning to his son, thus perpetuating the knowledge through *parampara*, meaning lineage, progeny, uninterrupted row or series, succession or tradition. Here we have the main elements of the oral tradition: the teacher or guru, the student or *shishya*, and the unbroken line of knowledge or parampara, in which the master and disciple are individual participants in a tradition which stretches beyond both.

Oral traditions for passing on knowledge are still very much alive in India today. Certain kinds of skill lend themselves most naturally to such transmission through direct contact between teacher and taught. The ancient system of medicine, Ayurveda, is one such branch of learning which holds to traditional teaching methods. Another is storytelling, where myths come vividly to life when elders relate them to their grandchildren. Similarly, drama, dance, and music depend on the ability of the older generation first to master them, then to nurture them in the next generation.

Continuity in the arts relies on human beings. Written texts may record certain principles, but the belief in the efficacy of the living teacher goes back to the time of the ancient sage and teacher, Narada. "What is learnt from reliance on books and is not learnt from a teacher does not shine in an assembly."[1] Moreover, since dance and music communicate through nonverbal means and their nuances of expression lie beyond words, these arts are especially indebted to the living oral tradition. Students rely on their chosen guru as the key to the rich world of creative endeavor.

In the Upanishads, it is stated that:

> *The syllable* gu *means shadows (darkness)*
> *The syllable* ru, *he who disperses them.*
> *Because of his power to disperse darkness*
> *the guru is thus named.*
> *(Advayataraka Upanishad, verse 5)*

A guru in the primary sense is someone who leads the student from the darkness of ignorance into the light of knowledge. Although this is an interpretive rather than an etymological definition, it suggests the symbolic power of the guru—the honored preceptor at the heart of traditional learning.

As with a spiritual guru, dance gurus are usually viewed as surrogate parents: they give birth to the dancer in each of their students. Exponents of certain temple dance traditions were actually adopted so that mother and teacher became one.

The one-to-one relationship between guru and shishya is the cornerstone of the learning system, and implies a close and lasting contact between the two based on love and devotion. Ravi Shankar names the teacher as the first of three concepts at the heart of the music tradition: guru, *vinaya*, and *sadhana*. For a serious artist, choosing a guru is more important than choosing a husband or wife. Then vinaya follows, which is "humility tempered with love and worship."[2] Not only reverence but also fear can be part of a student's attitude towards his guru—and can contibute to his learning. Modeled on a father-son relationship, rather than that of friends or equals, the ideal rapport in music is intimate and at the same time hierarchical. The third concept, sadhana, which means practice and discipline, involves complete faithfulness to the guru's tradition and absolute obedience to his instructions in art and life.[3] Humility, obedience, and dedication are all attributes of a good student who must for several years rely completely

> *on the guidance of his guru. This is because the guru teaches everything to the shishya individually and directly according to our ancient oral traditions, for very rarely do we use textbooks or manuals.[4]*

It is necessary for a guru to be in constant contact with his student in order to be able to nurture his artistic skills and attitudes. The ancient system arranged this through *guru-kula*, in which the student was incorporated into the guru's household, almost as a family member. *Kula* is the Sanskrit word for family, lineage or house; hence, guru-kula means learning "at the house of the guru." This custom of going to live with the teacher, central to the system of ancient education, was the prevalent manner of learning music for all previous generations in North and South India, but for most present-day students of dance, guru-kula belongs to an idealized past. Restrictions of time in the modern rhythm of life permit only a few months of residing and learning in the guru's home, seldom the years of full training as in the past.

One guru-kula situation does remain intact in *Kuthiyattam*, the Sanskrit drama form of Kerala. Although there are a small and declining number of exponents, one teacher, Sri Madhava Cakyar, instructed his nephew, the traditional successor to the art, in Sanskrit, grammar, the epics *Mahabharata* and *Ramayana*, and *abhinaya* (acting). But his primary task was to teach his student how to behave in society.

The royal family in Cranganoor formerly provided free instruction in traditional subjects: astrology, ayurvedic medicine, Sanskrit literature and abhinaya. With the patronage and personal interest of royalty and rich landlords, the traditional arts were sustained, and the guru who took students into his home could teach without financial interest or worries.

A serious and committed dance school, Kalakshetra, founded in Madras in 1936 by Rukmini Devi, was established on principles that tried to retain the qualities and atmosphere of guru-kula. It is a boarding school where teachers and students live and work together for most of the year, with students staying for a minimum four-year course. The last master Chandu Pannikar, who was the pillar of the Kalakshetra Kathakali department, commanded the utmost respect, demanded full attention, and exacted strict discipline. Those who studied under him, including his son Kuniraman, say that students today would not be up to the hardships and discipline:

> Whenever you would visit him, he would make you do some prac-tice—eyes, talam [rhythm], mudras. It was twenty-four hours work. … Afterwards I realized why he scolded us, why he would get angry, even if someone who was sitting and watching praised us.[5]

The guru would tell even tougher stories of his own teacher, who once took him by the knot of his long hair and threw him against the wall, simply because he had stopped doing the rhythm.

But student life was not all trial. The close proximity with the guru also allowed the creativity of the master to flow whenever the mood took him. The susceptibility to mood—most critical in expressive art—was preserved and allowed within a disciplined structure of learning. Even if inspiration came to the master in the middle of the night, he would not hesitate to call his students to him to impart his knowledge.

But the call of the guru did not always mean that dance instruc-tion would be given. Another very important aspect of the guru-shishya relationship, especially possible in a guru-kula setting, is the "service" the student performs for the master: washing clothes, preparing and carrying hot water for a bath, giving massage and oil baths to the teacher, cleaning dishes, doing shopping, and conducting *puja*, or worship, in the guru's house when he is away. Service and obedience in mundane tasks seem to demonstrate the dedication and humility in the student and worthiness to receive the knowledge and skill embodied in the teacher. It remains an important element in the guru-shishya relationship today.

There was no prior arrangement for fees in the ancient system of education and certain texts actually condemn teachers who stipulated payment as a condition for accepting students.[6] However, the idea of *guru-dakshina*, gift for the guru, is a long accepted and traditional practice. Early sources suggest the ideal—that the gift was simply to please the teacher, not an equivalent or compensation for the knowledge received. This ideal was based on the belief that knowledge was so sacred that even when a guru taught a single letter of the alphabet, he could never be adequately recompensed with worldly wealth. Nevertheless, *dakshina* was appropriate at the completion of studies. An ancient law, Manu II:245–246, states that when the student is about to return home,

> *he may offer his guru some wealth, the gift of a field, gold, a cow, or a horse, or even shoes or an umbrella, or a seat, corn, vegetables and clothes (either singly or together) may engender pleasure in the teacher.*[7]

Naturally this tradition of guru-dakshina has been perpetuated in contemporary situations. A guru who has given of his art and his love expects gratitude and respect in the form of gifts.

The major gift-giving still takes place at the time when basic training is completed, which in dance coincides with the occasion of a first performance, called *arangetram* in Bharata Natyam. The standard practice was to give according to the student's abilities and the teacher's needs.

Other occasions for guru-dakshina are particular auspicious events—for example, the beginning of study or the first class back with a guru after a certain absence. The Mysore tradition of Bharata Natyam demanded that a guru be propitiated (as a god) with betel leaves, areca nuts and coconut, and gifts of clothes on the first day of study.[8]

The other occasion for dakshina is Saraswati *puja* which falls sometime during the month of October. Saraswati is the goddess of the arts and learning, so this day is highly favorable for beginning any artistic or creative endeavor. Gifts at special times and occasions contribute to the harmony of the relationship between guru and student, and demonstrate that the disciple is prepared to make sacrifices and sincerely values the knowledge and skill of which he partakes.

Perhaps the concept of guru exists within oneself, as one holds the image and power of the guru in one's mind and heart. In the initial stages of the relationship, the teacher is responsible for giving birth to the artistic being of the student and for nurturing the pupil's skills by taking the role of second parent. But then in the end the guru and his tradition become assimilated, contained within the disciple.

When set against the backdrop of tradition, parampara (the relation-ship between guru and student) becomes more than just a meeting and exchange between individuals. It serves as the vital link in the continuity of the dance.

Notes:

1 P. V. Kane, *History of the Dharmasastra*, vol. 2, pt. 1 (Poona: Bhardarkar Oriental Research Institute, 1968), pp. 348–49.

2 Ravi Shankar, *My Music, My Life* (New Delhi: Vikas Publications, 1968), p. 12.

3 Odissi guru Debu Prasad Das emphasizes his loyalty to his guru with the words, "If I change, I die."

4 Shankar, p. 13.

5 Kuniraman now teaches in California; the author spoke to him at Kalakshetra school in India.

6 A. S. Altekar, *Education in Ancient India* (Varanasi: Nand Kishore and Brothers, 1965), p. 81.

7 Kane, p. 360.

8 R. Sathayanarayana, *Bharata Natya: A Critical Study* (Mysore: Sri Varalakashmi Akademies of Fine Arts, 1969), p. 159.

Parabola
Volume: 14.1
Disciples
and Discipline

THE ROAR OF AWAKENING

Retold by Paul Jordan-Smith

Once upon a time a tigress, big with young, prowled hungrily for many days without discovering any prey, when she came upon a herd of goats. She leapt ravenously upon them, but the strain of the leap brought on the birth of her cub, and she, from sheer exhaustion, died in the process. The goats, who had scattered, returned to their grazing to find a tiger cub, whimpering beside its mother's body. In compassion, they adopted the poor creature and raised it as their own.

At first, the goats suckled the tiger cub with their own young, and as time passed it learned with them the language of the goats, adapting its voice to their gentle bleating. At first it was difficult to nibble the thin grass blades with its pointed teeth, but in time it managed, and the vegetarian diet kept its form trim and its temperament meek.

One night, after some years had passed and the tiger cub had nearly grown to his full size, a fierce old tiger attacked the herd and again it scattered. The cub, however, completely unafraid, remained where he was. He had never seen another tiger since his birth, and he stared at the intruder with utter amazement. Then he began to feel a little self-conscious and, uttering a thin and forlorn bleat, he nibbled at a blade of grass while the old tiger stared at him in amazement.

Suddenly the old tiger roared, "What are you doing among this herd of goats? What are you eating?" The cub looked up and bleated, and then returned to his grazing. The tiger roared again, "What is this sound you make? Do you think you are a goat?" Then, taking the cub by the scruff of the neck and shaking him, he carried him off to the edge of a pond. Setting him down, the old tiger compelled the younger to gaze at the glassy surface, illumined by the moon.

"There!" he roared. "Do you see the two faces reflected there, yours and mine? Are they not the same? Like myself, you have the face of a tiger, and indeed you are one. Why do you imagine yourself to be a goat? Why do you utter only that miserable bleating sound and nibble pitifully on thin blades of grass?"

At first the young tiger did not know what to say. He stared at his reflection and at that of the old one. Troubled, he shift his weight from paw to paw, and bleated quaveringly. The old tiger seized him again by the scruff of his neck and carried him off to his den. There he gave the young tiger a piece of raw meat from a fresh kill. The cub, shuddering with disgust, turned away and bleated. The old tiger ignored his cries and turned him again to the meat. "Take it! Eat! Swallow!" the old one bellowed, and forced the bloody meat into the young one's mouth.

At first, the unfamiliar taste and texture of the food was unbearable to the young tiger. He chewed as best he could, but the muscles of his jaws were weak from grazing, and his teeth not used to anything tougher than grass. The old tiger was relentless however, and as he chewed, the young one began for the first time to taste blood. He was alarmed at the new taste, but then amazed. Eagerly he swallowed the first morsel and seized another and began to chew. And as he chewed, a strange sensation began to creep over him, a fiery strength flowed into his veins and nerves and muscles and throughout the whole of his body. An excitement and a kind of drunken joy filled his heart. He licked his jowls and opened his mouth in an enormous yawn, as if awakening from a long sleep. His tail swept from side to side, and then from the depth of his lungs, grown mighty from the surge of energy that now flowed in him, there burst the terrible, glorious and triumphant roar of a tiger.

As the echoes of that roar died away down the valley below, the old one said to the younger, "Now do you know who you are? Come, let us go to the hunt."

Retold by Paul Jordan-Smith, from the version by Heinrich Zimmer in *Philosophies of India*, edited by Joseph Campbell (Princeton: Princeton University Press, 1951), pp. 5–8; and from *The Gospel of Sri Ramakrishna*, translated by Swami Nikhilananda (New York: Ramakrishna-Vivekananda Center, 1942).

Parabola
Volume: 24.4
Evil

THE SNAKE WHO LOST HIS HISS

Retold by Kamla Kapur

The elders of a village went to the Saint where he was meditating in a cave in the mountains, and complained about Nagarajah, an evil snake that had terrorized the village.

"His hiss can be heard for miles around," they said. "He bites and swallows our cattle, our dogs, our children, our men, our women. Even the bravest among us have become afraid to venture out into the fields which are dry, parched, uncultivated. Our granaries are depleted and empty. Our numbers are dwindling from death by the snake, and by starvation. Help us, Guru, you alone can subdue and vanquish him."

The Saint, realizing the gravity of the situation, descended to the village, and went to the large, spreading bodhi tree. This used to be the tree under which children played, yogis meditated, and lovers lay in each other's arms in the moonlight. But no more. Now at its coiling, twisted roots, the snake lived in his burrow.

"Come forth, O Ancient One," the Saint called, and the snake crept out of his hole, slithering and undulating, his scales shimmering in the sunlight. He was dark and shining in his majesty, awesome in his length and his beauty. He glided to the Guru and coiled up meekly at the man's feet.

"Oi, what is this I hear about you being the scourge of the village? Leave your destructive ways. Be good. Don't kill needlessly. Stop biting them. Leave them alone," the Saint said.

Because the snake had good karma, because he could be made conscious of the consequences of his acts, and because he had the sense and the power to obey the Saint, he returned to his burrow, resolving henceforth to leave his evil ways and be good.

The fields yielded grain, the children came out to play, the lovers loved, the brave came out with their bows and arrows, and the villagers were once again at peace.

One day, several months later, the Saint passed by the tree in the village, and found the snake coiled near the root of the tree. He was utterly transformed. His scales had fallen off, he looked mangy, emaciated, innocuous, limp. He had sores all over his body. He seemed to be on the verge of death.

"Oi, what happened to you?" the Saint asked.

"This, O Guru, is the fruit of obedience, of being good. I obeyed you, I gave up my evil ways, I let the villagers alone, I stopped biting them, I stopped eating their livestock, and what happened? Look what they did to me. The children come and throw stones at me. Even the rats dance on my head. I haven't eaten for months. I am simply waiting to be eaten when I die."

"This is your own fault," the Saint replied. "I told you not to bite them, but I didn't tell you not to hiss."

Parabola
Volume: 15.3
Liberation

Maya

Retold by Heinrich Zimmer

The teacher said: "Everything is God—this precept is the 'End of the Vedas.'"

As he heard this, the adept understood: God is the only reality. The Divine moves in all things, unsuffering, intangible; everything in the world, subject or object, is but the veil of Its *maya*.

He was seized by an enormously powerful feeling; he felt as if he were a huge and luminous cloud, endlessly expanding until it filled the whole sky, and he walked along like a cloud, freed from gravity's sway. In total self-absorption he kept to the middle of the road when all at once an elephant approached, marching toward him. The driver, seated high on the animal's neck, shouted down at him: "Give way! Give way!" And the bells on the huge animal's body surrounded its silently heaving form with silvery laughter as it moved along.

The adept heard and saw the elephant clearly, in spite of his ecstasy, but he did not get out of its way. He said to himself: "Why should I stand aside? I am God, and the elephant is God. Is God to live in fear of Himself?"

Fearlessly he walked towards the animal—and at the last moment the elephant seized him, wrapping him up in its trunk, sweeping him aside and depositing him not very gently in the dust of the roadside.

The adept, completely crushed and covered in dust,

went to his teacher and told him of the encounter.

The guru said: "You are quite right; you are God and the elephant is God—but why did you not listen to the voice of God speaking to you from above, on the elephant?"

Translated by Gerald Chapple and James B. Lawson from the first chapter of Heinrich Zimmer's *Weisheit Indiens: Märchen und Sinnbilder* (1938), which retold stories from the *Teachings of Ramakrishna*.

Parabola
Volume: 30.1
Awakening

THE LIBERATING SHOCK

Paramahansa Yogananda

I made my way to my master's empty sitting room.

I planned to meditate, but my laudable purpose was unshared by disobedient thoughts. They scattered like birds before the hunter.

"Mukunda!" Sri Yukteswar's voice sounded from a distant inner balcony.

I felt as rebellious as my thoughts. "Master always urges me to meditate," I muttered to myself. "He should not disturb me when he knows why I came to his room."

He summoned me again; I remained obstinately silent. The third time his tone held rebuke.

"Sir, I am meditating," I shouted protestingly.

"I know how you are meditating," my guru called out, "with your mind disturbed like leaves in a storm! Come here to me."

Snubbed and exposed, I made my way sadly to his side.

"Poor boy, the mountains couldn't give you what you wanted." Master spoke caressively, comfortingly. His calm gaze was unfathomable. "Your heart's desire shall be fulfilled."

Sri Yukteswar seldom indulged in riddles; I was bewildered. He struck gently on my chest above the heart.

My body became immovably rooted; breath was drawn out of my lungs as if by some huge magnet. Soul and mind instantly lost their physical bondage, and streamed out like a fluid piercing light from every pore. My sense of identity embraced the circumambient atoms. The roots of plants and trees appeared through a dim transparency of the soil; I discerned the inward flow of their sap.

My ordinary frontal vision was now changed to a vast spherical sight. Through the back of my head I saw men strolling far down Rai Ghat Road, and noticed also a white cow who was leisurely approaching. When she reached the space in front of the open ashram gate, I observed her with my two physical eyes. As she passed by, behind the brick wall, I saw her clearly still.

All objects within my panoramic gaze trembled and vibrated like quick motion pictures. My body, Master's, the pillared courtyard, the furniture and floor, the trees and sunshine, occasionally became violently agitated, until all melted into a luminescent sea; even as sugar crystals, thrown into a glass of water, dissolve after being shaken.

An oceanic joy broke upon calm endless shores of my soul. The Spirit of God, I realized, is exhaustless Bliss; His body is countless tissues of light. A swelling glory within me began to envelop towns, continents, the earth, solar and stellar systems, tenuous nebulae, and floating universes. The sharply etched global outlines faded somewhat at the farthest edges; there I could see a mellow radiance, ever-undiminished. It was indescribably subtle; the planetary pictures were formed of a grosser light.

I cognized the center of the empyrean as a point of intuitive perception in my heart. Irradiating splendor issued from my nucleus to every part of the universal structure. Blissful *amrita*, the nectar of immortality, pulsed through me with a quicksilverlike fluidity. The creative voice of God I heard resounding as *Aum*, the vibration of the Cosmic Motor.

Suddenly the breath returned to my lungs. With a disappointment almost unbearable, I realized that my infinite immensity was lost. Once more I was limited to the humiliating cage of a body, not easily accommodative to the Spirit. Like a prodigal child, I had run away from my macrocosmic home and imprisoned myself in a narrow microcosm.

My guru was standing motionless before me; I started to drop at his holy feet in gratitude for the experience in cosmic consciousness which I had long passionately sought. He held me upright, and spoke calmly, unpretentiously.

"You must not get overdrunk with ecstasy. Much work yet remains for you in the world. Come; let us sweep the balcony floor; then we shall walk by the Ganges."

A master bestows the divine experience of cosmic consciousness when his disciple, by meditation, has strengthened his mind to a degree where the vast vistas would not overwhelm him. The experience can never be given through one's mere intellectual willingness or open-mindedness. Only adequate enlargement by yoga practice and devotional *bhakti* can prepare the mind to absorb the liberating shock of omnipresence. It comes with a natural inevitability to the sincere devotee. His intense craving begins to pull at God with an irresistible force.

Adapted from Paramahansa Yogananda, *Autobiography of a Yogi* (Los Angeles: Self-Realization Fellowship, 1998), pp. 141–45. Reprinted by permission.

Parabola
Volume: 17.3
The Oral Tradition

Stillness

Swami Chetanananda

Many myths, sacred stories, and rituals are attempts to recreate a sense of stillness. This is their essence. Indeed, without some awareness of stillness, ritual takes on only its external approximation, becoming heavy and solemn. On the other hand, ritual that arises out of the experience of stillness is a light and joyful thing.

This is not inertia, but the dynamic stillness of the Self, which Abhinavagupta, the thirteenth-century master of the Kashmir Shaivite tradition of India, described as pure consciousness. It is from here that our notion of "I" as an individual self coalesces and reveals the multiplicity of the universe. Stillness is not the same thing as silence, nor is it like quieting the mind. It does not operate on a simply personal level. The stillness we are interested in knowing is always within us, even as we are within it, and we find freedom through our contact with it. As we have become established in our contact with its power, we recognize that all our desires, wants, needs, insecurities, and tensions are nothing. Underlying every pursuit, and even our quest for meaning as a whole, is the longing for contact with stillness. When we have this, what more is needed?

We see this in the story of the Buddha when he sat down and resolved not to move until he had achieved enlightenment. Once he had made this commitment, all kinds of terrors and temptations overtook him. It was his ability to abide in stillness, even as everything within him intensified, that allowed for his awakening. The great stillness he discovered was the source of his enlightenment and liberation, and of all the Buddhist teachings.

The mind *does* have a connection to this reality, but not one that the mind itself can recognize. Through stillness, we discover over and over again that this is not what we thought it was. What we learn about it has nothing to do with accumulated knowledge.

So, what is the knowledge being conveyed by the different oral traditions? It is not spiritual *knowledge* because, practically speaking, this is useless. Rather, it is spiritual *experience*—an experience of stillness.

We are reaching for something deeper within us. When we come into its presence, our ordinary minds and capacity for language are useless. The transmission of the knowledge we seek occurs only obliquely through the spoken word, and more directly through silence, both of which constitute aspects of an oral tradition.

In India, the two kind of transmission are reflected in two terms for "teacher." One is *acharya*, the other is *guru*. Acharya means "instructor," or "transmitter of information," while guru is the "dispeller of darkness," or "giver of light." To interact with a guru is to participate in a shared learning experience of a different order.

It is the teacher, in this second sense, who is the locus of our contact with stillness. In Sufism, for example—and particularly among the Mevlevi dervishes—the teacher is referred to as "the post." In the rituals, he takes on the role of the still point at the center around which the students whirl and turn.

In many of the teaching traditions of India, awareness of the sacred is transmitted through the oral tradition of mantra. Usually this is taken to be a system of practices based on sound, but this is somewhat misleading. The knowledge that the master transmits is more subtle than verbal instruction about mantra or even the experience of sound itself.

When one receives a mantra in direct transmission from a teacher, it is the resonance of the teacher's awareness—his or her direct contact with dynamic stillness—that is being conveyed, not simply a word or syllable to repeat. This is why the explanation of the mantra must be oral and direct.

In the Kashmir Shaivite tradition, what is truly significant about a mantra is not its actual syllables, but what is present and unchanging between them. The syllables—their cadence, rhythm, and pitch—are all changeable, just as every breath we take is different. What is never different, however, is what lies between the syllables: that stillness which is beyond time and space, and beyond any kind of classification.

In the beginning, we practice speaking and breathing the mantra. In the end, the breath of the mantra practices us.

Parabola
Volume: 26.3
The Fool

Viddhi! Kooshmãndam

Translated by Reade Wood

In Kori-Kotta there lived an expert doctor who could save people from even the most venomous serpent bites. As was the usual practice, he would not go to the patient, the patient would be brought to him, for there is an agreement between poison-doctors and snakes—snakes won't bite poison-doctors, and doctors won't go to treat those who have been bitten. The patient would stay at the doctor's house until he was cured. The doctor would never accept money for his services. However, the grateful patient would leave an offering at the doctor's door. The doctor thus became a wealthy man and was known all over Kerala for his skill. Many students came to him, and to each he gave a divine mantra.

Just south of the doctor's home lived a once-prosperous family who now were so poor they could barely afford one meal a day. Their only son, Kocchu Rãman, decided to become a poison-doctor like his rich neighbor. Unfortunately, this was only a dream, for the youth was a numbskull; in fact, he even found the alphabet too hard to master.

One day he asked some of the doctor's students: "I want to be a doctor. What must I do?"

"You must first approach a teacher and request him to accept you as his student. Then offer at his feet the best offering you can give. If he is pleased with you, he will impart a divine mantra to you. Repeat that mantra with concentration over and over, day after day, and you will gain power. Once you have attained mastery, chant the mantra over some water and give this to your patient. The poison will leave his body."

Kocchu Rāman was overjoyed to hear this, it sounded so simple! But the next moment he was sad, for he had nothing to give the teacher. He walked back to his tumble-down house, and looking up saw a pumpkin entwined around the eaves. There were five pumpkins on the vine. Kocchu Rāman smiled: "I'll give these to the teacher!"

The next morning Kocchu Rāman woke before dawn, bathed, and plucked the pumpkins. He put them in a basket and carried them to the teacher's house. When the doctor walked of out his door that morning the first thing he saw was Kocchu Rāman standing before him with a basket of pumpkins on his head and a foolish smile on his face.

"Why have you come?" asked the doctor.

Rāman placed the pumpkins at the feet of the doctor and prostrated. "I want to be a doctor. Please teach me how to remove poison!"

"What's this, *viddhi! Kooshmāndam?*" [Sanskrit for "Idiot! Pumpkins?"]

Kocchu Rāman was so excited with the prospect of becoming a doctor that when he heard "Viddhi Kooshmandam" he thought the teacher had accepted him! He was filled with bliss and couldn't speak a word. He prostrated before his teacher again and ran off, leaving the doctor puzzled. As soon as Kocchu Rāman reached home he bathed again, lit a lamp, sat down before it, and began to recite the mantra, and such was his ardor, that after a few months he gained the power to cure.

For the first few days he had no clients, for no one believed him capable. Rāman didn't know that poison-doctors never go to see their patients, so he would go to wherever someone was bitten, chant his mantra over some water, and cure them. News of his skill spread and he became known as a great healer. People came from all over Kerala to take Rāman with them to cure victims of snake bite. He soon amassed much wealth, for he didn't now that a doctor should not accept gifts directly.

One day the King of Kori-Kotta was bitten by a very poisonous snake. All the best poison-doctors were called, but all of them failed to cure the king. The king grew weaker, and by the third day he could not move or speak. Preparations were made for his funeral. It was then that Kocchu

Rāman was summoned to the palace. As soon as he arrived he ordered rice gruel to be prepared. When the other doctors heard what this new doctor had asked for, they asked:

"What is this for? The king hasn't taken food for three days now. He is fated to die, no skill on earth can save him. Who is this fool?"

Kocchu Rāman chanted his mantra over some water and washed the king's face with it. The king opened his eyes. The doctor again chanted and sprinkled water over the body of the king. The king sat up in his bed and asked for some rice gruel. At once it was brought and the king ate it. A few moments later he felt completely well.

"Who removed the poison?" asked the king.

"This Kocchu Rāman who stands before you, sire," answered the courtiers. The happy king gave the doctor a thousand gold coins and two gold chain-bracelets of honor. He ordered his men to carry the great doctor home in the royal palanquin with a troop of musicians singing his praises. All the other doctors were ordered to walk behind the palanquin, acknowledging Kocchu Rāman's greatness.

The crowd of doctors who had gathered at the court were deeply shamed at their inadequacy, and asked one another who this new doctor was. One of them was Rāman's own teacher. But there was such a sea of people surrounding Kocchu Rāman that he did not recognize him.

The procession made its way through the city and into the countryside. Kocchu Rāman happened to turn around and recognize his teacher walking behind him. At once he descended from the palanquin, placed his presents before the feet of his teacher, and prostrated.

"What does all this mean?" asked the astonished teacher.

"All this is because of your blessings! I've been so busy I was unable to see you earlier. Please forgive me and accept this humble offering."

"But I never taught you anything!"

"The mantra that you gave me was my only instruction."

"What mantra?"

Kocchu Rāman whispered in his teacher's ear:

VIDDHI KOOSHMĀNDAM.

From *Folk Tales from Kerala* by Reade Wood.

Parabola
Volume: 15.3
Liberation

Walking on Water

Retold by Heinrich Zimmer

A Brahman had built his hermit's hut near the great river. Every day a milkmaid came over on the ferry and brought him some milk from the shepherd on the other shore. Sometimes she came rather late, which annoyed the Brahman. The milkmaid apologized, saying she often had to wait a long time if the ferryboat had just left or was on the other shore.

"Utter foolishness," cried the Brahman with scorn, "this ferryboat!" and he went on to say, somewhat hesitantly: "Child, a man of faith, with God's name in his heart and on his lips, is able to walk over the waters of the unendingly circling sea of innumerable deaths and rebirths unto the distant shore—and the mere waters of a river are supposed to stay his feet?"

The milkmaid stood before the holy man, silent and ashamed. Then she bowed down before him and, taking some of the dust at his feet, she placed it on her forehead.

The next day the milkmaid appeared promptly and so too on each day following. The Brahman was delighted by her zeal and finally asked her: "How is it that you are now always so punctual?"

The girl replied: "Master, I am doing as you told me to. With God's name in my heart and on my lips, I walk in faith upon the water; my foot does not sink, nor do I have need of any ferryboat."

•

The Brahman stood in silent amazement before the miraculous power of the name of God in so simple a creature; but he gave no sign of this and said:

"This is well and good. I shall go with you and watch you walk upon the water and I myself will walk with you across the river."

He wanted to observe the miracle working for the girl; if this young thing could do it, then it would have to work for him too.

When they came to the bank, the girl's lips were silently moving; gazing into the distance she constantly whispered the name of God and floated light as a feather on the water. The swiftly flowing water gurgled beneath her without splashing up on her; the soles of her feet seemed not to be touching it.

The Brahman was amazed and, quickly gathering up the hem of his garment a little, began to murmur God's name as he entered upon the water. But he was unable to keep pace with the milkmaid, who was continuously flying ahead with the supple flight of a swallow—he was in danger of sinking. The girl noticed this, gave a merry laugh, and called to him over the rushing water as she wafted away from him.

"No wonder, Master, that you are sinking! How is the name of God to bear you over the water when in the very act of calling to Him you lift up your garment for fear of getting the hem of it wet?"

Translated by Gerald Chapple and James B. Lawson from the first chapter of Heinrich Zimmer's *Weisheit Indiens: Märchen und Sinnbilder* (1938), which retold stories from the *Teachings of Ramakrishna*.

•

CHAPTER FIVE

The Four Aims of Life

Thus we may go so far as to assert …
that however a religion may be self-sufficient if it be
followed to the very end to which it is directed,
there can hardly be supposed a way so plain that it could not here
and there be better illuminated by other lights than that of the
pilgrim's private lantern,
the light of any lantern being only a refraction of the Light of lights.
A diversity of routes is not merely appropriate
to a diversity of travelers,
who are neither all alike,
nor start from one and the same point,
but may be of incalculable aid to any traveler who can rightly read
the map;
for where all roads converge,
there can be none of them that does not help
to clarify the true position of the center of the maze,
"short of which we are still in a duality."…

In the matter of direction towards the Kingdom of Heaven
"within you," the modern world is far more lacking in the will to
seek, than likely to led astray by false direction.

—A. K. Coomaraswamy

Now verily, a person consists of purpose. According to the purpose a
person has in this world, so does he become on departing hence. So let
him frame for himself a purpose.

—Chandogya Upanishad

Hindu thinkers have always recognized that a "diversity of routes" is "appropriate to a diversity of travelers," as A. K. Coomaraswamy says in the first epigraph. For everyone in the world truly is different, not only in character and circumstance but most important in aim; as the *Chandogya Upanishad* says, "According to the purpose a person has in this world, so does he become on departing hence."

The opening selection in this chapter, Karl Potter's "Four Indian Attitudes toward Money," frames the four "aims" or paths traditionally recognized in Hindu thought: *artha*, *kama*, *dharma*, and *moksha*. Potter interestingly differentiates these paths in terms of the relative concern those who follow them have for others, and of their attachment to the affairs of the world.

The artha point of view is generally characterized by the pursuit of wealth and, in Potter's terms, minimal concern for the objects and people one interacts with in daily life. Kautilya's *Arthashastra*, the Indian equivalent of Machiavelli's *The Prince*, gives advice on how to achieve the aims of artha; it is not cited anywhere in this volume. One whose aim is defined by artha is essentially manipulative, and there have not been any articles in *Parabola* exploring this path. Sri Aurobindo's "The Role of Money," in fact, advocates abandoning the aims of artha even when handling money.

Kama, loosely translated "desire," involves passionate attachment and "growing but weak concern" for the objects of one's desire. It is perhaps the most slippery of the aims of life to address, for although attachment to things of the world ultimately leads to misery, as told in many stories and in the teachings of the Buddha, attachment to and desire for the divine are the very foundation of *bhakti*, devotional worship, which is the most widely practiced spiritual path of Hindus. (In this case, of course, concern for that which is desired is very strong.)

Erotic love, that most salient manifestation of kama, is well known as a disturber of the peace of mind, society, and even the cosmos. The power of love to disturb even a sage—and the renewed life such love can lead to—is explored in "The Triumph of Desire." Next, Diane Wolkstein retells the great myth of the love of Shiva and Sati, in which love literally makes the world go round and loss makes it stop, in "The Eternal Dance of the Universe." The power of love, parental or erotic, to open us to divinity is a truth inextricably bound to the stories of

Krishna's childhood. This is the theme of John Stratton Hawley's "The Thief in Krishna."

The third aim of life, dharma, often translated "duty," implies adherence to traditional norms of behavior. How these expectations of order are handed down within the family is suggested by Lizelle Reymond in her account of personal experience in "Laws and Customs in a Brahmin Family." But adherence to dharma, famously advocated by the charioteer Krishna in his speech to Arjuna in the *Bhagavad Gita* (translated in "Selfless Service") also allows space for, even mandates, a respect for one's fellow actors in the drama of life. As Karl Potter says, "the attitude of dharma is an attitude of concern for others as well as a fundamental extension of oneself." Glen Kezwer's "Inviolate Action," in which Gandhi's understanding of Krishna's words is discussed also revolves around this theme. As Kezwer points out, however, Arjuna and Gandhi had a "more profound motive" for their actions than just to follow dharma. They "desired to attain the highest state of liberation."

Moksha or liberation is, as Potter says, the "most worthwhile kind of attitude" in the Hindu tradition. In moksha one is attached to nothing, and thus "free to show universal concern for others." In practice, this is most apt to result in an oceanic sense of the oneness of human souls rather than an impulse to feed the poor and heal the sick. It is the path of the renunciate, the *sannyasi*, as explored by Wayne Teasdale in "Dweller in the Cave of the Heart." Teasdale estimates "conservatively" that there are twenty million renunciates in India. Even in a population of one billion, this is a critical mass that profoundly affects the society. There are many, many more individuals who, while not becoming full renunciates, structure their lives in such a way as to allow time and space to pursue the knowledge necessary for eventual liberation. An interview with one such spiritual seeker, Shri Parthasarathi Rajagopalachari ("A Terrible Longing in the Heart") gives a taste of the attitude of one on the path of moksha.

Finally, Heinrich Zimmer's retelling of the story of "Krishna and King Mucukunda: The Sleeper Awakened" opens up the cosmic dimension of moksha—release from the endless round of rebirths that is mankind's usual fate.

Parabola
Volume: 16.1
Money

Four Indian Attitudes Toward Money

Karl H. Potter

The love of money is, according to the Christian New
Testament, the root of all evil. That is a typically Western
point of view, supported by the amount of attention given
to acquiring material wealth, particularly in American
society. It is interesting to compare this form of attachment with the "four aims of life" in traditional Hindu
thought, and thus to relate a specific viewpoint toward
money to the implications of a standard classification of
human concerns handed down for over two millennia.

When reflecting on man's situation the classical
thinkers of ancient India had recourse to a series of four
notions frequently called, in contemporary accounts of
them, "aims of life." The Sanskrit terms for these four
notions are *artha, kāma, dharma*, and *mokṣa*. The proper
understanding of the meaning of these terms, though
essential for understanding classical Indian philosophies,
is by no means easy.

To call these four things "aims" suggests that they are
states toward which one aims. Now in some sense perhaps the last of the four, mokṣa or complete freedom, is
a state, but the sense in which this is so is one which
makes it inappropriate to apply the same description to
the other three. There is no state of artha, of kāma, or of
dharma which a man may come to realize and rest in.

Rather these terms are to be construed more subtly, perhaps as attitudes or orientations.

Artha is usually said to have to do with material prosperity. Kāma has specifically to do with sexual relations—and incidentally with aesthetic value. Dharma is said to concern the duties of one's station in life, the requirements laid down by one's involvement in family, caste, or class. It is certainly not at all easy to see the underlying rationale for this list, and calling them "aims," that is, attitudes or orientations, may not seem in any very evident fashion to help us understand the notions better. Nevertheless, if we take time to explore the concepts, I think the reader will see why calling them attitudes is perhaps the least misleading way of assessing them.

Consider first the kind of attitude one tends to take toward material objects that one has to handle from day to day in the routine of making a living—say, toward the door to one's office. How concerned are we for the door? That is to say, do we identify ourselves with the door and care what happens to it? Yes, but minimally. We care that the door opens and shuts when operated. We may care what it looks like, that it not have an unpleasant appearance. Beyond that, it would not occur to most of us to have a concern for the door. It is, therefore, an object of minimal concern for us, and it is the attitude of minimal concern which is the attitude marked out by the word *artha*.

Now such an attitude can, in principle, be taken toward any item in the world. Most people take an attitude of minimal concern toward some animals, or even all animals. Most of us take this attitude toward some people, reserving our attitudes of personal concern for relatives and close friends. A few people have no close friends, and treat their relatives impersonally. There have even been cases where we might be justified in suspecting that a person has taken an attitude of minimal concern toward himself, although this has an air of paradox about it; nevertheless, one who kills himself in a fit of despair may well be thought to have, at least at the suicidal moment, considered himself as of minimal concern. When the Indians have said that artha has to do with material prosperity, I think they have had in mind that those things which are manipulated in making a living, including in some places people or even oneself, that *those* things are typically things toward which we take an attitude of minimal concern. But it is the kind of attitude that the Indians were interested in, and the identification of this attitude by reference to material prosperity was merely a convenient way of marking down contexts in which this attitude is most frequently taken. It is not a defining characteristic of the attitude of minimal concern, artha, that it be directed toward those things with which we come in contact in our search for material prosperity, although it is in fact true that we tend to see this attitude exhibited frequently toward those things.

To take the artha attitude toward things is to exhibit maximal attachment coupled with minimal concern. With specific relation to the attitude toward money, the case that comes to mind is the seeker after wealth, the concupiscent miser or spendthrift. Such a person sees money as an end in itself or a means of fathering more material goods, of displaying more things' dependence on himself. He aggrandizes the things he desires, caring little for how their wishes or interests (if any) are served in so doing. His attachment is measured by his dependence on money; without it he views his own worth as negligible. As a result, but without his seeing it, he is completely dependent on things other than himself. If his wealth should perish, he surely would also be doomed.

The attitude one tends to take toward those to whom one is passionately attracted has a very distinct feeling from the attitude of minimal concern. Again, one may take this attitude of kāma or passionate concern toward anything in the world. The little girl who hugs her teddy bear takes it toward an inanimate object, while the grown man who loves a woman passionately takes it toward an animate one. Again, it is possible to take this attitude toward oneself, as may be the case in narcissism. The mark of this attitude is an element of possessiveness in the concern one has for the object of one's attentions, coupled with a partial identification of oneself with that object.

In the kāma relationship one depends upon the object that is loved and therefore guards it jealously, restricting if need be its habits or wishes (if it has them) in one's own interest. This is also true, to be sure, of the artha attitude, for one who takes an attitude of minimal concern toward a thing may guard it jealously and not hesitate to restrict its habits or wishes. But in the kāma attitude, unlike the artha one, there is a feeling that at some moments, at any rate, one is enlarged by becoming one with the loved one or thing. The little girl projects herself as the teddy bear and talks and feels on its behalf and receives satisfaction therefrom, as does the successful lover who in making love projects himself as the beloved and acts, for the moment, as if he were she or the two were one. Again it is paradoxical to speak of the narcissist projecting himself into himself; this seems to involve two uses of the word "self," for the self that projects is distinct from the self into which it is projected. But the paradox will be recognized, I think, as reflecting something essentially true. As before, when Indians describe the kāma in terms of sexual relations they do not mean to restrict the operation of this attitude to just those objects with which one can come into a sexual relationship, but are rather pointing to sexual relationships as typically involving instances of the taking of this kind of attitude.

To take the kāma attitude, then, is to exhibit a strong attachment coupled with a growing but weak concern. Applying this to money, one can see that the lover sees money as a means of winning the affection of loved ones. But real love, one may well respond, requires maximal concern, unqualified commitment to another's welfare. To put a price on sharing must surely qualify in some fundamental way that extent of one's concern for one's beloved. Maximal concern, in turn, is a state free from dependence—on money, on the beloved's affection, on anything else but one's pure concern for others. So the kāma attitude, though more admirable than that of the life of dependence and attachment characteristic of the artha-oriented person, falls short of true or real love insofar as it constitutes a claim on the other and thus a dependence on him or her.

When we turn to the dharma notion, we find again that it is an attitude to which the term has primary reference. It is an attitude of concern greater than that involved in artha or kāma. In taking the dharma attitude, one treats as oneself things commonly thought of as other than oneself; not, however, in the way that the kāma-oriented man treats himself—in a spirit of passion and possessiveness—but rather in a spirit of respect. That is, not only do we in the dharma orientation project ourselves into others, but we do so with a certain conception of ourselves which precludes either using others or depending on them as the artha- or kāma-oriented person does. It is customary to render dharma as "duty" in English translations of Sanskrit works dealing with the "aims of life." This rendering has the merit that it suggests, following Kant's use of the word "duty," the crucial aspect of respect for the habits and wishes of others. It has the drawback, however, that it suggests to many people a rather stiff, perhaps even harsh, attitude, from which one tends to withdraw to something halfway between possessive love and "righteous" minimal concern. As a result, there is a supposed irreconcilability between an ethics of passionate concern for others and an ethics of duty which operates independently of such concern. But we need not wish this difficulty upon Indian thought; dharma does not mean "duty" in any sense of lack of concern for others—quite the opposite. The attitude of dharma is an attitude of concern for others as a fundamental extension of oneself. To see more clearly what this means we do well once more to appeal to examples.

Like the others, the dharma attitude can be taken toward anything, but the Indians mention certain things in the world as being more frequently its object. The attitude of a wise and loving mother toward her child is a case in point: The mother is concerned for her child as a fundamental and (within this orientation) indistinguishable part of herself. Her own self is enlarged by this identification. But since she respects herself—i.e., she respects her own habits and wishes, unlike one who takes an artha or kāma attitude to herself—she must also respect her child's habits and wishes, so that she neither uses the child for her own devices nor does she depend on the child in the way the passionate lover depends on his beloved. This is because the child is part of herself within this orientation. And generally speaking, since Indians have a strong feeling for the sacredness of family ties, relations of parent to child and grandchild, of child to parent and grandparent, are primary areas where one may expect to find the dharmic attitude exemplified. Not far removed, too, are the relations between oneself and the rest of one's clan, or caste, or class. Here, too, one may hope to find dharma instances, although all too frequently—especially in this day and age, so degenerate according to classical Indian tradition—one will be disappointed.

This dharma attitude involves weakening attachment and strengthening concern. Such a one sees money as a means of helping others to gain ends one views as worthwhile for them. He is willing, indeed eager, to part with his money to help others, provided he views their aims as right and their cause as just. He is able to love, showing concern for others, though this love is still tempered by judgments about relative worth, relative to *his* ends. These claims on him are, though, when he is being honest with himself, subject to doubt and suspicion—and when he is not so honest, the claims may be met with defensive insistence coupled with a refusal to succumb to the doubts and suspicions. Still, the dharmic person is, as has been frequently recognized by psychologists, less at the mercy of unwanted developments, more able to bear up under strain and hardship. His money is not everything to him, as it is to the miser, nor is it something he depends on for everything he holds dear, as it may be for the passionate lover who needs money to keep the attention of the beloved. Loss of such a one's money may (though unfortunately it may not) be the catalyst to propel him forward to the state of liberation, the fourth state which I am about to discuss.

The route to superior control, to the fourth and most worthwhile kind of attitude, mokṣa or complete freedom, lies in the mastery of attitudes of greater and greater concern coupled with less and less attachment or possessiveness. In fact, the fourth orientation is well understood by extrapolating from this route. In moving from artha to kāma, we move from lack of concern to concern, and from more attachment to less. Mokṣa or freedom is the perfection of this growth. When one attains freedom, one is both not at the mercy of what is not oneself (that is to say, one is free from restrictions initiated by the not-self), and one is also free to anticipate and control anything to which one turns one's efforts, since the whole world is considered as one's self in this orientation. The *freedom-from* corresponds to one's lack of attachment, and the *freedom-to*, to one's universal concern.

The mokṣa attitude is one of maximal concern and minimal attachment. One is not attached to money or to making it; one is not at the mercy of any need for money, one is not dependent on having it. That is to say, then, that one is free to show universal concern for others. One's own needs are completely subjected so as to leave room for the needs of others, to behave so as to strengthen their concern and lessen their attachment. Indian myths and histories are full of examples illustrating behavior reflecting this combination of attitudes. Indian traditions covering the expectations about the behavior of holy men underscore their conception of such a one's nature. As examples one may consult the *Jātaka* stories of the Buddha's former births, stories which range over the gamut of stages of his lives but include several in which he displays undemanding sympathy and understanding of others coupled with complete sacrifice for their betterment.

It is, of course, far too easy to misrepresent this ultimate stage of spiritual advancement. Nonliberated folk, among other shortcomings, are understandably incapable of accurately distinguishing the really liberation person from the consciously fake or unconsciously self-deluded display of some of the presumed features of liberation. The notion of liberation has the capacity to hoodwink the best-intentioned sympathizers, and people uncompelled by any vision of spiritual perfection find this a mark of the shortcomings of this entire way of viewing human aims. It is probable that current movements in India are undermining the classic theory of the aims of life and its implication of complete freedom—minimal attachment with maximal concern—as being the fundamental aim and purpose of life. Yet that way of thinking about human purposes still sways some of the ordinary folk in Indian villages, and in the now-distant past has moved ancient wise men to produce some of the most stupendously rich literature on human life and its ultimate purpose that has ever been composed. Perhaps it is not *passé* even now.

Adapted by the author from Karl H. Potter, *Presuppositions of India's Philosophies* ([1963] Westport, Conn.: Greenwood, 1972), pp. 5–10.

Parabola
Volume: 16.1
Money

The Role of Money

Sri Aurobindo

Money is the visible sign of a universal force, and this force in its manifestation on earth works on the vital and physical planes and is indispensable to the fullness of the outer life. In its origin and its true action it belongs to the Divine. But like other powers of the Divine it is delegated here and, in the ignorance of the lower Nature, can be usurped for the uses of the ego or held by Asuric[1] influences and perverted to their purpose. This is indeed one of the three forces—power, wealth, sex—that have the strongest attraction for the human ego and the Asura and are most generally misheld and misused by those who retain them. The seekers or keepers of wealth are more often possessed rather than its possessors; few escape entirely a certain distorting influence stamped on it by its long seizure and perversion by the Asura. For this reason most spiritual disciplines insist on a complete self-control, detachment and renunciation of all bondage to wealth and of all personal and egoistic desire for its possession. Some even put a ban on money and riches and proclaim poverty and the bareness of life as the only spiritual condition. But this is an error; it leaves the power in the hands of the hostile forces. To re-conquer it for the Divine to whom it belongs and use it divinely for the divine life is the supramental way for the Sadhaka.[2]

You must neither turn with an ascetic shrinking from

the money power, the means it gives and the objects it brings, nor cherish a rajasic[3] attachment to them or a spirit of enslaving self-indulgence in their gratifications. Regard wealth simply as a power to be won back for the Mother[4] and placed at her service.

All wealth belongs to the Divine and those who hold it are trustees, not possessors. It is with them today, tomorrow it may be elsewhere. All depends on the way they discharge their trust while it is with them, in what spirit, with what consciousness in their use of it, to what purpose.

In your personal use of money, look on all you have or get or bring as the Mother's. Make no demand but accept what you receive from her and use it for the purposes for which it is given to you. Be entirely selfless, entirely scrupulous, exact, careful in detail, a good trustee; always consider that it is her possessions and not your own that you are handling. On the other hand, what you receive for her, lay religiously before her; turn nothing to your own or anybody else's purpose.

Do not look up to men because of their riches or allow yourself to be impressed by the show, the power or the influence. When you ask for the Mother, you must feel that it is she who is demanding through you a very little of what belongs to her and the man from whom you ask will be judged by his response.

If you are free from the money-taint but without any ascetic withdrawal, you will have a greater power to command the money for the divine work. Equality of mind, absence of demand and the full dedication of all you possess and receive and all your power of acquisition to the Divine Shakti[5] and her work are the signs of this freedom. Any perturbation of mind with regard to money and its use, any claim, any grudging is a sure index of some imperfection or bondage.

The ideal Sadhaka in this kind is one who if required to live poorly can so live and no sense of want will affect him or interfere with the full inner play of the divine consciousness, and if he is required to live richly, can so live and never for a moment fall into desire or attachment to his wealth or to the things that he uses or servitude to self-indulgence or a weak bondage to the habits that the possession of riches creates. The divine Will is all for him and the divine Ananda.[6]

In the supramental creation, the money-force has to be restored to the Divine Power and used for a true and beautiful and harmonious equipment and ordering of a new divinized vital and physical existence, in whatever way the Divine Mother herself decides in her creative vision. But first it must be conquered back for her, and those will be strongest for the conquest who are in this part of their nature strong, and large, and free from ego; and surrendered without any claim or withholding or hesitation, pure and powerful channels for the Supreme Puissance.

Notes:

1   *Asura* designates the demon or anti-god.

2   Seeker.

3   Rajah-[like passionate—ed.]

4   The Divine Power.

5   Another name for the Divine Power.

6   Grace.

Parabola
Volume: 20.4
Eros

Triumph of Desire

Retold by D. K. M. Kartha

Once, during the reign of Lomapada, drought ravaged the kingdom of Anga. Season after season the rains failed, and distress overwhelmed the land. When respectfully consulted, Lomapada's advisers told him to seek out Rishya Shringa, the son of sage Vibhandaka, who lived in the forest adjoining Anga in total devotion to spiritual practice. If this young man would set foot in the land, the soil would cool and the clouds would gather to rain over the sanctified kingdom, for he had amassed vast redemptive powers through his pure, austere life.

There was one difficulty in seeking to bring Rishya Shringa to the kingdom. He was being brought up in a peculiar way by his father Vibhandaka: the boy had never seen another human being except his father; he had never tasted a sweet fruit or smelled a flower; he had never heard a note of music except for the three-tone chant that pacifies the senses and the mind; and he had never embraced anyone. His father had a reason for banishing all sensuous experiences from the boy's life. When Vibhandaka himself was young, he had lived a celibate life of spiritual pursuits, but then one day he happened to see Urvashi, the dancer of the heavens, as she bathed. His seed spilled and was swallowed by a doe that was drinking from the river. Thus Rishya Shringa was born from the doe and had a single horn on his forehead.

Because Vibhandaka wanted to avoid such mishaps in his son's life so that his spiritual power might become colossal, he arranged for his son to be totally secluded from all worldly distractions from birth. Even bushes with sweet berries were uprooted from the vicinity of their hermitage.

The king asked his courtiers, "Can anyone think of a way to bring Rishya Shringa to our land?"

After a long silence, an elderly courtesan, who was an adviser to the king in matters of strategy, spoke up:

"Allow me, your majesty, to send my beautiful daughter to the holy young man so that she may try to entice him to come to Anga. I know the task is perilous, for these sages in their celibacy have great power that could be used to curse us and send us to our destruction. But we courtesans have mastered the art of seduction, which in itself is quite potent.

"Please arrange a boat for us. It should have a spacious deck with an artificial garden, and in the garden a hermitage just like the real one. We will go to Vibhandaka's hermitage when he is away, and we will see if we can kindle desire in his young son."

A short while later, Vibhandaka returned to his hermitage after a day's absence and found Rishya Shringa sitting in a corner, lost in thought. He saw that his son had not lighted the fires; nor had he collected sacred grasses for the evening ritual. The father asked for an explanation.

Rishya Shringa replied, "Father, as soon as you left, a radiant being came to the hermitage. He said he was a spiritual seeker like myself, but he looked so different from us. He had no hair on his face or chest, but on his head there was luxuriant hair, wavy, long, and unmatted. He wore garlands of flowers that I have never seen, and their scent was so different from that of holy basil. His clothes were so smooth and soft to the touch that I felt ashamed of the tree-bark clothes I wore. He gave me fruits to eat that were neither sour nor bitter, and the liquid he gave me to drink produced ecstatic feelings that were superior to the rapture I feel in our meditations.

"The aspirant then put his lips on mine, and I nearly fainted with happiness. His chest was so sweetly rounded, and as he pressed me against himself I felt a wave of spiritual insight race through my veins. Then he took me to his hermitage where he initiated me into the many rituals of his order. But before I could embrace and experience more divine joy, he said he had to leave, and his hermitage disappeared from sight.

"Since then, my heart has been yearning for his company. Father, I want to pursue his kind of spiritual practice and join his order. I believe his way will bring me to realization much faster than ours!"

Vibhandaka was deeply disturbed by his son's words and said, "Rishya Shringa! That visitor was not a sage or a spiritual seeker. That was a demoness! What she gave you was intoxicating liquor, and what she made you do were unholy things. Forget about that incident, and let us go back to our way."

From that evening onward, however, the young sage's heart only grew heavier with longing for that mysterious and wonderful visitor and the mysteries to which she had introduced him. At last, when his father had once again left him alone, the courtesan's daughter returned and took him to the hermitage on the boat, and the boat was rowed into the kingdom of Anga.

As soon as the sacred one alighted from the boat onto the land, rain began to come down in torrents that cooled the ground and filled the air with the smell of wet, fertile earth. King Lomapada immediately arranged for the lawful marriage of his daughter Shanta to Rishya Shringa, whose heart had been made ready by the persuasive arts of the young courtesan.

When Vibhandaka returned after his journey, he saw that his son was missing. Through his spiritual vision he found out what had happened, and he rushed to the king's palace to redeem his son and to set a curse on the king and his land.

Advised by his wise courtiers, the king had taken precautions to avert the wrath of the sage Vibhandaka. He had lined up as presents for the sage thousands of milk cows on both sides of the path. When the raging old man saw the well-groomed cows, and other signs of abundance and welcome along his way, he calmed down considerably. And when he saw his son standing at the door of the palace with his bride Shanta shining like the moon with the star Rohini cradled in its crescent, all his anger melted into tears of joy. After all, his spiritual practices had not completely parched the soil of his heart, and he blessed the son and daughter-in-law who were reaching down to touch his feet.

Thus it was that desire triumphed and brought fertility to the kingdom of Anga.

Parabola
Volume: 5.4
Woman

THE ETERNAL DANCE OF THE UNIVERSE

Retold by Diane Wolkstein

The Creator Brahma sat in serene meditation. Around him in a circle stood his ten mindborn sons and the ten world guardians. They watched as Brahma sank into himself with a vision, and each time an apparition appeared in bodily form.

Brahma plunged suddenly into the depths of his own darkness, and to the surprise of the assembly there stood a beautiful, young, naked woman. She was Dawn—with glistening blue-black hair, eyes like dark lotuses, a face as round as the moon, and upturned, dark-tipped breasts.

The assembly stared at her in astonishment. She, in turn, laughed a soft rippling laugh which brought Brahma out of his trance so that he wondered, as did all who gazed at her, for what purpose in the unfolding of the creation this amazing apparition might have been summoned.

Then a second surprise. From Brahma's wonder another creature came into being. He was a youth—dark, strong, and splendid—with powerful and beautifully formed limbs and the aroma of blossoms about him. In one hand he carried a banner with the emblem of a fish; in the other, a bow and five flowery arrows. As Brahma and his ten mindborn sons and the ten world guardians stared, desire crept into each of them—the desire to possess the woman, Dawn.

So Desire entered the world. In his first moment he turned and spoke boldly to Brahma, "What is my name? And what am I to do? Each being flourishes when doing the work for which he is designed. Give me my name, and since you are a Creator, give me a wife!"

Brahma was silent a moment. What had he done? Who was this creature who had slipped from his being? Then Brahma gathered his consciousness and brought his being to center. And because he was Brahma, the divine original consciousness, when he saw the truth he spoke the truth, even if it meant that his own power might be lessened.

"You will wander the earth with your bow," Brahma said, "and no creature will be able to escape the aim of your arrows. Your task is to send your arrows into the hearts of men, women, and gods, arousing bewilderment and delight and thus assuring the continual creation of the world."

Then Daksha, the lord of the ten world guardians, said to the youth, "Your name is Kama, God of Love, and your arrows will be stronger than those of Brahma, Vishnu, and even Shiva. You are the All-Pervader. We are all in your power."

When Kama heard these words, he turned toward the assembly, drew his bow taut, and let his arrows fly:

> *Intoxicating breezes permeated the assembly;*
> *Heavy scents of spring flowers brought rapture.*
> *The gods stumbled ... they reeled from side to side.*
> *They stared at the woman Dawn ... they quivered ...*
> *One by one ... the gods went mad:*
> *They gaped ... they groaned ... Brahma broke into a steam ...*
> *Daksha and the world guardians began to smoke*

The quivering and shaking caused a rumbling in the firmament, and in the far distant mountains, the arch-ascetic of the universe, Shiva, was disturbed in his concentration. He drifted toward the Love Constellation and when he beheld the infatuated Brahma and the gaping flock, he burst into laughter. "Well, well! And what is all this? Brahma, have you forgotten that you yourself revealed the laws in the *Rig Vedas*? 'The sister shall be as the mother and the daughter shall be as the sister.' The universe is founded on constancy. How can you permit yourself to lose your balance at the mere sight of a woman?"

At these words Brahma's mind split in two. He returned to his True Being; yet a part of him was still gripped by desire and lust. Waves of heat streamed down Brahma's limbs. Sweat poured down the bodies of the world guardians. From Daksha's sweat a woman, gleaming like burnished gold, appeared. Daksha gave her to Kama as a wife, and called the first wife "Rati" which means delight.

At last Brahma was cleansed of his lust. But though Shiva had withdrawn to his place of meditation, the string of Shiva's words did not leave him. He had been rebuked before his holy sons. He burned with humiliation.

"Why was it that Shiva was not moved by a woman?" he fumed. "If Shiva continued to remain aloof from all the universe, how would he be able to carry out his appointed task? If he remained forever in a rocklike state of meditation, how would he be able to destroy the great ones of the earth when renewal was necessary?"

As Brahma came out of his meditations he saw the young God of Love, Kama, joyfully united with the beautiful Rati, and he spoke to them: "How blissful and radiant you are. What joy there is in seeing you together. You must go to the mountain tops where Shiva lives and set him on fire with love so that he, too, will take a wife and join us in the eternal dance of the universe."

Kama answered, "If you order it, I will go. But if I succeed in stirring the rocklike Shiva, where is the woman who can arouse him? Nowhere do I behold such a woman for Shiva."

"I shall create her," Brahma replied. "Now go."

When the Love God had departed, Brahma spoke with Daksha: "Who can Shiva's future wife be? What possible woman does he hold in the depths of his spirit? Yet there is only one. She is Maya—The World Illusion—The Enchantress. She is Shakti, the Energy of the World; she can take on any form. She is the one who will beguile him. Daksha, you must go and with proper offerings persuade Shakti to be born as your daughter and then to become Shiva's bride."

Daksha understood the wisdom of Brahma's suggestion and took himself to the other side of the divine Milky Ocean, across the timeless sea where Vishnu sleeps and dreams the dream of the world. There he prepared himself to make offerings to the Great Goddess who is the manifestation of Vishnu's dream. With the image of the Enchantress in his mind and heart he went into deep meditation so that by his heat he might be able to animate her image and see the Goddess with his own eyes. For 36,000 years, Daksha remained in a state of prodigious and prolonged concentration, creating his vision of the Goddess.

While Daksha sat meditating the mighty Brahma took himself to the holy mountain, Mandara, and there for 36,000 years he praised with potent syllables the Mother of the Universe. He called to Shakti in her myriad forms:

> *Maya—Enchantress—Everlasting Divine Drunkenness of Dream— Lady of the Spheres—Smoky One—Weaver of the World—Wisdom— Compassion—Delusion—The One Who Releases—Maya ...*

At the end of 36,000 years Maya appeared.

She was dark and slender, with her hair hanging free; and she was standing on the back of her tawny lion.

Brahma greeted her, "Kali, Oh Dark One, oh Goddess, I have called to you because of your power. The Lord of Spirits, Shiva, remains solitary. If he takes no wife the world creation will not continue in its appointed course. Only you can entice and bewitch him into the eternal dance of the universe."

Kali replied, "It is true what you say. I am the Divine Energy of the Universe. From me comes the food of the universe—all that has breath, all that speaks. I make each one what that one wishes to be—great and powerful, weak and helpless, passionate, or full of dreams. Yes, for the sake of the creation I will agree to entice Shiva. When Shiva meditates and goes into the innermost kernel of his heart he will find me there. I will have melted into his heart."

She disappeared, and on the other side of time Daksha saw the Goddess, and she appeared to him on her lion. Her body was dark, and her breasts were mighty. Daksha bowed to her and announced his wish. She answered, "For the sake of the well-being of creation I will grant your wish. I will become your daughter and the wife of Shiva. But if for a single moment you lose proper reverence for me, I will not remain on earth. I will leave my body, whether happy or not."

Full of joy that his wish would be granted, Daksha descended to earth. He married a beautiful woman named Virani, the daughter of Virana, the fragrant grass. Vriani conceived at once from the vision of Daksha's soul.

When the child was born and she was a girl, flowers descended from the heavens. Virani did not know that her daughter was Maya, the Mother of the Universe, the Great Enchantress. She only knew a little infant was wailing, and she took the child in her arms and gave her the breast to suck.

So the child grew. When she played with her small friends she delighted in drawing pictures of Shiva, and when she sang, her child-like songs were of her love for Shiva. Shiva was always in her heart. Her father gave her the most beautiful name. He called her "Sati" which means "She Who Is."

When she became a young woman, she went to the mountains to meditate. Then Brahma with his divine wife, Savitri, and Vishnu, with his divine wife, Lakshmi, went to visit Shiva in his place of peace.

When Shiva saw them, a strange thing happened. The Paragon of Peace was moved by the radiance and bliss in the faces of the two joyous couples, and the smallest trace of desire for woman entered his spirit.

"We have come to you," Brahma said, "for the sake of the creation. I am the Creator, Vishnu is the Preserver, and you are the Destroyer. But if you remain in your state of rocklike meditation, how will you understand passion and be able to destroy when the moment for destruction comes? We have come to ask you to take a wife."

Shiva said, "At every moment I behold the supreme eternity of the True Being. At every moment I keep it before me. Where is the woman who is as consecrated to my work as I am, who is as dedicated to the Highest Vision? If for the sake of the universe I were to take a wife, where is there a woman who could be capable of absorbing my incandescent power, shock by shock?"

Brahma was elated. He said, "She exists! At this moment she is waiting for you and longing for you! Her name is Sati!"

The two couples departed.

Shiva descended to earth to the place where Sati was meditating alone in the mountains. When she opened her eyes and saw Shiva standing before her she was flooded with joy and fell to the ground worshiping his feet.

When Shiva saw Sati he was pleased. "What do you wish?" he asked. "Speak."

But Sati could not utter a word. She could not speak before the one who had moved her heart since she was a child.

Shiva was filled with a longing to hear the sound of Sati's voice and that was the moment Kama, the God of Love, drew his arrow and shot Shiva through the heart. Shiva shuddered. He forgot his True Being and he cried, "Be my wife!"

And she said, "Speak to my father."

Shiva thundered, "Be my wife *now*!"

Sati trembled and ran toward her home.

Shiva, the Paragon of Peace, returned to his mountain abode. He directed his thoughts to Brahma, and Brahma appeared.

"Brahma," he said, "you have won. I am powerless. Maya has caught me in her web. Now all I can be, all I can become, is Sati's husband. You must arrange it. Brahma, speak to Daksha, ask him if he will permit me to marry Sati."

So the wedding of Shiva and Sati was arranged. It was held on the day and at the hour that was most propitious according to the stars.

The bridegroom Shiva arrived accompanied by divine musicians and dancing girls. He wore a loincloth of tiger skins and a live serpent draped from his left shoulder to his right hip. In his hair rested the young moon and a garland of skulls.

The dancing girls whirled, and the divine musicians played. The lesser and greater spirits, all incarnations of the great Shiva, danced. Flowers poured down from the heavens. The whole firmament was gay and brilliant, blown with sweet-scented breezes. All the trees stood forth in blossom.

Solemnly, Shiva received Sati's hand. The gods gave praise and recited verses from the holy vedas.

Then Vishnu spoke and blessed Shiva and Sati, "Sati gleams blue-black and Shiva is fair. Together you will be a protection to the gods and men."

"So be it!" echoed Shiva, and Sati laughed with happiness.

Then Shiva lifted Sati onto his white bull Nandi, and they rode to the tops of the Himalayan peaks. And there they dwelt, and there they played, night and day, and all their play was love.

Shiva went and gathered wildflowers for Sati. He let down her nightdark hair and played with it. Then he knotted it up so that he might loosen it again. He painted her pretty feet with scarlet lac so that he might hold them in his hands, and he whispered in her ear what he could have just as well have said aloud. But in this way he could be closer to her.

In the bowers and by the banks of high mountain streams they tasted each other and played with each other and loved each other. Shiva put a spot of musk on her beautiful lotus breasts and lifted off her necklaces of pearl and set them back again just to touch her softness. He drew off her bracelets and opened the knots on her clothing and tied them back again. He decked her whole body with chains of flowers and swallowed the nectar of her mouth, and Shiva and Sati's desire never ceased. The fountain of their passion was watered continuously by their love.

And so they loved, and the days and nights of 9,000 years passed quickly by.

Once before the rainy season Sati asked Shiva to build a house where they could find rest and shelter.

And the Great God said, "With what would I build it? I have only a loincloth, the serpents that decorate my body, and a skull for a begging bowl."

Still he lifted her up and carried her high above the clouds and there he united with her in love.

Then when the rainy season was over, Shiva asked Sati where she would like to go.

And Sati said, "Let us go to Mt. Himalaya."

And there they dwelt for 3,600 years, and Shiva's heart was held entirely by Sati.

Now Sati's father, Daksha, decided at this time to hold a Great Offering to the Supreme Being. He invited every living being in all the reaches of space: the gods and the demons, the spirits, clouds and mountains, the rivers and oceans, the men, beasts, birds, trees, and grasses—all beings. There were only two creatures he did not invite, and they were Shiva and Sati.

He thought that Shiva who meditates among corpses and carries a skull for a begging bowl would not be fit to attend such an Offering. And, of course, he could not invite his beloved daughter, Sati, if he were not to invite Shiva.

Then Vijaya, the sister of Sati, came to see Sati who was alone.

"Dear Vijaya," Sati said, "you have come by yourself. Where are your sisters?"

"They are preparing for the great celebration. All the women in the universe are on their way. I have come to fetch you. ... Are you and Shiva not coming?"

"Celebration? Where?"

"Oh Sati! Have you not been invited? Your father, Daksha, is holding a Great Offering. Everyone in all the worlds has been invited. Oh *Sati*!"

Sati was struck as if by a bolt of lightning. Anger began to burn in her, and her eyes hardened. She said, "It is because my husband carries a skull for a begging bowl."

And she thought to blast Daksha to ashes with a curse. But then she remember her words to Daksha: "If ever, for a single moment, you do not show proper reverance for me, I shall leave my body, whether I am happy or not."

As Sati's eternal form became visible to her, she thought, "I will leave this body. I will not stay. The gods will not have what they wish this time. But one day I will return to Mt. Himalaya where I have dwelt so long in happiness with Shiva, and I will be born as the daughter of Menaka. I will play, and then I will marry Shiva and complete the work the gods have wished for."

With that she closed the nine portals of her body. She withdrew her breath and braced herself. Her life force shot up through her body and ripped through the top of her skull, and her body slumped to the ground.

When the gods above saw this, they lifted a universal cry of terror. And Vijaya cried, "O Sati! Sati! What have I done? Your poor mother will be shattered by the pain—and how will your heartless father survive? Never to see you dancing eyes and hear your sweet words? O Sati, you were a mother to me. Sati, I am crying. Sati, who but you will ever have such loving kind words for me? O Sati. And who will care for Shiva? *Shiva*! Oooooh!"

In his meditations Shiva heard Vijaya's shriek. He returned at once to their mountain top where his beloved Sati lay crumbled dead on the earth. But love would not allow him to believe she was dead.

Gently he stroked her cheek. "You are asleep?" he said. "Beloved, what has sent you to sleep? Sati, wake up …"

Then Vijaya told Shiva that something inside of Sati seemed to have burst when she had told her that neither she nor Shiva had been invited to the Great Offering.

With these words Shiva's entire being was filled with wrath, and he transported himself to the place where the Great Sacrifice was being held. There he saw that every living creature had been invited: the gods, the planets, the beasts, the fish, the worms, the seasons, the ages of the world. And each was reverently carrying out his role. Only he and Sati had not been asked.

Shiva stepped into the sacred place to destroy the Offering. The Offering, the animal that was being sacrificed to the gods, was so terrified it changed itself into a gazelle and fled away into the skies, seeking refuge in Brahma's realm. Shiva followed. The gazelle sought asylum in Vishnu's realm. Shiva followed. At last the frightened animal darted back to earth and disappeared on a mountain top.

The hiding place it had found was the corpse of Sati.

When Shiva stood once again before the dead body of Sati, he forgot the gazelle. He forgot the Offering. He saw only Sati. And then a great cry of grief came up from his throat, and his heart broke.

He looked at Sati—at her lips, her cheeks, her beautiful, dark hair. Her laughter, her kindness, her touch rushed through him, and he broke with grief like a common mortal.

He flung himself to the ground. He crouched by her corpse. Then he got up and ran, but he returned and reached out and touched her body. It was stiff and cold.

He caressed her forehead and cheeks and lips. He undid her clothes, then fastened them up and opened them again. Then he picked Sati up in his arms and began to walk. He sobbed and he walked, and he sobbed, and he would not let her go.

Vishnu and Brahma watched Shiva, and they knew that Sati's corpse would never decay as long as Shiva held her. So by their craft, Brahma and Vishnu hid themselves in Sati's corpse and as Shiva walked they began to dismember Sati's body.

Her two feet fell, and the place they fell was called "the Mountain of the Goddess." Not far from there her two ankles fell. And then to the east her womb fell, and nearby her navel: then her two breasts together with a golden necklace, and her shoulders and her neck. Every place a part of her fell became a sacred place and a blessing to the children of the world.

When her head fell, Shiva stopped. He stood and stared and broke into a terrible groan of pain.

The gods drew at once around Shiva and wished to comfort him. When Shiva looked up and saw the gods, he was ashamed and transformed himself into a rock in the shape of a lingam.

The gods praised Shiva, hoping he would return to himself. "Light of all Lights, Shiva, you understand the impermanence of all things, in your form of lingam you are the Highest Being We tremble before your grief. Shiva! Let your anguish pass. Shiva!"

Shiva remembered his Highest Self that had always been the object of his meditations, but he could not bring his powers to focus. His grief was overwhelming.

At last Shiva opened his eyes. When he saw Brahma, he said, "Brahma, what am I to do?"

And Brahma said, "You must let your pain go. You must let your anguish go. It is only Maya. Return to your True Being. In the whirling dance of the Universe you will find Sati again."

And Shiva said, "Brahma, I can do nothing. Brahma, stay with me until the pain passes, until I come up from the ocean of my loss. Do not leave me, Brahma, stay by me and give me comfort."

And Brahma said, "So shall it be."

Blind with suffering, Shiva took Brahma's hand, and the two gods departed into the solitude of the mountains. They walked until they came to a lake. It was surrounded by holy hermits who were meditating. The lake was quiet, clear, and peaceful.

Shiva sat by the lake and looked into the waters. He saw fish swimming, darting in and out among the lotus stems.

It was beside the waters of this lake that Shiva found his rest. He released himself from suffering and centered himself in the eternity of his True Being. So he remained in deep peace and meditation until Sati was reborn as Parvati, the daughter of Manaka, Queen of the Mountain.

And by her long sustained meditations, Parvati was able to stir Shiva from his deep place of peace and bring Shiva to her, so that once again, they were united in love.

And once again, the rebirth of the world was assured.

Adapted by Diane Wolkstein from Joseph Campbell's translation of Heinrich Zimmer's "Four Episodes from the Romance of the Goddess," published in *The King and the Corpse.* ([1948], Princeton: Princeton University Press, 1971). This version was originally told in the series, "Winter Tales for Adults" at the New School in New York City.

Parabola
Volume: 9.2
Theft

THE THIEF IN KRISHNA

John Stratton Hawley

India is the land of the lock. Nothing is too small or
humble to go without protection: biscuits, stamps, paper
clips, toe rings—all are commonly held under guard; and
at railway stations you cannot check even a torn backpack
unless the zipper is secured with a tiny padlock. Houses,
temples, museums, offices, libraries bear gigantic locks, and
if the important individual entrusted with the key does not
happen to be in view, there simply is no admission.

Behind every lock lies the fear of a thief, and in India
that fear has become a national obsession. No issue of
the Benares daily newspaper is sent to press without an
account of how some outlying village has been ravaged
by robbers the night before; no movie marquee goes long
without promising such favorites as *Three Thieves* or *Thief
of Thieves*; and when Phoolan Devi, the bandit queen, was
at large some years ago, it made the headlines every day.

Some of this attention is justified. Phoolan's band not
only looted but killed, and dacoit gangs such as hers have
acted with sufficient daring over the years to cause the
importation of words like *loot* and *thug* from Hindi into
English. But Phoolan Devi attracted as much fascination
as fear. One heard stories of how stunning she was, stories all the more remarkable because, in a country where
light complexions are prized above all other signs of
beauty, Phoolan Devi's was jet black. In truth, the tone of

Phoolan's skin often served to heighten rather than decrease her appeal, as did the reports of her sexual abuse as a child. Here was a thrilling figure in whom fear and love met as dangerous bedfellows.

India has a god who shares with Phoolan Devi a dark skin and a mysterious allure. This god is Krishna, whose very name means "black," but who, in keeping with recent Indian taste, is often depicted in a somewhat more acceptable midnight blue. His thievish episodes provide the land with some of its most vivid mythology. Krishna doesn't use force, but his skill in stealing away what people hold dear is unparalleled; and he doesn't kill, but he manages to unburden people of their ordinary lives. Once they've seen him, they lose the self-possession that makes for coherent biography in the first place.

Krishna's brand of thievery is all tied up with love. He is the great romantic here of Indian legend—the Casanova, the Don Juan—but he is at once more simple than these and more grand: in the most celebrated aspect of his earthly self-manifestation, he is plain cowherd lad, yet in actuality he is God. At the center of his activity on this earth is the dance he enjoys with the cowherd girls (*gopīs*) of his native Braj, just south of Delhi on the banks of the River Jumna. By means of the haunting notes he plays on his flute, he lures the gopīs away from all their worldly occupations. However far away they are, they drop their brooms and pails, turn from the demanding voices of their mothers-in-law, even catapult themselves from the marital bed. Off to the forest they run, far from the structures and confines of home and family, to dance with Krishna. And although by legend there are sixteen thousand in this *rās* dance, each one is made to feel as though Krishna is her partner alone, and that she is the sole object of his attention. In that moment they are his, soul and body, yet at the same time they are drawn into a circle, a community with each other that they could not have known in the profane world from which they were so abruptly summoned.

And then, like a thief, he slips away. He leaves them with a common memory of fulfillment beyond anything they had ever imagined possible, but a memory that makes them feel hollow to the core. Even the community they had attained is now one of longing and waiting, a shared impoverishment. And that, the theologians point out, is the rub in our human condition: we can know God, to be sure, but soon after the moment of truly knowing, we are ineluctably separated from the divine presence.

Hindu appraisals of who is responsible for this estrangement differ from Christian and Jewish ones. Hindus place the blame not only on human sin but on the nature of God, who sets—who indeed comprises—the conditions that ultimately structure our lives. But these same Hindus stress that the awareness of the loss of God is itself a powerful way of experiencing the divine. The gopīs' apprehension of Krishna is hardly dispersed by his absence; if anything, it is heightened. All of us are Krishna's milkmaids, wallflowers for life, who yearn to return to the dance floor just one more time. When these gopīs complain of their undeserved fate, we naturally join their lament. Here is voiced on their—and our—behalf by the sixteenth-century Hindi poet, Sūr Dās:

> Gopal has slipped in and stolen my heart, friend.
> *He stole through my eyes and invaded my breast*
> *simply by looking—who knows how he did it?—*
> *Even though parents and husband and all*
> *crowded the courtyard and filled my world.*
> *The door was protected by all that is proper;*
> *not a corner, nothing, was left without a guard.*
> *Decency, prudence, respect for the family—*
> *these three were locks and I hid the keys.*
> *The sturdiest doors were my eyelid gates—*
> *to enter through them was a passage impossible—*
> *And secure in my heart, a treasure immeasurable:*
> *insight, intelligence, fortitude, wit.*
> *Then, says Sūr, he'd stolen it—*
> *with a thought and a laugh and a look—*
> *and my body was scorched with remorse.*

Though Krishna's departure from their midst is a terrible blow to the gopīs, they ought to have been prepared. Krishna is hardly famous for his reliability—he often steals off to a new bed at night and comes back with scratches of passion on his chest——and the poem quoted above could refer to any number of occasions. No wonder, then, that the friends of Radha, Krishna's favorite gopī, frequently warn her about what may happen if she falls under his spell. In the following poem, for instance, we hear one of Radha's confidantes describe the dangers of consorting with

Krishna. Referring to him by several of his affectionate titles—Kānh and Śyām—she portrays his lover's thrall as a principality ruled by thieves and tyrants:

No justice reigns in this realm, Rādhā.
Lust is King and Kānh is in charge;
strange and cruel are their customs.
The swirl of curls that swarm round his ears
and the eyebrows in league with his eyes
Serve as spies; they ferret out secrets
and glean every word that you say.
They sit as a council of sycophants,
fearlessly following the lead of King Lust.
Poor friend, you've newly encountered alone
the despotic ways of this desperate place,
Where his gentle laugh and gentle speech
and gentle moves engender love:
As the heart is stolen, the body follows,
as minions mimic their king.
So since you embody the treasures of beauty,
and handsome Śyām has heard your fame,
While he remains the ruler, says Sūr,
force will forge his victory.

This sense of unjust power bubbles up at a number of points in poems and stories about Krishna, and in one of the best-known tales it is symbolized as an act of thievery. As the episode begins, we find the gopīs bathing in the Jumna at dawn one wintry morning. They have vowed to engage in a month of self-mortification in the Jumna's frigid waters to win the favor of the goddess Kātyāyani. They hope that the goddess will grant them in return a good husband—someone to care for and protect them the rest of their lives—and many cannot help hoping that it will be Krishna.

Their prayers are answered a bit sooner than they had planned, for Krishna appears on the banks as they bob in the water. He sees that the girls are naked, and immediately gathers up their saris from the river's edge and takes them up into the branches of a nearby kadamba tree. There he perches while he festoons the kadamba with all the stolen saris.

At first the girls notice nothing, but when they have finished saying their mantras and are prepared to head for shore, they see that their clothes have disappeared. As their eyes scan up from the bank to the branches, they see what has happened. They excoriate Krishna for his mischief and beg him to return the clothes and get on his way. But he refuses, and in some versions of the story he taunts them with further outrages: he pretends to understand nothing about what they are saying and wonders out loud how they can imagine that the lovely new flowers on the kadamba tree are in reality their saris. In other renditions, he claims that the gopīs deserve this fate since they have been so brazen as to bathe in the nude. But whatever his first response to their recognition of their predicament, the condition that he sets for ending it is always the same: they must come out on the bank with their hands above their heads. Then he will be only too happy to return their garments.

This and similar tales have caused quite a flurry among theological commentators anxious to make sure that devotees of Krishna understand that such provocative behavior on Krishna's part can only be excused in the realm of the gods and ought never to become a model for mortal actions. But whatever clearings of the theological throat this episode has caused, there has been no shrinking from its importance. It has traditionally been regarded as the test of the gopīs' true love for Krishna, their readiness to leave everything—every possession, every shred of female decorum—for his sake. To have him, they must give up all else; in short, they must appear before him naked. Then only can they earn the right to join in the ultimate act of intimacy, his rās dance.

It is the same with all of us. There's no fooling God with postures, pride, and the garments of civility. We appear before God naked or not at all, and the timing is not usually what we would choose.

That Krishna has a special talent for catching people off guard is made clear in stories that reach back into his childhood. In fact, his own mother (or to be exact, the foster mother who has raised him from the day he was born, believing him to be her own son) is his very first victim. Yaśodā does everything she can to provide him with the nourishment and comforts that every growing boy needs. She is happy to bake for him an array of sweets and goodies—*gujiyās, pāpadīs, lāddus, mohanthārs, mohanbhogs*—everything that would satisfy any ordinary child a hundred times over. But Krishna is no ordinary child. His favorite food is simpler than any of these; it's pure, creamy, white, and delicious. He insists on butter.

Krishna is wild for butter, and Yaśodā would be glad to give it to him, though she cannot understand why he shuns her more elaborate preparations. The difficulty is, however, that he never wants to take it when she wants to give it. Instead, his hunger always strikes when she is out of the house or otherwise occupied, and then, driven by an insatiable appetite, he goes to any length to obtain his favorite food. If she has hidden pots of butter in a dark storeroom, he finds them with unerring instinct. If she has suspended the pots from the ceiling, so that he cannot ransack her supply, he reaches them nonetheless, perhaps by climbing on a big stone mortar. Or he may take advantage of the shoulders of some of his little friends and let them share in the spoils. Krishna doesn't respect any closed doors, any fences or boundaries: he would just as soon perpetrate his wanton acts in the homes of any of the women of Braj. If he is caught in the act, he often claims he didn't know the difference.

The milkmaids of Braj, including Yaśodā, react with a certain ambivalence. On the one hand, they would love to have this lovely child eating out of their hands; sometimes they almost seem to invite him to come. On the other hand, they cannot abide his lawless independence, which is sometimes expressed by his spattering the walls with whatever he and his cohorts do not care to eat themselves, or by offering the leftovers to monkeys. On other occasions, Krishna and his friends recklessly smear their loot in the faces of any hapless children left at home to guard the house.

What is one to do with such a thief? The gopīs and Yaśodā made countless efforts to tie him up, but it is always futile. Either he manages to play on the emotions of one so that the other will have pity, or even worse, he tangles them in their own efforts at order. In one episode much celebrated in the modern-day Krishna dramas of Braj, a gopī manages to apprehend the little marauder and vows to tie him to a pillar. But it turns out that she doesn't know how to tie a very good knot, and Krishna is easily able to wriggle free. Finally he comes to his captor's aid and offers to teach her how to tie a decent knot. But he demonstrates on her, and by the time he has finished, it is she who is the captive, not he.

Such escapades of the butter thief are told all over India, and wherever they are told, it is remembered that butter is not all that is at issue. For the butter Krishna eats builds not only his strength but also his character; hence these episodes have a lasting effect. Long after he has put away childish things, Krishna remains the thief he was as a boy, only with far more serious consequences. Many years later we find a gopī—again in the words of Sūr Dās—lamenting this legacy:

> This is more than simply butter stealing.
> *Once we were happy to see your thieving face;*
> *we gladly gave, and the loss was small.*
> *For in those days you were little Kānh, our prince,*
> *and we were simple country maids.*
> *Kānh, you were a child in a family of kings*
> *so we kept your little butter thefts purely to ourselves.*
> *Now you've grown, and we've grown too,*
> *wise in the ways of the world.*
> *What, now, you'd go, you'd disappear,*
> *after stealing all the treasures of my soul?*
> *Heart thief, head to toe you've gone*
> *and stolen everything—and now you'd wrench away!*
> *Says Sūr, you've come and robbed my every part,*
> *and still I am tied and strung to your heart.*

What does this fund of stories mean? Why must Krishna steal? Why does he have such a special taste for butter? Why can he never be caught? Any why do Hindus affirm that this obstreperous, heedless thief is none other than God himself?

I have asked these questions of Indians many times, and though the answers I receive are not always the same, they always point back to the central affirmation made in the mythology of Krishna: this is a god of love, and love is at the heart of his story. Butter itself is love. It is the concentrated form of milk, the substance on which all human life depends for its beginning. And milk, in turn, issues from love. The cow is the great symbol of mother-love in India, and though we have grown accustomed to milking our cows with metallic milking machines, Hindus still do it the old-fashioned way. They put the cow in the vicinity of her calf and watch the juices begin to flow. So boundlessly loving is the source, they point out, that even an effigy of a calf will suffice to stimulate the cow's desire to give. Milk is synonymous with love, and butter is its densest form.

Krishna loves love, and he insists on having it in the concentrated, unadulterated measure that butter symbolizes. Anything that would separate him from it—whether the walls of a pot, the refinements of good cooking, the threads of a garment, or the confines of marriage—must be set aside. So he confounds all barriers, traps, and entanglements that are put in his path, sometimes turning them back on those who place them there. Such a trap is the rope with which the gopī tries to tether Krishna in the play depicting the butter thief, and indeed this rope is called "the rope of love." But love is not the sort of thing that binds or sets boundaries; if the gopī tries to use it that way, she will find herself tangled in her own cord.

God is not to be limited, and neither is love. Because we have such a desperate penchant for order, even in games of love, God has no choice but to confront us in the guise of someone who does not play by the rules. He steals our love away, or so we think, and in doing so confronts us with a reality that is unpleasant, but that forces us to ask why we are so anxious to hold onto our love and its objects in the first place. The presence of the divine and the reality of love are such things as cannot be ordered and possessed; they always exceed what we are willing to allow. When God is pictured as a thief, then, it is to ask just who the thief really is in this tug-of-war between the human and the divine. Is God so unruly, or is it our own ordering process that robs reality of its inalienable freedom and ease?

We live in an era of savage order. We have seen bureaucratic finesse used to cause and at the same time justify unimaginable extremes of human suffering, and we are daily aware that with every further winding of the technological clock the possibility of our total destruction draws nearer. These realities, though especially terrifying in their twentieth-century form, have deep roots in history and are as endemic to India's society as our own. But India's longer experience with the structural oppression of society has produced a notion of God that is peculiarly liberating. To perceive God as the sort of being who roams about outside our walls of reason and discretion, looking for a chance to make a raid, is to question the ultimate sense and authority of the structures we erect in such glorious and proud detail. These machines of the mind, these boundaries and perimeters, often cost us dear; hence it seems little wonder that as we watch them crumble in the mythology of Krishna, we register a certain glee. And the more so if we sense, as many of the stories of Krishna teach us to do, that the divine enemy is within—and is no enemy, but an uncanny, hidden ally who has been with us all the while.

Two fundamental intuitions about the nature of religious truth accord with this sense of apparently unwarranted delight. The first is that some of our most powerful experiences of the divine come in the form of surprise. The experience of God often has a deft, unexpected, intrusive quality about it. It is elusive, it defies description, it is not quite known, yet it sweeps us off our feet. Though we do not know quite what has hit us—or because of that fact—we say that we have known revelation. It overtakes us like a thief in the night; and we say, though we are not always sure afterward, that we are glad.

The second intuition about religious awareness is as powerful as the first, but it has very little glee associated with it: we find that we often know the truth at just those times when we experience loss. It sometimes seems, in fact, that it is only when we lose that we truly gain. Even more unsettling, our sense of loss sometimes seems precisely to have been caused by having had a brush with the truth, since the new knowledge leaves us with the feeling that our ordinary perceptions are vacuous. In either sense there is the realization that in some measure, like it or not, to know God is to lose the world.

The mythology of Krishna breathes this sadness. We sometimes laugh at what happens when the thief is on the scene. But it is not so easy to laugh when the thief steals himself away, for we understand that to have been visited by the holy angel is, like Jacob become Israel, to limp forever after. Krishna's gopīs are fulfilled in their love, but at the same time they are maimed.

For thousands of years people have asked how God can be God if there is suffering in the world. It is the old problem of theodicy, and it will never go away. But there is a chance that by allowing ourselves to experience God as a thief, this debate can be stood on its head. Instead of expecting God to validate our convictions about what is orderly and right, we may begin to admit what our ordering leaves out. Instead of expecting God to be the answer to all our problems with the world, we may begin to sense that God is the question that puts them all in perspective.

The poems that appear in this article are selected from *Krishna, the Butter Thief* by J. S. Hawley (Princeton: Princeton University Press, 1983), and are based on critical editions of poems from the *Sūr Sāgār* of Sūr Dās. I am grateful to Mark Juergensmeyer for his help in improving the quality of these verse translations, and to Laura Shapiro for her steady hand with the prose.

Parabola
Volume: 2.4
Relationships

Laws and Customs in a Brahmin Family

Lizelle Reymond

About twenty-five years ago, I lived for a considerable period of time in an orthodox Brahmin family, at Almora in the Himalayas. It was an unexpected opportunity which had a deep and lasting influence on me. I can speak of it for there is still a living bond between us beyond the Laws and Customs that separate us.

My participation in the work of translating sacred texts having to do with the series of volumes "The Great Masters of Contemporary India" had brought me to live in Almora. It is a town in the mountains whose name is mentioned by Swami Vivekananda as indicating a magical point, in the North, from which a large range of possibilities opens up.

The pilgrimages towards Kailas and Manasarova start from Almora. It is crossed by the routes down which the Chinese pilgrims of old entered into India and up which, in times of oppression, the sacred books were carried in flight to Tibet. The Brahmins of the plains went up there during the Moslem invasions and took possession of these "High Hills." The relatively isolated position of Almora, legal capital of the Northern Borderlands, has contributed to the flourishing of spiritual disciplines even far into the heart of the valleys of the whole district.

The Joshi, strict Brahmins of Almora, invited me to live with them after the astonishing "intelligence service" covering all of India had been functioning around me for an entire year without my being aware of it. "Who is this foreign woman? She never leaves her house; she never receives anyone; she is served by a Singh; she eats neither meat nor eggs?" The head of the Joshi family came to visit me with the priest of his house to inquire about me. Surprisingly, the invitation was extended and I accepted it.

The Joshi mansion is called "Ishwaribhavan," which means "Abode of the Divine." In front of the house there is a rose garden. The room that was given to me opened up on a gallery facing the mountains, with an outside staircase to the garden. It was the guest apartment, without any communication with the inner court around which lay the private apartments of the family.

On my table, three books awaited me: *The Laws of Manu*, *The Grammar of Panini* and *The Aphorisms of Patanjali*, which set forth the Laws and Customs of all Brahmins of high rank.

A young boy of fourteen, stammering with shyness, came to greet me in the name of his father and announced that Narain, the Brahmin at the service of the family, would bring me all my meals to my room. Next morning, Pandit Joshi came to visit me to make sure I was comfortable, and left. My isolation was beginning. By inviting me, Pandit Joshi was satisfying his idea of being liberal; by accepting, I had chosen a difficult, unknown situation.

In the garden, I saw two little boys of eight and ten playing with a ball and another little boy who, without showing any displeasure, did nothing but pick it up for them. Obviously he was the son of a servant. From the other side, I was hearing the calls of women, the sounds of a conch and of the rhythmic bells accompanying Sanskrit recitations. The house was living, vibrating.

The practical teaching which I supposed was given in the family came to me, in the first place, through an uncle of Pandit Joshi. He offered to explain to me The Laws of Manu in their higher, absolute meaning down to the details of everyday life and the necessity of knowing everything forbidden so that the thought does not stray.

He said: "From the time of the Vedas, Manu has once and for all determined the conduct of the human being. For is we observe human relationships, we see that Manu is that very Cosmic Intelligence who dictated them for all family events: birth, marriage and death. We can invent disobedience but as everything is put down in the Laws, we necessarily come back to them on discovering the essence of our life."

There is a Brahmin pride that, defying time and history, obeys only the "Law and Order" of the Spirit. And what has become of this Tradition since Western progress has spread in all its forms over India? The great traditional families are not particularly affected since this situation of apparent rupture has occurred before, in fact several times, during certain periods of invasions or of religious intolerance. The living Tradition has not been touched. During times of danger, it contracts and hides itself, gets temporarily scattered—and reappears, when the time comes, in all its strength and purity.

There still remains, as in the past two or three thousand years, the custom of choosing certain boys of brilliant intelligence, and of sending them to be educated in a Gurukul, a monastic school. There, separated from any contact with their families for twelve years, they learn the sacred texts by heart, becoming thus the "reserve" of traditional knowledge, preserving it even if all the written texts should be destroyed. When they have passed their final examinations they have the choice of staying as teachers in the Gurukul or of going back to the world to bring up a family according to the required Order of things. The Laws ordering such a discipline are not discussed. They are respected. All Brahmin families are proud to have a son or relative among the pandits or pupils of a Gurukul.

On the whole men and women follow the Laws of Manu in an apparently passive way, but they are also very conscious of the advantages inherent in them. Today, in modern life, their customs are, by experience, still more powerful than laws dictated by the government and the Constitution of India, which abolish the castes. They weave an invisible net that protects all the members of any Brahmin family belonging to the same *gotra*, i.e., having the same family origin, going back to the first *rishis* of the Vedas.

The genealogical tree of the Joshi family covered the wall of a large hall. A very fine writing, framed within medallions, described every father, every son and their male descendents, giving a short chronological account of their activities. Each sannyasin, who had voluntarily dedicated his life to God and to asceticism, was written up in red ink. Women were not mentioned. This genealogical tree is known by the family priests, who consult it for arranging a marriage; but more often it is the grandmother who chooses the bride and discusses the propitious time for the marriage and the dowry. In 1976, the Joshi's fourth son was married in accordance with Tradition, thus determining that his *dharma*, i.e., his destiny, remains linked to that of the family. It is in fact an insurance on all levels. Certain men bear heavy loads on their shoulders for, should a young wife become a widow she would be sheltered and her children brought up by their uncles as if they were their own sons. It sometimes happens that a son refuses to meet his share of obligations. He is nevertheless tolerated in the family, without being subject to any reproach. In this case the grandmother will speak of the unity of the group to avoid any dissension, because Manu, the Legislator of the Cosmic Laws, has set up the family in divine time and space.

I was very moved by the education of little boys. Every morning I saw their master as he arrived and soon after I heard a rhythm, given by a bell and a wooden rule, for the scanning of verses. It lasted a long time. On several occasions Pandit Joshi brought one of his younger children or a visiting cousin to see me, so that I could share their "knowledge." First the child would greet me by touching both my feet, then standing, he would recite in a loud, somewhat strained voice one of the sections of the eight chapters of Panini's *Grammar*. What did he understand of what he was saying? Apparently nothing. I gave a present to the child to congratulate him and remained with my question.

A long conversation with Pandit Joshi would follow. Indeed Panini, the rishi par excellence, full of wisdom and knowledge, had impressed on classical Sanskrit his own method of thinking, his logic, structure and rules. He gave an appropriate name to everything known—so much so that nowadays the natural living impulse has no place to express itself! I defended the child. The father would listen to me until I confusedly felt my ignorance in front of Tradition.

In am indebted to Pandit Joshi for having taught me, every morning, the construction of Sanskrit words through the play of roots, using a parallel to logical thinking as stylized by Panini, who referred to the "divine thousand years" when sounds, letters and words created the world. In Panini, life blooms: the far horizons, the places where things happened, social life; everything which has a name and a shape, from the good Northern wine to the white Southern rice, sports, games, arts, music and dance. Pandit Joshi said: "Five centuries before our time are in our hands today, as is every word with all its possible derivations. Facing no matter what difficulty in life, we know, thanks to Panini, what is appropriate to think and to do. The child lives in a forest of impressions where he learns unconsciously all that he will need to know consciously later on."

I only met the women of the family after having passed a serious examination, and was then again to be observed and discussed by these women.

When I first arrived I had sent a gift to Pandit Joshi's mother, who had replied with sweets "made by her own hands." One day though, she invited me to get acquainted. This happened ceremonially in the Reception Hall. She greeted me with a smile. A widow, dressed in white, with the bunch of all the keys of the house attached to her sari, she pointed out my place to me—a cushion on the floor in front of her. She didn't speak English well and I spoke a poor Hindi, but we understood each other well. She wanted to know what spiritual discipline I was following. Did I have a guru to guide me and follow my progress, in order to prepare within me the place of the living experience which is the meeting with God? Nothing else for her was important. I noticed that several women had slipped in surreptitiously and sat down at the back of the Hall. They were watching my every movement.

From that day on, although I had never been inside the family apartments, Pandit Joshi's wife came to see me with her close relatives and later with young girls, who were friends; they all wanted to ask me questions. Several times I was invited to their parties, where only women could come and which were extremely elegant with music, dances, poetry and more particularly with daring pantomimes that revealed the elder's oddities—an unexpected letting go!

Between women we could speak of weddings, studies, careers, as so many facts existing on another planet. I understood the reason—perhaps it was unconscious—for my having been invited to Ishwaribhavan. Amidst the rigid customs having to do with caste, I was a bridge between two ways of thinking, while I remained deeply respectful of the Brahmin Laws and Customs. Pandit Joshi trusted me.

He had told me: "Do not teach anything to anybody. Do not speak of your life, or of your journeys. Actually nobody would believe you.

Incidences are mere anecdote, do not create them. Your attitude alone will determine who you are. It is linked with the freely accepted sacrifice which establishes a constant relationship between oneself and the Law that is lived."

Every day he stressed the fact that in the family cosmology where everything was organized around him—he belonged to the Chandra dynasty (moon)—everyone played his role in a voluntarily impersonal way. This made possible a neutral space where spiritual discipline entered in an active way. If detailed rules of behavior created restrictions, on the other hand, they permitted an individualized research; one could withdraw for a time with everybody's approval. Nothing was left to chance.

One spoke of death, for instance, in as simple a way as of a birth—natural events in life where everything is transitory. Of a young widow of twenty, mad with grief, Pandit Joshi said to me: "In a few years from now, her pain will have become the nourishment of her serenity. It is she herself who will discover the expansion of her inner being. One can only support her active perseverance."

I found myself related to a certain way of living that led me to a constant awareness of my movements: never go out alone, never buy anything, not even stamps or sweets. No alms are to be given. Always be able to receive anybody. And there were more refined rules such as: never address somebody with a question, never speak except when questioned, stifle reactions and worries heavy in one's heart.

It was Patanjali's Yoga that gave the key to the observation of one's character. A pandit regularly came to comment upon the Aphorisms of Patanjali and tell symbolic tales to the younger ones in the family. Beside this general teaching everyone had his personal discipline, his way of meditating, often very profoundly, related to one or another of the particular Aphorisms that determine a precise technique for achieving an equilibrium between the inward life and the phenomena of outer life. An extreme discretion protected secrecy as regards the essential.

The women knew very well how to approach yogic techniques in the middle of life, in spite of husbands, servants, traders, gardeners, children, visitors, without any impatience—in the middle of the discomfort of Hindu life, which was almost of the Middle Ages in these mountains. They were supported by the rites and pujas and mainly by an adoring attitude toward the Supreme Divine. They knew the detailed scale of sensations to reach a vibration of the whole being. Since life was considered as a means of purification, the obstacles and revolts—and there were some—became finally gradually diminished.

On certain days, there took place a veritable jousting around Pandit Joshi—an assemblage of Brahmin judges and lawyers, all experts on exegesis. Their way of speaking was deeply influenced by an atheist Samkhya, and they discussed for hours such subjects as dualism, the matter-Spirit disassociation, or the struggle that each being must sustain to liberate himself by his own means. They finally reached a state of harmony with the theist Yoga thanks to the techniques of concentration and meditation coordinated by Patanjali.

Every three years I meet again the elder son of Pandit Joshi, who has become the head of the great family of Almora since his father's death. He is an active man who travels a lot. He is the father of three daughters, and one day they will have a university education instead of a dowry and gold jewelry. Such is the only decision influenced by modern life that I have discovered.

At Ishwaribhavan, I still have my guest room facing the outside, while Tradition is hidden inside, within the hearth of the home.

Parabola
Volume: 17.1
Solitude and
Community

SELFLESS SERVICE

From the *Bhagavad Gita*

Translated by Eknath Easwaran

Arjuna: *O Krishna, you have said that knowledge is greater than action; why then do you ask me to wage this terrible war? Your advice seems inconsistent. Give me one path to follow to the supreme good.*

Sri Krishna: At the beginning of time I declared two paths for the pure of heart: *jñāna yoga*, the contemplative path of spiritual wisdom, and *karma yoga*, the active path of selfless service.

He who shirks action does not attain freedom; no one can gain perfection by abstaining from work. Indeed, there is no one who rests for even an instant; every creature is driven to action by his own nature.

Those who abstain from action while allowing the mind to dwell on sensual pleasure cannot be called sincere spiritual aspirants. But they excel who control their senses through the mind, using them for selfless service.

Fulfill all your duties; action is better than inaction. Even to maintain your body, Arjuna, you are obliged to act. Selfish action imprisons the world. Act selflessly, without any thought of personal profit.

At the beginning, mankind and the obligation of selfless service were created together. "Through selfless service, you will always be fruitful and find the fulfillment of your desires": this is the promise of the Creator. Honor and cherish the *devas*[1] as they honor and cherish you; through this honor and love you will attain the supreme good. All human desires are fulfilled by the devas, who are pleased by selfless service. But anyone who enjoys the things given by the devas without offering selfless acts in return is a thief.

The spiritually minded, who eat in the spirit of service, are freed from all their sins; but the selfish, who prepare food for their own satisfaction, eat sin. Living creatures are nourished by food, and food is nourished by rain; rain itself is the water of life, which comes from selfless worship and service.

Every selfless act, Arjuna, is born from Brahman, the eternal, infinite Godhead. He is present in every act of service. All life turns on this law, O Arjuna. Whoever violates it, indulging his senses for his own pleasure and ignoring the needs of others, has wasted his life. But those who realize the Self are always satisfied. Having found the source of joy and fulfillment, they no longer seek happiness from the external world. They have nothing to gain or lose by any action; neither people nor things can affect their security.

Strive constantly to serve the welfare of the world; by devotion to selfless work one attains the supreme goal of life. Do your work with the welfare of others always in mind. It was by such work that Janaka[2] attained perfection; others, too, have followed this path.

What the outstanding person does, others will try to do. The standards such people create will be followed by the whole world. There is nothing in the three worlds for me to gain, Arjuna, nor is there anything I do not have; I continue to act, but I am not driven by any need of my own. If I ever refrained from continuous work, everyone would immediately follow my example. If I stopped working I would be the cause of cosmic chaos, and finally of the destruction of this world and these people.

The ignorant work for their own profit, Arjuna; the wise work for the welfare of the world, without thought for themselves. By abstaining from work you will confuse the ignorant, who are engrossed in their actions. Perform all work carefully, guided by compassion.

All actions are performed by the *gunas*[3] of *prakriti*.[4] Deluded by his identification with the ego, a person thinks, "*I* am the doer." But the illumined man or woman understands the domain of the gunas and is not attached. Such people know that the gunas interact with each other; they do not claim to be the doer.

Those who are deluded by the operation of the gunas become attached to the results of their action. Those who understand these truths should not unsettle the ignorant. Performing all actions for my sake, completely absorbed in the Self, and without expectations, fight!—but stay free from the fever of the ego.

Those who live in accordance with these divine laws without complaining, firmly established in faith, are released from karma. Those who violate these laws, criticizing and complaining, are utterly deluded, and are the cause of their own suffering.

Even a wise man acts within the limitations of his own nature. Every creature is subject to prakriti; what is the use of repression? The senses have been conditioned by attraction to the pleasant and aversion to the unpleasant. Do not be ruled by them; they are obstacles in your path.

It is better to strive in one's own *dharma*[5] than to succeed in the dharma of another. Nothing is ever lost in following one's own dharma, but completion in another's dharma breeds fear and insecurity.

Arjuna: *What is the force that binds us to selfish deeds, O Krishna? What power moves us, even against our own will, as if forcing us?*

Sri Krishna: It is selfish desire and anger, arising from the guna of *rajas*;[6] these are the appetites and evils which threaten a person in this life.

Just as a fire is covered by smoke and a mirror is obscured by dust, just as the embryo rests deep within the womb, knowledge is hidden by selfish desire—hidden, Arjuna, by this unquenchable fire for self-satisfaction, the inveterate enemy of the wise.

Selfish desire is found in the senses, mind, and intellect, misleading them and burying the understanding in delusion. Fight with all your strength, Arjuna! Control your senses, conquer your enemy, the destroyer of knowledge and realization.

The senses are higher than the body, the mind higher than the senses; above the mind is the intellect, and above the intellect is the Atman. Thus, knowing that which is supreme, let the Atman rule the ego. Use your mighty arms to slay the fierce enemy that is selfish desire.

Notes:

1 The thousands of lesser (i.e., non-supreme) gods or divinities of Hindu mythology.

2 A legendary and exemplary Hindu king.

3 The three qualities which make up the phenomenal world: *tamas*, inertia, ignorance; *rajas*, energy, passion; and *sattva*, harmony, purity, law.

4 Nature, the basic energy comprising both the mental and physical worlds.

5 Usually defined as "duty," but Easwaran points to a deeper meaning, "the essential order of things" or "that which supports," i.e., the inner virtue or essence which generates the sense of duty.

6 Passion.

From *The Bhagavad Gita*, translated by Eknath Easwaran (Tomales, Cal.: Nilgiri Press, 1985). Reprinted by permission of Nilgiri Press.

Parabola
Volume: 27.7
War

INVIOLATE ACTION
Blunting the Arrows of War

Glen Kezwer

Nonviolence, known in Sanskrit as *ahimsa*, is one of the injunctions at the heart of the Indian tradition of yoga. The philosophy of yoga consists of eight limbs. The first limb is *yam*, guidelines for the purification of the mind. Ahimsa is the first of these guidelines.

The concept of nonviolence is multifaceted. It means not killing or inflicting injury or pain on any other person or living creature by thought, word, or deed. The scope of nonviolence includes other injunctions, such as non-deception or truthfulness, refusal to seal, and non-acquisitiveness. If these are not practiced along with the nonviolence, then the nonviolence remains impure. It is said that people and creatures that are normally inimical to one another become amicable in the presence of one in whom ahimsa has been perfected.

It is important to note that ahimsa must also include the idea of nonviolence against oneself. We all have bodies and minds that are to be cherished, for they are the only tools we have for attaining the highest level of consciousness, which is our birthright. Ahimsa is based on the recognition of the unity of all life. That conscious force which animates every living being, which shines from every pair of eyes, is one and the same in all. Therefore, any injury caused to a so-called other being is really an injury to oneself.

The notion of nonviolence is intimately connected with the question of war. Two Hindu points of view, embodied by Mahatma Gandhi and Lord Krishna, take what appear to be radically different approaches to this issue.

Gandhi promulgated and practiced a philosophy of nonviolence. Along with *satygraha*, truth, ahimsa was a cornerstone upon which his political system was built, and was his most effective tool in a decades-long campaign to end British rule in India. Gandhi realized that the English were far outnumbered in his country. "We in India," he wrote, "may in a moment realize that one hundred thousand Englishmen need not frighten three hundred million human beings."[1] But he was also acutely aware that India's overlords were heavily armed and possessed a strong military presence, whereas the Indian people where almost without weapons. Gandhi had to devise a strategy to counter the military superiority of the British. The strategy he formulated was nonviolence.

As Gandhi practiced it, nonviolence was a political, economic, and social tool. It's component were many: civil disobedience, passive resistance, noncooperation, fasting, the spinning of one's own cloth and the creation of many other cottage industries, the boycotting of imported goods, and self-government right down to the level of the individual village. In practical terms nonviolence meant: let us march to the sea to evaporate water and produce our own salt rather than pay an unjust tax; let us sit peacefully and block access to factories rather than submit to impossible conditions; let us practice social noncooperation, such as withdrawing from public offices and the civil service, boycotting courts and other government agencies, and removing our children from government schools; let us refuse to eat, even to the point of death if necessary, in order to force the hand of those who govern us against our will; but never let us raise a hand in violence against our oppressors.

In a letter written in 1941, Gandhi gave one of his most definitive statements of nonviolence.

Our resistance ... does not mean harm to the British people. We will ... not defeat them on the battlefield. Ours is an unarmed revolt. ... We are determined to make their rule impossible by nonviolent noncooperation. It is a method in its nature undefeatable. It is based on the knowledge that no spoliator can compass his end without a certain degree of co-operation, willing or compulsory, of the victim. Our rulers can have our land and bodies, but not our souls.[2]

In Gandhi's view, nonviolence was by no means a tool to be used by the weak; instead it was a sign of strength. In his own words,

It does not mean meek submission to the will of the evil-doer, but it means putting of one's whole soul against the will of the tyrant. … I am not pleading for India to practice nonviolence because she is weak. I want her to practice nonviolence being conscious of her strength and power. … I want India to recognize that she has a soul that cannot perish.[3]

And again,

Nonviolence is not a cover for cowardice, but it is the supreme virtue of the brave. Exercise of nonviolence requires far greater bravery than that of swordsmanship.[4]

Gandhi waged a nonviolent war and in the end he succeeded, for on August 15, 1947, India achieved the status of a free and independent nation.

In seeming contrast to Gandhi's philosophy of nonviolence are the teachings of Lord Krishna, found in the *Bhagavad-Gita*, which forms part of that timeless work, the *Mahabharata*. The story of the *Bhagavad-Gita* unfolds on the battlefield of Kurukshetra where two large armies are arrayed against one another. One is that of the Pandavas, commanded by Arjuna, and the other is the army of the Kauravas, whose leader is Duryodhana. The Pandavas and the Kauravas are two royal families of cousins who have come into conflict over the question of land.

Duryodhana and his father Dhritarashtra were always jealous of the Pandavas, and to deprive them of the half of the kingdom that was rightfully theirs, they invited the eldest of the Pandava brothers, Yudhishtira, to come to their capital city Hastinapur to play a game of dice. Yudhishtira had doubts about Dhritarashtra's motives, but since Dhritarashtra was not only his uncle but had also raised him from a young age, he felt he had to accept. Bound by the rules of his caste, Yudhishtira, along with his family, proceeded to Hastinapur to participate in the game of dice.

Yudhishtira's forebodings proved to be well-founded. He was pitted against Duryodhana's uncle Sakuni, who had loaded the dice in his own favor. Sakuni described the wager: "All our fortune depends on this one throw of the dice. The winner will be lord of the entire Kuru land. The loser will have to live in the forest for twelve years. One year more will have to be spent in disguise. No one should be recognized. If, however, the identity is revealed, twelve years more will have to be spent in the forest."[5]

Yudhishtira was defeated, and he and his family dutifully forfeited their kingdom and marched off into exile. Thirteen years later they returned to claim their lost realm, but Duryodhana refused to return anything to the Pandava brothers. "Not even land which can be covered by the tip of a sharp needle," he replied, "will be surrendered to the Pandavas by us."[6]

The stage was set for the battle between the Kauravas and the Pandavas. Before the battle, Duryodhana and Arjuna each approached Krishna for help. Krishna offered them two choices: his well-equipped army of millions, or himself alone, unarmed. Allowed to pick first, Duryodhana chose Krishna's army. Arjuna, confident that Krishna's wisdom was far more valuable than armed might, was more than pleased to have Krishna alone as his advisor and charioteer. All the elements were in place on the field of Kurukshetra.

Arjuna rode up to the front lines with his charioteer Krishna. There he surveyed the enemy ranks and realized that they contained many of his nearest and dearest—relatives, friends, and even his respected teachers. Despite the fact that it was he himself who had declared war, Arjuna was paralyzed by the thought of the death and destruction about to take place. Arjuna threw away his bow and arrows and sank into the back of his chariot, overcome by a state of total confusion.

The only thing that Arjuna was capable of doing was asking Krishna questions. Krishna's first admonition to Arjuna is clear: "O scorcher of foes, arise and fight!" After all, Arjuna was a warrior who had declared a just war against an enemy who had transgressed the norms of human behavior. His duty as commander-in-chief was to lead his army into battle.

Krishna then told Arjuna the deepest truth, which is the fundamental message of the Gita. The true nature of each soldier on both sides, and of every human being, is the Self. The Self is eternal, unborn and undying. It is imperishable, and therefore does not undergo birth and death. The Self is the reality underlying manifest creation, and is one and the same everywhere. It cannot be burned by fire, dried by the wind, wet by water, or destroyed by weapons. Only to the mortal being are birth and death inevitable. "Neither he who thinks that the Self causes killing, nor he who thinks that the Self is killed by someone has realized the truth, for the Self neither kills nor is killed."[7] Knowledge of this universal truth is Self-Realization; the inability to understand it is called ignorance.

Arjuna was duty-bound to take up his weapons and fight, and thus the Gita is, on the obvious level, advocating war. But the circumstances must be borne in mind. Krishna did his utmost to avoid a confrontation and to convince the Kauravas to restore to the Pandavas the half of the kingdom that was rightfully theirs. Only when he saw that the Karuavas had become blinded to truth and justice did he accept Arjuna's declaration of war and agree to participate. He sought to destroy the collective ignorance of the Pandavas.

It is important to realize that Krishna's teachings were given in the middle of a battlefield, not in the comfort of Arjuna's sitting room. They pertain to a situation in which war has already been declared and the opposing armies are facing one another.

In his personal struggle, Gandhi was following Krishna's advice and doing his duty. The means he chose to wage his war was nonviolence, but wage war he did, and succeed he did. Yet like Arjuna, Gandhi had a deeper, more profound motive for his actions. He too desired to attain the highest state of liberation.

> *What I want to achieve—what I have been striving and pining to achieve these thirty years—is self-realization, to see God face to face, to attain Moksha. I live and move and have my being in pursuit of this goal. All that I do by way of speaking and writing, and all my ventures in the political field, are directed to this same end.*[8]

Gandhi understood Krishna's deepest teaching that the achievement of self-realization is the ultimate goal of all action. In the self-realized state, there is no war and there is no peace. There is only the Self alone.

Notes:

1 M. K. Gandhi, *Young India*, August 11, 1920.

2 M. K. Gandhi, letter to Adolph Hitler, reproduced in *My Non-violence* (Ahmedabad: Navajivan Publishing House, 1960), p. 159.

3 M. K. Gandhi, *Young India*, August 11, 1920.

4 *Ibid.*, August 12, 1926.

5 Kamala Subramanian, *Mahabharata* (Bombay: Bharatiya Vidya Bhavan, 1982), p. 177.

6 *Ibid.*, p. 387.

7 *Bhagavad-Gita*, chapter 2, verse 19.

8 M. K. Gandhi, *An Autobiography, or, The Story of My Experiments with Truth* ([1927] Ahmedabad: Navajivan Publishing House, 2002), p. x.

Parabola
Volume: 17.1
Solitude and
Community

Dweller in the Cave of the Heart

Wayne Teasdale

The mystical life of India has always emphasized the solitary path of the wandering ascetic who is called a *sannyāsi*, a figure dating back to the oral tradition of the *rishis*, the forest sages of Indian antiquity. Whereas the Greeks in a later age epitomized the good life as the pursuit of wisdom or philosophy, the rishis saw the good life in much larger terms: an encounter with the Divine, the Ultimate Mystery, or Brahman. Thus they retired from society, devoting themselves to spiritual realization through meditation.

Their quest for the Absolute has always been understood as an inner journey. Indian mysticism, though including a cosmic, external revelation of the Divine, strongly recommends introversion, interiority, the inner search for the Absolute known as *Atman*, the eternal Self. This Self abides in the *guhā*, the "cave of the heart," one of India's enduring metaphors for such contemplation. The way to it is open to all, and spiritual fulfillment requires realization of the Self in the cave of the heart. The Self is one with God, with the Brahman, and the aim of the exterior and the interior journeys is the same.

The sannyāsi is pre-eminently the ascetic monk who seeks integration with the mystery in the cave; he is in search of what dwells in this cave, and so he or she becomes a dweller there. This metaphor aptly captures the personal nature of Hindu spirituality, which is very much a matter of individual effort, unlike the more collective approach of Semitic or Buddhist traditions, which are organized into churches, mosques, synagogues, temples, and monasteries. Such single-minded commitment to spiritual life translates into the ideal of the hermit, the solitary who finds his or her own rhythm of growth on the path to enlightenment. Solitude is thus an essential value of Hindu asceticism, while community is primarily a concession to the spiritual needs of a master's followers and the material needs of monks. Community is also the matrix for learning the tradition through the study of scripture and the teaching of a guru: the place where transmission of mystical wisdom from a master to his disciples takes place.

Sannyāsa in Sanskrit means to abandon totally, to let go or give up, and so implies complete renunciation of all attachments, such as family ties, responsibilities, religious duties, power, money, social position, and all earthly ambition. Renunciation frees the person to pursue the Absolute, the Divine, and liberation. Only the one who actively dwells in the cave of the heart can reach enlightenment, the final realization in mystical consciousness. One who lives as a renunciate is thus a sannyāsi (a monk) or a sannyāsinin (a nun).

Sannyāsa, the most ancient ascetical, mystical, and monastic tradition, is at least 7,000 years old. Its existence is first recorded in the Vedas. India's early hermits, the rishis, founded not simply a monastic system, as did the Desert Fathers in the Christian world of the third century, but also the "Eternal Religion" itself, as Hinduism is called, and therefore the very culture and civilization of India. The historical role of the rishis, however, is dwarfed by their spiritual importance, and it is here that we must look for their ultimate value.

In the *Rig Veda* a long-haired sannyāsi, called a *muni*, is a silent ecstatic and an intimate of the gods. He practices silence, a kind of interior quiet facilitated by the silence of speech. The muni's relationship with the Divine frees him to seek the depth and development of mystical union. He enters into this relationship through ascetical practices which augment a meditative regime. Through his spiritual practice he achieves an inner freedom, similar to his external freedom from social norms and religious obligations, and so is free *to be*, to transcend this world. By transcending the cares of society, he is able to discover the forms and principles of all things which are accessible to his inner gaze. Because he is unbound he has the time and environment to explore the mystical realm within.

Though not everyone becomes a sannyāsi, there are four distinct successive stages or orders which mark a person's development in Hindu tradition. The first is the student period, beginning at twelve and lasting twelve years. During this time the individual becomes proficient in Sanskrit and the scriptures; he participates in the daily temple sacrifices and other rites. The second is that of the householder, when the person marries, raises a family, works, and looks after his parents. This stage is considered the most important because it is the basis of Hindu society in the support it gives to the other stages. When a person's hair turns white and he sees his grandchildren, he may enter the third stage, that of the forest-dweller or hermit. This order is a time of retirement and preparation for sannyāsa. The forest hermit reflects on the mysteries of life and follows a more rigorous schedule of meditation fortified by ascetical practices. The final stage is that of sannyāsa itself.

These stages are defined and discussed in great detail in the *Laws of Manu*,[1] an ancient legal code and source of norms written probably during the first century AD, but whose principles have much greater antiquity. *Manu* gives a fairly clear picture of what a sannyāsi should be in his external life. The fundamental rule of the ascetic is to wander. Speaking of this, *Manu* says: "Let him always wander alone, without any companion, in order to attain (final liberation), fully understanding that the solitary (man, who) neither forsakes nor is forsaken, gains his end."[2]

Solitude is indeed indispensable to this path. The solitary way of the monk facilitates his inner realization as he frees himself from all social and religious responsibilities; his growth in mystical consciousness is greatly accelerated. This solitude is the ideal in Indian monasticism, though ashramic community is also an important dimension of the tradition. Even so, every sannyāsi, just by virtue of having this path, values solitude. It is closely connected with his or her spiritual understanding and self-knowledge. It is what supports his discipline in meditation, guaranteeing it a permanent place in his practice, a practice which community life, with all its demands, can weaken.

The sannyāsi is not bound to society in any way, other than to have his needs met. He must be free of all desires, especially self-seeking. True renunciation is, as Bede Griffiths remarks, a "renunciation of the self ... inner renunciation. The man (or woman) who works without attachment, free from self love is a true sannyāsi ..."[3] Detachment and renunciation are, in a deeper sense, essentially a freedom from the ego, a point made by most spiritual masters. This interior freedom allows one to seek intimacy with the Divine through one's spiritual practice of inner silence, a transcendence of the senses and imagination, meditation, solitude, mendicancy, wandering, and repetition of the name of God. One lives a life of purity of heart, holiness, and interiority. The sannyāsi practices austerities, disciplining his body and his will, so that he can keep his inner focus. Ultimately sannyāsa is a mystery of interiority and of transcendence, a return to the Source.

The practice of these disciplines gives the sannyāsi a certain inner freedom which makes possible his exploration of the mystical realm, his association with the gods, as the Veda expresses it,[4] and more accurately, his unitive relationship with the Divine. But Raimundo Pannikar suggests that the price the sannyāsi (muni) pays for his station is that he "ceases to be a normal man."[5] He must often endure loneliness, darkness, and misunderstanding. He is, after all, an ascetic who is actually dead to the world. He does not relate to it on its terms; he cannot, because his task is different. He must be able to devote his time, energy, and focus to the Ultimate Mystery. He is a full-time mystic, and like the monk in any tradition, he is a pioneer of the Spirit, exploring remote territories of consciousness, breaking new ground.

Other than as the last stage in life, there are two further ways a person may enter the state of renunciation: through inner experience (*vidvat-sannyāsa*) or aspiration (*vividisā-sannyāsa*). The former is a call from *within*, the latter a call from without. *Vidvat* comes from the Sanskrit root *vid* which means "to know," but this kind of knowing is profoundly experiential, mystical, and deeply interior, happening within the cave of the heart. Vividisā-sannyāsa, on the other hand, starts not with inspiration or experience, but with an aspiration and a conscious decision: it implies a striving after contemplative wisdom and transformation, much as in Western monasticism.[6]

Vidvat-sannyāsa provides a key to life and vocation. If one is given such a powerful mystical experience, then one is called to a life of pure contemplation and renunciation, in order to seek the Absolute. The Hindu tradition regards such an initial experience as an awakening, a kind of initiation by the Spirit, and the person so privileged is not free to ignore its implication for his life—that he is meant for the mystical path.

Ramana Maharshi (1879–1950), a South Indian sage, was a vidvat-sannyāsi who was mystically awakened at the age of seventeen and left the world behind to embrace the solitary life, seeking the Absolute in poverty, simplicity, and obscurity. He came to dwell at Arunachala, the holy mountain in Tiruvannamali in Tamil Nadu in the south. After some years there, disciples flocked to him and built an ashram around him.

Ramana Maharshi's inner awakening was sparked by an imagined experience of his own death in which he realized that though his body, with its senses and functions, and his mind, with its faculties, might die, the immortal consciousness of the Self would remain. He *knew* he was not his body or mind, that he was the Self. This is the inner reality of all things,[7] pure awareness, the nature of which is existence-conscious-ness-bliss,[8] or *Saccidānanda*, the great metaphor for mystical realization of the Godhead in the knower as the experience of bliss in the total consciousness of being.

Vividisā-sannyāsa, that which comes by choice or aspiration, some-times overlaps the last of the four stages of life, that stage where one takes sannyāsa to achieve liberation as part of the natural course of events. But this form usually comes earlier in life, as a conscious decision or at the instruction of a guru.

An example of a vividisā-sannyāsi was Henri Le Saux or Abhishik-tananda (1919–1073),[9] a French Benedictine monk who came to India in 1948 and sat in the presence of Ramana Maharshi. Although the two never exchanged words, Abhishiktananda claimed to have been awak-ened within by this encounter. With another Frenchman, Jules Mon-chanin (1895–1957), he founded Shantivanam Ashram, near Trichi in Tamil Nadu. The retreat, though nominally Benedictine, was established to be a center of deep ecumenism and reconciliation between the Hindu and Christian traditions.

Abhishiktananda immersed himself more and more deeply in Hindu spirituality and, along with Monchanin, became a sannyāsi as well as a Benedictine monk. Near the end of his life, he spent more and more time in the caves of Arunachala and in 1968 turned Shantivanam over to another Western monk and vividisā-sannyāsi, Bede Griffiths, and spent his own final years in a hermitage in the Himalayas.

Abhishiktananda has written that vidvat-sannyāsa "comes upon a man of itself and, whether he likes it or not, he is seized by an inner compulsion. The light has shone so brightly within, that he has become blind to all the things of this world, as happened to Paul on the road to Damascus."[10] Speaking of vividisā-sannyāsa, he observes that this "other kind of sannyāsa ... is taken ... in order to get *jñāna* (spiritual wisdom) and *moksha* (liberation)."[11] Jñāna is something akin to gnosis in the Christian tradition: an inner, experiential knowledge of the Divine. Moksha refers to final enlightenment and release from life: liberation, but with the mystical awakening of jñāna as a prerequisite.

Although the ideal of sannyāsa emphasizes the solitary path, the community dimension is also prominent. Conservatively, in India, there are some 20,000,000 sannyāsis and sannyāsinins, and around 5,000,000 ashrams. Most ashrams normally have a few sannyāsis, with one of them as the guru at the center of the community. Some continue to be centered around a particular guru even after his or her death.

Though some of these communities are composed almost entirely of renunciates, ashrams are not necessarily monasteries. These communities are more like houses of prayer in which spiritual teaching, practice, and the communication of the tradition through the scriptures take place. An ashram is a special environment where monks and laity live together united in their common spiritual focus under the guidance of a spiritual master.

When sannyāsis are very holy, wise, and in possession of jñāna, they will inevitably attract disciples, who in turn often build ashrams as centers where spiritual masters may teach and guide others. These communities may vary in size from three or four members to several hundred, but they always center around a guru who is normally a monk.

Community life there, for the renunciates, is a kind of practical concession to the needs of others, especially the profound need for inner guidance to awakening, which in most cases a teacher must initiate. Even hermits often group together, at least at certain times of the year, to support each other in their solitude and to meet practical needs.

Solitude and community are not opposed but internally related, since everyone and everything are grounded in unity. Nothing is actually separate, although distinctions are certainly real. This is the mystery of the *advaita*, or non-duality, non-separateness, or unity: it is the mystery of distinction-within-unity. True community is rooted in this mystery of advaita. The sannyāsi chooses solitude to realize experientially the unity of everyone and everything, the truth that all is within him, and his guru is similarly within him, in the cave of his own heart. There he finds:

> *... that mystery of glory and immortality*
> *hidden in the depth of the heart,*
> *beyond the firmament,*
> *which cannot be won either*
> *by ritual, or by begetting*
> *offspring, or by giving one's wealth:*
> *but which only they can enter*
> *who have renounced all.*[12]

Notes:

1 *The Laws of Manu*, translated by G. Buhler, in *Sacred Books of the East*, edited by Max Müller ([1886] Delhi: Motilal Banarsidass, 1964), vol. 25.

2 *Ibid.*, Chapter 6:42, p. 206.

3 Bede Griffiths, *River of Compassion: A Christian Commentary on the Bhagavad Gita* (Warwick, N.Y.: Amity House, 1987), p. 108.

4 *Rig Veda* 10:136:2, 4 and 5. From *The Vedic Experience: An Anthology of the Vedas for Modern Man and Contemporary Celebration*, edited and translated by Raimundo Pannikar (Pondicherry, India: All India Books, 1977, pp. 436–37).

5 *Ibid.*, p. 436.

6 See *St. Benedict's Rule for Monasteries*, translated by Leonard J. Doyle (Collegeville, MN: Liturgical Press, 1948), chapter 58.

7 *The Spiritual Teaching of Ramana Maharshi* (Boston: Shambhala, 1988), p. xiii. See also Abhishiktananda, *Saccidānanda: A Christian Approach to Advaitic Experience*, revised ed. (Delhi: ISPCK, 1984, revised), pp. 19–29; and *The Collected Works of Ramana Maharshi*, edited by Arthur Osborne (New York: Samuel Weiser, 1972), especially pp. 17–47.

8 *Spiritual Teaching of Ramana Maharshi*, p. 3.

9 For a profound treatment of his life, see James Stuart, *Swami Abhishiktānanda: His Life As Told Through His Letters* (Delhi: ISPCK, 1989), but for an account of his own awakening, see his *The Secret of Arunachala* (Delhi: ISPCK, 1979).

10 Abhishiktānanda, *The Further Shore* (Delhi: ISPCK, 1975), p. 11.

11 *Ibid.*

12 *Māhānārāyanha Upanishad* 12, 14.

Parabola
Volume: 29.3
The Seeker

A Terrible Longing in the Heart

An Interview with Shri Parthasarathi Rajagopalachari

Born on July 24, 1927 in South India, Shri Parthasarathi Rajagopalachari (Chariji) is the president of Shri Ram Chandra Mission (SCRM) and the third living master in the lineage of spiritual masters of the Sahaj Marg system of Raja Yoga. Besides the main ashrams in Chennai, South India, and at Satkhol, in the Himalayas, he spends a considerable amount of time traveling to various SRCM centers in India, Europe, America, South Africa, and Oceania to meet with his abhyasis *(i.e., Sahaj Marg meditation practicants) and teach them the benefits of heart-centered meditation. His books include* Heart to Heart, Down Memory Lane, The Fruit of the Tree, In His Footsteps *and* My Master *(Shri Ram Chandra Mission).*

> *This interview was conducted on a bright, sunny afternoon in Fremont, California. Our conversation was casual, informal, and joyful—from the beginning to the end.*
> *—Rama Devagupta*

Rama Devagupta: *What impulse moves one to search? What influences our search?*

Parthasarathi Rajagopalachari: The impulse is a terrible longing in the heart which says, "I must know the truth"—truth in terms of spiritual values. If your material circumstances are too good, too comfortable, too glamorous, they take you away from your search. When you are over-protected, you lose sight of the search. However, if your interest in the search is burning in your heart, you will eventually break out of it—like the chick breaking out of the shell.

RD: *Are there different ways of conducting a spiritual search?*

PR: At the beginning, you are guided more by the strength of your inner longing. But that longing may not be intense enough. The confusion between what you are seeking and what you find can lead you astray unless the inner search is so powerful that it can say, "Not this! Not this!" You may become momentarily trapped into situations which seem to fulfill your search—like drugs, alcohol, even sex. If that fulfills you and you stop there, it means that your seeking was not intense enough, nor was your goal defined. You may stop with sensory or social fulfillment at a particular level, but the longing will lie dormant and something may spark it off again.

When the search is a real search, the flight toward the goal becomes very direct, what we call the *Shuka* path. Shuka is the Sanskrit name for the parrot, which flies straight like an arrow—no meandering here and there. The Shuka path depends on your strength of purpose, your ability to reject temporary goals, to withstand the temptation to experiment with temporary goals, thinking, "Suppose this is it!" In the true seeker's path there isn't any "suppose this is it!" There may be a pause for a day or two but then you move on, whereas others get lost in a jungle of pos-sibilities for years.

RD: *Does the search have a direct relation to the level of attainment of the seeker?*

PR: No, no, it only relates to the strength of purpose. The moment you are satisfied with a temporary goal, say, "Stop." For example, consider the migration of birds. A truly migrating bird flies thousands of miles, often from one continent to another. Many are lost in the ocean, caught in a storm, not able to fly, and fall into the sea. But an enormous number of them do make it, so, it is possible.

Now, birds have the power of "instinct" to guide them. At the human level, we have the instrument of the intellect, but unless we cultivate wisdom, intellect doesn't take us anywhere except in the pursuit of material goals—scientific, artistic, commercial, economic, but not spiritual.

RD: *Is it necessary to have a teacher?*

PR: Yes. A teacher is one who shows the way.

RD: *What is the place of practice and technique?*

PR: Everything is a practice if it is used in the right way. Even a man who becomes a drinker, thinking that it will fulfill his dream of nirvana, can benefit from it. If he is able to get out of it quickly, it will have had its place, and it will no longer attract him. If he is satisfied and says, "This is it," however, he is lost. Your inner fire must tell you what it is and what it is not.

RD: *What is the role of spiritual literature and sacred texts?*

PR: Spiritual literature gives you intellectual satisfaction, and it is easy to be satisfied intellectually. You may read about something and feel you know what it is, but spiritual values have to be *felt*, not known about. Knowledge of that kind has no place in spiritual life. Many people are easily satisfied—they read a lot of literature and say, "I know all about nirvana. I have read about sixty-eight different varieties of nirvana in Buddhism, Hinduism, Taoism, and Sufism." The question is: Have they ever *felt* anything?

Spirituality needs a certain bravery, a bold approach. It is not for cowards. That is why my Guruji said, "I want lions, not sheep." We have to stake all to get all. It is not a gamble where you can put in a penny and expect a pound in return. That is why Jesus says, in Matthew 16:25, "For those who want to save their life will lose it, and those who lose their life for my sake will find it."

RD: *Is it necessary to be part of a spiritual school?*

PR: What is a school? It is something which offers you an education. We have the school called "life," and when you learn in life depends on what you are seeking. So we come back to the seeker. You look for mundane satisfaction, you will find it. You want sensory pleasure, you can find it. You want to become a millionaire, you can become one. Life offers everything.

RD: *How does a teacher decide if a seeker is genuine or not?*

PR: The teacher must assume that everybody who comes to him or her is a genuine seeker. Time itself will select the true seeker from the false. Those who are there for fun, drop off. Those who are true, remain. They may drop off at various stages, depending on their inner fire and how far it will take them.

"Seek and you shall find," doesn't mean "Seek and it shall be found immediately." When you find it and where you find it depends on the integrity of your search, and the power behind that search. You may discover it just where you are, or you may go around the universe and come back to the place where you started and find it just there. That is why the spiritual search always begins and ends within your *self.*

RD: *So a genuine teacher would accept everybody?*

PR: He has to! Because he doesn't know! I had a vision once, between the waking and sleeping states. In the vision, I am looking at a packet of seeds in a shop, trying to pick out the good seeds for planting. Then, something tells me, "How do you know that the seed that looks good is going to germinate and the seed that you are throwing away will not?"

So we don't know the inner life potential that is in the seed: apparently weak, it may be strong on the inside; the other one is apparently strong, but weak on the inside. The guru lets his students evolve and helps them according to his own ability to do so, at the right time. But the guru can never judge. He must not judge.

RD: *Does the seeker change and evolve in the search?*

PR: Naturally. If you put your hand in the fire, will it not get roasted? A spiritual seeker is said to be something like a metal, which is put into the fire to be melted and purified so that all the dross is burnt away. Like the purification of gold.

RD: *Must one renounce the world to become a seeker?*

PR: The spiritual practice of Sahaj Marg says that you must fly with two wings, like the seagull—the wing of spirituality and the wing of materiality. There is no question of renouncing anything except obstructions to achieving the goal.

RD: *When did you become aware that you were a seeker?*

PR: I don't think I was ever a conscious seeker. Perhaps it began in a past life. I never looked for a teacher; I *found* him. There must have been some inner preparation, but it seems that I must have wasted several lives searching for what I could have found in one life. My Master once told me that I had been associated with him in an earlier life.

The teacher's task is to continue to teach and help others evolve. He may come life after life, highly achieved, but with a duty to come back to teach us, whereas the seeker comes only to seek and to find. In a sense, the teacher's search is to find seekers—having finished his search himself and found what he sought.

RD: *Is finding the Teacher the beginning of our journey or is it the end of our quest?*

PR: If a bird lays an egg, it has given the possibility of a new life. But it all depends on the bird within the egg—whether it is able to break out of the shell. That final purpose has to come from the chick in the egg, pecking it from inside and breaking the shell to come out.

So there is an element of fulfillment when you find your guru; it is a big part of our journey. But what is left? My guru once told a very senior advanced disciple, "Now your journey is very short." Then he laughingly said, "It may be very long too." Another disciple who was present with my master became puzzled. "How can short become long?" he asked. My master replied, "One percent of infinity is still infinity, and if you stumble there, you can go back all the way—to the point where you started."

RD: *What pitfalls might face a seeker?*

PR: Everything is a pitfall for the unwary and the faithless. And nothing is a pitfall for the courageous seeker who just shakes it off like a bear.

RD: *Having found a spiritual technique, a master, and having become established in the practice, how can a seeker assess his progress? What criteria should he use?*

PR: A seeker can never assess his own progress. Even my Guruji used to say, "What I am and where I am, only my Master knows." This is going back to that Heisenberg principle in physics, "If you know its location, you won't know its velocity. If you know its velocity then you won't know its location." This principle applies much more profoundly and truthfully to spiritual matters.

RD: *We are so used to assessing our progress at school or at work.*

PR: There, it is assessable. But here, we cannot. When you fly, you need an altimeter to tell the height. If you are out in space, you need ground control because there is no barometric pressure to tell you the altitude. You are in vacuum. So you rely on another source. Ground control tracks you, and your obedience must be total. In spiritual matters, the more you grow, the more you rely on your guru's wisdom. It is a matter of survival.

RD: *Does the spiritual seeker ever reach a stage where he can consider that he has reached the goal?*

PR: There is so such thing as a fixed goal in spirituality. It is ever changing. Learn to love and do not seek love for yourself. Things break down when you want everything for yourself and you are not concerned for others—whether it is in individual, or a country, or the whole world. "I want to be powerful." "I want to be rich." "I want to be wealthy." Where there is "I," there is always destruction.

Never be diverted away from your course by the enticements of life: whether they are material, mental, or even apparently spiritual. The so-called spiritual world is full of enticements. All has to be renounced because spirituality is, ultimately, becoming nothing, where "nothingness" is what matters.

Parabola
Volume: 7.1
Sleep

Krishna and King Mucukunda: the Sleeper Awakened

Heinrich Zimmer

King Mucukunda is not a king in the historical Western understanding of the term. He is a mythological antecedent of human monarchs, a titanic warrior who fought bravely with the gods (deva) *at an early stage in the Hindu cycles of time called* yugas. *His "sleep" can be likened to a cosmic coma which takes a hero out of action for aeons. His awakening occurs in an age which is substantially different from the one he left through his self-induced slumber.*

From a Hindu perspective, King Mucukunda's sleep was merely a rest-stop in the soul's long journey through existence. It is not the goal of life, for this deep sleep is not the same as the highest realization known as moksha. *Sleep prevents the king from achieving the stage of* sanyasin, *the final crucial stage* (ashrama) *which all twice-born individuals should pass through prior to death. In his playful manner, Krishna spurs the ancient king onward toward total conscious absorption in God.*

Professor Campbell used the story of King Mucukunda

as an example of "refusal of the return." Instead of following the full round
of the monomyth, which brings the hero back into the familiar world with
his prize, Mucukunda elects to retreat still farther into the mountains. Many
signs, such as the diminutive size of men, reveal to Mucukunda that the
final time cycle (kaliyuga) *has dawned. The ancient warrior, his deep sleep*
abated, leaves to pursue a higher awakening in the solitude of the mountains.
As Campbell concludes, "And who shall say that his decision was altogether
without reason?"
                                                        —J. Michael McKnight

A king is slumbering inside a mountain, sleeping his long sleep in the
dark of his cave—a motif we find in the myths and legends of many
peoples. But what induced so profound a sleep? What bade him seek
rest instead of the vigilance for kingly deeds? What compels his sleep
and what wakens him once more? What is to happen, what will he do
when he awakes?

Myths and legends yield an array of answers to these questions. India
recounts the myth of King Mucukunda, the hero of prehistory who slept
away countless ages in a cave. Mandhatr, his father, had come into the
world by a miracle and been nourished by the divine finger of the King
of the Gods, Indra himself. Destined to be the only king among men
to attain Indra's size, he grew larger by suckling the god's index finger;
for since he was not of woman born, no mother could nurture him. His
father had been pregnant with him a hundred autumns long until the
child could burst forth from his father's left side (the childless Indra had
accidentally drunk of the magic potion prepared by the priests to make
his wife fertile).

In those days when the world was young, gods and men still inter-
mingled freely and physically. Wise seers gazed into the secret powers
to discover potent spells and powerful new rites; and there were also
priests, filled with the fire of asceticism, who could perform magical acts.
These two groups helped the gods come to power. Now, the dawn of the
world is turbulent and shrouded in mystery: the gods are not yet the
true rulers of the world—"immortals" and "dwellers in heaven." They are
competing for divine rank with the titans, their half-brothers by the same

father, the "Lord of All Progeny" (Prajāpati), the primordial Tortoise-Man (Kaśyapa); humans give help to both sides. In the end it is the gods who have the good fortune to ascend to power and order the world: they surmount the back of heaven; they gain the sun, the seat of everlasting life; they drink the potion of immortality (*amṛta*, "ambrosia"). In the same way that Zeus defeats the titans, and the gods of the Eddas conquer the giants, these gods master their rivals; by their cunning and resourcefulness they lay low the brute but superior force opposing them, reducing it to mere demonic strength, effective only in the form of anti-gods.

But in their battles with these demonic anti-gods, the gods need assistance from humans and their sacerdotal magic arts. Side by side with Indra and the gods stand the mighty archer kings on their chariots. Now Mucukunda was one of those heroes who helped the gods of old to victory. The battle won, the gods allowed him to make a wish: he could wish for anything within their power to give him. Whereupon he wished to be able to sleep forever—so tired was he from fighting, or so the story has it. And anyone who might disturb his sleep was to be burned to ashes by the first gleam from the eyes of the awakening king.

His wish was granted. He slept in a cave through three of the world's ages. Then, at the dawn of the fourth and final one, Vishnu, the God of the Universe, came down to earth in the form of Krishna, the Savior-Hero, to do battle with the world's demonic forces (who were in the guise of human fiends and tormenting monsters) and to announce to the fourth age, in the *Bhagavadgītā*, his way of salvation. And not until that moment was Mucukunda roused from his sleep.

By conquering the demons in all kinds of shapes, Krishna, from his obscure beginnings, had risen to become the foremost hero of the tribe which Vishnu, the God of the Universe, had honored with his incarnation. Soon he saw his people being threatened by barbarians from the northwest. As if it were mere child's play, he vanquished them in a manner befitting his divine nature: with a crafty ploy. He crowned himself with lotuses and, like the new, waxing, crescent moon, he walked unarmed out of his fortified city to lure the king of the enemy army into trying to catch him. Fleeing from him, he enticed him into a cave. There the king found someone lying asleep and thought: "Has he lured me all this way so that he can play the harmless sleeper?" He gave the person lying there a kick. And then did Mucukunda arise from his age-old sleep and slowly open his eyes. His gaze took measure of the cave until it fell upon the man standing there—who then burst into flames and was reduced to ashes.

Then Mucukunda's gaze full upon the God of the Universe in his human shape who had playfully hidden himself from his pursuer and, mindful of the ancient prophecy, the hero recognized Krishna by his shining splendor. Now fully conscious, Mucukunda found himself reluctantly abandoned once again to the aimless play of successive incarnations, to the senseless alternation of longing and loss, to the deceptive pleasures of the self-conscious ego and its despair, from which the god's eternally glittering *māyā* is woven. At this moment the true meaning behind his wish for unceasing sleep becomes clear: it was not exhaustion from the cosmic struggles and victories he had taken part in that compelled him to disdain god-like splendor and delight in the world. He realized what human life was: he was achieving a sense of its endless flux and aimless alternation of delight and pain; this led to the revelation of the reason why he wanted to turn to ashes anyone who dared waken him. He speaks these words to Krishna:

"For eternities I have been wandering around in the ring of this *saṁsāra*; the fire of great suffering has been overwhelming, and nowhere have I found peace and rest. Pain I thought pleasure. Mirages on the desert sands I took for refreshing waters. I reached out for joys; they brought me torment. Royal power and dominion over the earth, might and wealth, friends, children, a spouse and a royal retinue and all things of the senses—I embraced them all because they seemed to me joy, yet all was transformed and its essence turned into tormenting fire. I managed to ascend into the company of gods who wanted me as their companion—but where was here the peace of eternal rest? Deluded by your māyā, Lord, all creatures stumble into birth, old age, death, and every manner of misery. They behold amongst all these the god of the dead and find, in their individual hells, unmitigated suffering in every conceivable shape—all comes from you. Dazzled by your māyā, I have fallen completely into the clutches of the world and am wandering aimlessly in the depths of the bottomless pitfall of the self. And so I seek my refuge in you, the Unbounded One, the Venerable One. I yearn for release from all of this."

Mucukunda's pious plea for salvation finds an ear to hear. In a state of grace through the promise of salvation, the ancient hero falls at the feet of the Lord of the Worlds. Then he comes out of the cave, which had been sheltering him dreamless like a thing unborn; he emerges from the earth's maternal womb born anew, destined for transitory reincarnations in divine glory and the world of men, as was prophesied by the mouth of Krishna. And these rebirths will make him forget the infinite number of his previous incarnations and will raise him toward the state of dissolution in the highest god—the god who gives birth in play to the whole world and all the creatures therein, who then reabsorbs them into himself, and who transcends all things.

He emerges from the jaws of his cave—into a world transformed! How tiny have men become since the dawn of the world's beginning when last he saw them! Suddenly it strikes him: The world's final age is now dawning, and he sets forth into the solitude of the mountains where as a fervent ascetic he undergoes constant purifications in the approach to his god.

What had been happening while he slept? We recall that, at the beginning of the world, the gods had come forth from its seething surge of energy and gained power in victorious struggle, whereupon Mucukunda had fallen into his timeless sleep. Now since then, the divine order which Brahma initially imposed on the world has become feeble and obscured. Stunted and stale, the world is standing at the threshold of its ultimate age, when it will waste completely away.

Translated by Gerald Chapple and James B. Lawson from Zimmer's *Maya: Der indische Mythos* (1936). This rendering of the story first appeared in *Eranos Jahrbuch*, 1934, as a part of a longer Zimmer article that compared the Indian king Mucukunda with Shakespeare's Hamlet.

•

CHAPTER SIX

Modes of Experience

The Lord said: I have known many past births,
and so have you, Arjuna.
I remember them all,
while you do not, enemy-burner.
Although indeed I am unborn and imperishable,
although I am the lord of the creatures,
I do resort to nature, which is mine,
and take on birth by my own wizardry.
For whenever the Law languishes,
Bhārata, and lawlessness flourishes, I create myself.
I take on existence from eon to eon for the rescue
of the good and the destruction of the evil,
in order to reestablish the Law.
He who knows thus the divinity,
as in fact it is, of my birth and work, no more returns to rebirth
when he dies—he returns to me, Arjuna.
There have been many who, rid of passions,
fears, and angers, and made pure by the austerities of insight,
have immersed themselves in me,
resorted to me, and become of one being with me.
I share in them in the manner in which they turn to me;
for in all their various sways men do follow my trail, Pārtha.

—Bhagavad Gita

The previous chapter touched on the four "aims of life," general attitudes of concern and attachment taken by an individual in the conduct of life. This chapter and the next deal with a very few of the myriad ways Hindus find to live with the realization of the limitations of the life they are granted at birth. The next chapter will present some views on the practice of meditation and the discipline of yoga. Here we take up other ways in which people seek meaning in their lives by opening themselves to the unseen powers in the world, primarily through periodic ceremonies and in pilgrimage. Very little has been published in *Parabola* about the role of personal devotion and daily worship in the path of most Hindus, so that is missing from our material here.

Belief in rebirth, driven by the inexorable law of cause and effect called *karma*, underlies the Hindu understanding of experience in this world. As the epigraph implies, rebirth and the law of karma apply without exception to humans and gods alike. Only the great God, called by various names (Krishna, Shiva, Brahma, according to one's preference), is conscious of the entirety of transcendental and immanent reality. An individual may aspire to liberation from the sorrows and pains of worldly existence, endlessly repeated. This may come by melding the individual consciousness with that of the great, transcendent God. But the theme of most seekers' lives is the search to expand their consciousness of divinity immanent in the real world.

"Chagrin at the memory of previous mistakes and despair at the realization that one will make them all again in this life, is what makes the baby cry as he enters the world." So writes Wendy Doniger in "Wake-up Calls." Here the fundamental impact of experience on our fates in this life and future lives, through karma, is placed side by side with our forgetfulness of both our past experience and our true nature.

The pain of life is perhaps most poignantly expressed as a sense of separation and of longing, as David Dean Shulman writes in "Modes of Meaning and Experience." He says that "the terms of *samsara* [the round of rebirth] are such that revelation can be, at best, but partial and paradoxical; the transcendent god can never be contained by our reality." However, he writes, "the tragic world is bounded, fragmented, and full of meaning," and truth is to be found on the boundaries between the experienced world and the transcendental one.

The meaning of events in daily life is illuminated by the rich ocean of stories in India. And stories also surround and enliven the frequent celebrations observed in both temples and households. The festival best known in the Western world is the fall festival of lights, Dipavali or

Diwali. One story explaining what is being celebrated is given in "The Slaying of Narakasura," retold from the *Bhagavata Purana*. Others are told by Rama Devgupta's "Kindling the *Deepa*."

One reason that the widely varying regions of the Indian subcontinent have through history formed a single cultural subcontinent is the almost universal practice of pilgrimage, an act of adventure and search, as vividly described by Lizelle Reymond in "Intimate Journeys." A pilgrimage is often taken in connection with a vow: "If so-and-so is granted to me, I shall journey to such-and-such a holy place to give thanks." Or it is undertaken in order to seek the advice or blessing of a wise man, as is recounted in the story "Giving and Grace," retold from a story by the great medieval poet Kalidasa.

Finally, transcendent experience in the form of brief but powerful moments of freedom from one's ordinary life is a gift sought by seekers in many contexts. Ravi Ravindra muses on this experience in "Unless It Is Wonderful, It Cannot Be Holy." A saint for whom such ecstasy was nearly continual was Ramakrishna Paramahansa, the nineteenth-century Bengali holy man (and there have been many others in the rich history of Indian saints). Marvin Barrett gives an account of Sri Ramakrishna's life in ecstasy in "Seeking the Transcendent."

Parabola
Volume: 30.1
Awakening

Wake-up Calls

Some Ancient Hindu Myths

Wendy Doniger

In the mythology of reincarnation, the signals we send to ourselves from our former lives are wake-up calls, like the message that Chippendale Mupp, one of the creatures in *Dr. Seuss's Sleep Book*, sends to himself: at bedtime, he bites the end tuft on his *very* long tail, so that the ouch will work its way up the whole tail and, finally, wake him up in the morning.

These myths ask: Where is memory, in the mind or in the body? How can our bodies remember things that our minds have forgotten? Indian philosophy locates memory in the *manas*: like the heart, it is a physical organ in the body, and like the mind, it is where you learn calculus, and like both mind and heart, it is where you fall in love—thus doubly blurring the Cartesian distinction between mind and body. Hinduism assumes that when the body dies, the soul transmigrates, taking with it the dead person's karma, the moral record of good and bad actions committed in all former lives. Although the transmigrating soul usually loses its memory as it crosses the boundary of rebirth and sheds its body, some particularly gifted people can remember their previous births. Some branches of Indian philosophy, therefore, locate memory along with karma in (or more precisely on) the soul, without, however, totally divorcing it from the body.

Belief in reincarnation has long appealed to non-Hindu consciousness. Karmic thinking continues to surface among us in what might be
called American folk belief. And many people grant the theory some
degree of useful wisdom, at the very least as a powerful metaphor and at
the most as an expression, *mutatis mutandis*, of ideas that we, too, hold
about the compelling force of the past.

All of us are subject to what the Hindus call *vasanas*, "perfumes,"
scents that are the impressions of anything remaining unconsciously
in the mind, the present consciousness of past perceptions. This force
accounts for our sense of déjà vu, among other things, the sense that one
sometimes has, on seeing someone or someplace for the first time, that
one has seen it before. These are the "impressions of lingering emotions"
that a king in a Sanskrit play (a man who has forgotten his wife) has in
mind when he says:

> *Even a happy man may be overcome*
> *by passionate longing*
> *when he sees beautiful things or hears*
> *sweet sounds.*
> *Perhaps he is remembering something*
> *he was not conscious of before that moment,*
> *the loves of a former life, firmly rooted in*
> *the impressions of lingering emotions.*[1]

The bits of experience that Hindus call the karmic memory traces cling
to our transmigrating souls even in new bodies, loose threads trailing not
merely from a former life within this lifespan but from a previous life, a
previous incarnation. (One commentator remarks that it is impossible to
shake off these impressions even after thousands of lives.[2])

The unconscious memories of past lives, the vasanas, predispose the
transmigrating soul to act in one way or another in its new life. Similarly,
the transmigrating soul in the myth of Er in Pluto's *Republic* (c. 375 BCE;
Book 10, 613–620) retains some sort of magnetic attachment to its old
body and, with it, to its old personality, like Eeyore to his detached tail.
For before our minds are washed clean as we drink the waters of Lethe,
we are given the choice of who to become in our next life; but we choose
to become the same sort of person we were before or, as the case may

be, the very opposite of the sort of person we were before. One way or another, the force of our previous personality constrains and skews our rational choice:

> *The choice was both laughable and amazing, since most people chose according to the habits of their former life. The soul that had been Orpheus chose to be a swan, because he so hated the race of women—at whose hands he had met his death—that he did not want to be conceived and born of them. And Er saw a swan changing into the life he chose as a man. When all the souls had chosen their lots, they went to the Plain of Oblivion and drank from the River of Forgetfulness, and then they all fell asleep.*

Plato describes many other, similar cases, each choice based on the experience of a previous life: Atalanta, seeing the great fame of an athlete, is unable to resist temptation; the jester Thersites chooses the form of a monkey; and so forth. Agamemnon becomes an eagle; does he remember that he was symbolized by an eagle in Aeschylus's eponymous play about him? So, too, Augustine (in the *Confessions*) speaks of habit as a kind of internalized necessitating power of the past, a chain that drags you into the past; and the *contrapposto* in Dante's *Inferno* dooms many sinners to an eternity whose torment consists primarily in being forced to do forever in Hell what they chose to do on earth—or its diametric opposite. Even if we cannot remember who we were, we are reborn in the shadow of our previous personality. The soul gets typecast.

Orpheus's choice of a swan may have been influenced by Plato's knowledge of the importance of that animal in Indian theories of transmigration, in which the swan (*hamsa*)—more like a wild goose, really—symbolizes the transmigrating spirit that returns year after year. A Hindu text from about 700 CE imagines the reincarnating soul meditating on its next life not on the far shore of Lethe but in the womb of the soul's future mother, where it (not yet he or she) not only remains fully conscious but remembers its previous lives in agonizing detail:

> *Then it begins to remember its many previous existences in the wheel of rebirth, and that depresses it, and it tosses from side to side, thinking, "I won't ever do that again, as soon as I get out of this womb. I*

will do everything I can, so that I won't become an embryo again." It thinks in this way as it remembers the hundreds of miseries of birth that it experienced before, in the power of fate. Then, as time goes by, the embryo turns around, head down, and in the ninth or tenth month it is born. As it comes out, it is hurt by the wind of procreation; it comes out crying, because it is pained by the misery in its heart. When it has come out of the womb, it falls into an unbearable swoon, but it regains consciousness when the air touches it. Then Vishnu's deluding power of illusion assails him, and when his soul has been deluded by it, he loses his knowledge. As soon as the living creature has lost his knowledge, he becomes a baby. After that he becomes a young boy, then an adolescent, and then an old man. And then he dies and is born again as a human. Thus he wanders on the wheel of rebirth like the bucket on the wheel of a well.[3]

Chagrin at the memory of previous mistakes and despair at the realization that one will make them all again in this life, too, is what makes the baby cry as he enters the world. *The Laws of Manu* (c. 375 CE), the classical Sanskrit text of Hindu law, promises many upwardly mobile transmigrations, but not for everyone: "Through the repetition of their evil actions, men of little intelligence experience miseries in womb after womb in this world."[4]

Reincarnation is generally regarded as a fresh start, but the tabula is not always quite so rasa as more simplistic treatments of the doctrine assume. The goal of liberation theology, Hindu style, is to untangle the knots of karma, to achieve *moksha*, freedom from the same old same old in life after life. For a Hindu, this means to break out altogether from *samsara* (the cycle of transmigration), but it could also mean to be free to go forward without the compulsion for self-imitation. For in our culture, too, people find it difficult to kick the Lethe habit. In many ways the vasanas that return to the reborn soul correspond not just to the unconscious as we have come to understand it but more particularly to the repressed unconscious that *returns*, in Freud's formulation. Freud himself likened this process to reincarnation, citing (as an example of the "remoteness of time" over which the repression operates) a line from Goethe about the survival of love: "For you were, in times lived through before, my sister or my wife."[5] Freud also referred (in "The

Unconscious") to a "memory trace" (*Erinnerungsspur*) that was not yet a part of conscious memory.

The Man Who Forgot He Was God: The Monk's Dream

A complex pattern of self-impersonation through reincarnation, and a circular model of the survival of consciousness, is formulated in the *Yogavasishtha*, a Sanskrit text composed in Kashmir between the tenth and the twelfth centuries CE, a time when Hindus and Buddhists were in close contact. This is the tale of a man who dreams he is the god Rudra, a form of the god Shiva who is, in this text, the supreme god:

> One day a monk decided to imagine what happens to ordinary people. And so he imagined that he was a man named Jivata, who lived for a long time until one day he drank too much and fell into a heavy sleep in which he saw a Brahmin who read all day long. One day that Brahmin fell asleep after a hard day's reading and dreamed that he was a prince; the prince fell asleep one day after a heavy meal and saw himself as a powerful king. The king, having gorged himself on his every desire, fell asleep and saw himself as a courtesan who fell into a deep sleep in the languor that followed making love; she saw herself as a doe who fell asleep and dreamed she was a clinging vine (for animals dream too, and they always remember what they have seen and heard). The vine saw herself as a bee who was trampled by an elephant and dying, saw himself as an elephant in rut; that elephant in rut was cut to pieces in battle, and, dying, saw a swarm of bees and became a bee again. The bee became a goose who was shot by a hunter and died and was reborn as the swan on which the god Brahma, the Creator, rides.
>
> One day the swan saw the god Rudra and realized, "I am Rudra." And he became Rudra, living in Rudra's palace, and as Rudra he could see every one of his former experiences. Then he went to the place where the monk was sleeping and woke him up; and the monk realized that he had been mistaken to think he was Jivata. Then Rudra and the monk found Jivata asleep and woke him up, and the three of them went to wake up the Brahmin, and so forth, until they reached the swan of Brahma. Then Rudra said, "Now go back to your

own places and enjoy yourselves there with your families for a while, and then come back to me. And at doomsday, all of us, the bands of creatures who are part of me, will go to the final resting place." And they all went back, but after a while they will wear our their bodies and unite again in the world of Rudra.[6]

The swan, a natural and cross-cultural symbol of periodic return, is the emblem of both the individual soul and the mind of god, in this case Rudra. The very substance of this god is (according to a doctrine that begins in the Upanishads, c. 600 BCE) the stuff that our own consciousnesses are made on—*brahman*, a kind of world-soul (sometimes translated godhead) which is distributed within each of our individual souls or selves (*atman*). In this metaphysical world, we remember both our dreams and our rebirths—much the same thing—when we awaken from our primary amnesia, which makes us forget that we are god.

The story does not reveal to us the entire rebirth of each of the characters; none of them is born, and most of them do not die within the story. Significantly, the first person the monk dreams of is named Jivata, a word derived from the word for a life or a soul, *jiva*. Some of the subjects are women (and female animals), with whom the male actors have no lasting attachments, merely brief physical encounters. These people dream and become what they have habitually dreamed about and are thinking about as they die. We awaken from ignorance, or from sleep, or from life; the same verb (*budh*) covers all three.

The creatures in the monk's dream form a pattern that is a masterful combination of order and chance. Though anything *can* happen, certain things are more *likely* to happen; this is how karma skews and orders the chaos of the universe. The text tells us: "Again and again these lives revolve in creation like the waves in water, and some [rebirths] are strikingly similar [to what they were before], and others are about half the same; some are a little bit the same, some are not very much alike at all, and sometimes they are once again just the same." This flexibility, together with the elements of pure chance and the gravity of karmic tendencies, makes certain coincedences not only possible but probable. For the text tells us that after the bee had become an elephant and was then reborn again as a bee, he went back to the same lotus pond where he had previously met with his unfortunate accident, "because people who are not aware of their karmic traces find it hard to give up their bad habits." So, too, the beautiful woman becomes a doe because she envies the beauty of the doe's eyes, and the text remarks, "Alas, the delusion that results from the karmic traces causes such misery among creatures."[7] Each of the people in the dream chain is reborn in a particular form *because they all want something.* There is a hunger, unsated in their present lives, that propels them across the barrier of death into a new birth where this still unfulfilled longing leads them to do what they do. By extension and implication, all of us, too, helplessly spin out of our desires the lives we have inherited from our former selves. And so in each new life, we pretend, once again, to be who we are, repeating lines from an earlier script even when we think that we are improvising or that we are not performing at all. We cannot escape from our own previous character, our desire, which sticks like tar to the transmigrating soul. Our memory of those ancient desires is also partly accidental, partly not so accidental; Hinduism offers several different praxes designed to help us remember our former lives, just as psychoanalysis claims to help us remember our dreams. For most of us, however, such memories remain largely unconscious and inaccessible.

The God Who Forgot He Was God

All of us tend to forget that we are god, according to the doctrine of Hindu idealism in the *Yogavasishtha.* But divinity is a continuum; some creatures are more divine than others, and some gods are more divine in certain texts than in others. The philosophical and mythological assertion that all humans are (conscious or unconscious) incarnations of a deity is enacted in the many rituals in which the worshipper masquerades as the god (through the use of masks, for instance). The *Yogavasishtha* depicts humans who forget that the god Shiva, as Rudra, is the very substance of consciousness, but in other texts, Shiva himself forgets who he is and engages in unconscious self-imitation when his wife Parvati tricks him by masquerading as another woman.[8] The chain continues when Shiva and Parvati become incarnate not merely in all human beings but in particular human beings (called partial incarnations) who slip in and out of their incarnational status.

A Sanskrit text composed in Assam in the tenth of eleventh century

CE explores the human complications that can arise out of such a partial (re)incarnation.[9] In this text, Shiva and Parvati impersonate a human king and queen on three, increasingly specific levels: First is the general philosophical doctrine that all creatures are made of *brahman*, and hence the king and queen are part of the godhead embodied in Shiva and Parvati. Second is the implicit metaphysical incarnation based on the belief that all men and women are forms of Shiva and Parvati, rather than of other deities, for human beings are all marked with the signs of the god Shiva and his consort, the male and female sexual organs, *lingam* and *yoni*.[10] And third, the proximate cause, is the explicit impersonation of the king by Shiva, necessitated by a sage's curse,[11] a common cause of the incarnation of Hindu gods as humans.

The incarnations (or avatars) of the god Vishnu, particularly Rama and Krishna, have a more particular awareness of their own divinity, yet even they often forget their divine natures. In the *Mahabharata*, Krishna often forgets he is god until someone else remembers—a mortal or, occasionally, another god, or Krishna himself. In later texts such as the tenth-century *Bhagavata Purana*, however, Krishna never forgets. Indeed, when Krishna is still a little child, he sometimes remembers not only that he is god but that he was previously incarnate as Rama, recalling, when he is drifting between sleeping and waking, his earlier birth as Rama.[12] He is also firmly in control of his knowledge of his own divinity when he deals with other people (including his mother) whom he allows to forget who he is because they cannot sustain the intensity of their brief visions of his true nature.[13]

Rama, too, often forgets his divinity. When Rama publicly doubts that his wife Sita remained faithful to him while the demon Ravana held her captive, the gods ask how he can do this, adding, "Can you not know that you are the best of all the gods?" Rama, uncomprehending, says, "I think of myself as a man, as Rama the son of king Dasharatha. Tell me who I really am, and who my father is, and where I come from."[14] Sheldon Pollock has argued convincingly that in order to achieve his purpose of killing the demon Ravana, Rama must become truly human, for Ravana has secured a boon that no one but a human being can kill him. And to be truly human is to forget that you are god, which Rama must do—at least until after Ravana's death. Moreover, taking on a human body is the consequence of wrong knowledge,[15] for true knowledge would have brought enlightenment and freedom from the wheel of rebirth. The very act of incarnation would destroy the incarnation's true knowledge of his divinity, but, in addition (as we have seen), in the process of being born, the newborn child must lose his knowledge. Therefore an embodied avatar cannot possibly remember who he has been; the very fact of human birth robs him of the capacity to remember his past existences. Other commentators argued that Rama had intentionally become ignorant or that he merely pretended to forget who he was.[16] In other retellings of the narrative, too, Rama insists that they merely pretended to subject Sita to an ordeal and, presumably, pretended to forget that he was god.[17] If the gods themselves are subject to this constant forgetfulness of their true nature and equally constant reawakening to it, how could we mere mortals hope to do any better?

Notes:

1   Kalidasa, *Abhijnanashakuntala* (Bombay: Nirnaya Sagar Press, 1958), 5.2.

2   *Raghavabhatta* 9, cited by Robert P. Goldman, "Karma, Guilt and Buried Memories: Public Fantasy and Private Reality in Traditional India," in *Journal of the American Oriental Society* 105.3 (1985): 423.

3   *Markandeya Purana* (Bombay: Venkateshvara Steam Press, 1890), 10.1–7, 11.1–21.

4   *Laws of Manu*, translated by Wendy Doniger, with Brian K. Smith (Harmondsworth, U. K.: Penguin Books, 1991), 12.74.

5   Sigmund Freud, *Moses and Monotheism*, translated by Katherine Jones (New York: Vintage Books, 1939), p. 162.

6   *Yogavasishtha* [*Yogavasishtha-Maha-Ramayana* of Valmiki], edited by W. L. S. Pansikar (Bombar: Nirnaya Sagara Press, 1918), 6.1.62–64; Wendy Doniger O'Flaherty, *Dreams, Illusions, and Other Realities* (Chicago: University of Chicago, 1984), pp. 207–209.

7   *Yogavasishtha* 6.1.66.22–24, 6.1.62.32, 6.1.63.17

8   Wendy Doniger, *The Bedtrick: Tales of Sex and Masquerade* (Chicago: University of Chicago Press, 2000), pp. 17–20.

9   *Kalika Purana*, edited by Sri Biswanarayan Sastri (Varanasi: Chowkhamba Sanskrit Series Office, 1972), pp. 49–52; Wendy Doniger O'Flaherty, *Siva: The Erotic Ascetic* (New York: Paperback Galaxy, 1981), pp. 206–207.

10   *Mahabharata* (Poona: Bhandarkar Oriental Research Institute, 1933–1969), 13, app,

1, no. 5, 69; Doniger, *The Bedtrick*, p. 397.

11 This text takes basic themes from the story of Rama: Shiva is cursed to become human as Vishnu is cursed to take on a human incarnation in the *Ramayana*, and Chandrashekhara is born as Rama is born, out of portions of a god (there Vishnu, here Shiva) distributed to a group of queens. But instead of producing multiple children (as Rama's borthers are produced), the portions here come together to make a single composite child, as Jarasandha, the enemy of Krishna, is created in the *Mahabharata* 2.16–17.

12 Goldman, "Karma," p. 240.

13 O'Flaherty, *Dreams, Illusions, and Other Realities*, pp. 109–10.

14 *Ramayana* (Baroda: Oriental Institute, 1960–1975), 6.105.8–10.

15 Sheldon Pollock, "'*Atmanam Manusam Manye*': *Dharmakutam* on the divinity of Rama," in *Journal of the Oriental Institute* (Baroda) 33.3–4 (March-June 1984): 233.

16 Pollock, "'*Atmanam Manusam Manye*'," pp. 234–35, 42.

17 Wendy Doniger, *Splitting the Difference: Gender and Myth in Ancient Greece and India* (Chicago: University of Chicago Press, 1999), pp. 9–27.

This article was adapted from the author's book *The Woman Who Pretended to Be Who She Was* (New York: Oxford University Press, 2004).

Parabola
Volume: 11.3
Sadness

MODES OF MEANING
AND EXPERIENCE:
VIRAHA AND VIḶAIYĀṬAL

David Dean Shulman

The vision of life articulated in medieval South Indian literature clearly included a dimension of feeling that we need not hesitate to call "tragic." The point is not, of course, to project an Aristotelian terminology upon an exotic set of ideas; rather, we need to analyze an intuition that achieved a unique cultural expression in the particular context of a given time and place. India, from earliest times, has shown a remarkable sensitivity—some would say, a hypersensitivity—to the pain and sorrow inherent in existence. Life, we are told, is a sacrifice—a violent process of cleavage within the unity of being, a process inevitably entailing suffering and sadness in various forms. But the medieval Tamil perception of the world develops this general Indian sensitivity in certain new directions, which are closely linked to other basic notions prevalent in the culture—notions about the divine in its relation to men and women, about the function of symbols in our awareness, about the nature and limits of human love, and so on. Together, these ideas, worked out in varying contexts of song, commentary, and story, present a coherent picture of the inner world of the Tamil court poet during the Chola centuries (ninth to thirteenth centuries).

Two concepts in particular may help us to enter into this world—
viraha, "separation," and *viḷaiyāṭal*, "play," "amusement." If, in the eyes
of the Tamilians, everyday life is in some sense "tragic," the reason lies
in its being suffused by the experience of viraha (Tamil *pirivu*). As
Friedhelm Hardy has shown, viraha is for the Tamil devotees of Viṣṇu
(especially Nammālvār) perhaps the predominant mode of experiencing
the divine:

> *They opened themselves to the beauty of the temple images and ritu-*
> *als and to the eros of the myths and tried to communicate them in*
> *turn through their sensual poetry. But the more they took in from this*
> *sense-and-emotion-filling nature of Krishna, the closer they thereby*
> *came to him and the more they thus fulfilled themselves and human*
> *beings—the more they suffered. This peculiar experience of suffering*
> *in one way could only be explained as due to Krishna's very presence*
> *in their hearts, and in another way they saw this as the reflection of*
> *human incapability to contain or encompass the transcendental.[1]*

This conceptualization is not, I would argue, by any means limited to
the Tamil Vaiṣṇava poets—among the Śaivas, the *Tevāram* poets present
similar notions—nor, for that matter, to the realm of religious feeling. Life
itself, in its ordered, normative aspect, is conceived as an arena of separation, which may be experienced on various levels—the metaphysical
separation of man from his divine source; the more generalized sense of
limitation and partiality inherent in mundane reality; and the emotional
torment involved in separation from those whom one loves. This latter
category has, in itself, several distinct levels: there is the everyday experience of loss (through absence, temporary or permanent, and above all in
death); the ill-defined longings which arise so mysteriously in the course
of our normal lives and which may have no conscious object;[2] and—here
we find what appears to be the most profound development of the theory
of separation in South India—that amazing sense of separation, loneliness, and loss that accompanies the *possession* of the object of one's love.
This is the feeling described by Hardy in the passage quoted above: the
very presence of the deity, his revelation before our eyes, evokes in us the
unbearable sense of his absence—of our finitude, our inability to hold
the god here, our frustration at the awareness of his total transcendence.

But the same emotion is present in any kind of loving, even, the medieval Tamils would argue, in the moment of ecstatic union with the beloved. The closer we approach the other, the more clearly do we realize the ultimate unknowability of another person and our inability to cross, once and for all, the border which divides us. Love, in its different aspects, is as much a form of separation as of merging.

This metaphysic of paradoxical separation-in-union apparently first developed self-consciously in Tamil Nadu in the *bhakti* traditions of the early medieval period. Its roots may lie in the much earlier Cankam love poetry, which shows a pronounced fondness for tragic images of love: of the five main phases of the conventional lovers'-drama, correlated, respectively, to five external landscapes (*tiṇai*), four contain explicit situations of separation. Thus *mullai*, the forest region, is the setting of the beloved's patient waiting for the lover's return; *nĕytal*, the seashore, is connected with anxious waiting; *pālai*, the desert wasteland, is the landscape of separation par excellence; *marutam*, the alluvial plains, the landscape proper to married union, is the scene of quarrels and infidelity—here we often encounter the wife whiling away the night in loneliness, as her husband is away with the courtesans. Even the fifth landscape, *kuriñci*, the mountainous setting of the joyous premarital union (*kaḷavu*) of the lovers, contains the seed of suffering—for kaḷavu, as its very name indicates, is at best a stolen pleasure, fleeting and laden with anxiety. The medieval poets, starting with this rich legacy, have expanded upon its hidden premises: separation now becomes not only a common, concrete reality in the lives of nearly all lovers, who are forced into a physical or, more painfully, an emotional distance from one another; rather, it is seen more and more as the outstanding characteristic of love even in—or especially in—its fulfillment in union.

Beyond this, separation serves as a many-faceted metaphor for man's normal state of being in the world, a state characterized by actual or potential loss and by ever-present fragmentation and limitation. Herein lies, it would seem, much of the affective power of Kampan's Tamil version of the *Rāmāyaṇa*, the *Irāmāvatāram*, large portions of which are devoted to expressing the trauma of separation that the heroes, Rāma and Sītā, must undergo. Many of Kampan's most powerful passages explore what he perceived as this most basic human experience. Thus when Rāma first returns to his hut in the forest and finds it empty—for

Sītā has just been kidnapped by Rāvana—he is overwhelmed by confusion and bitterness: the poet compares him to "a life which has left its containing body and returned to seek it—but in vain" (3.8.158); or to a man whose life depends upon his only treasure, which he has hidden in a box buried in the earth—only to discover that thieves have made off with it (159). Rāma's loss calls up in him a cry of existential protest, in a moment of total antagonism and outrage at the world:

> *That great one trembled—*
> *was he raging against* dharma*?*
>   *or against mercy* (aruḷ)*?*
> *or against the gods, or the sages,*
>   *or the prowess of the evil?*
> *How would it all end?*
> *Was he raging against the Veda itself?*
>   *(3.8.161)*

Note how the overwhelming reality of separation induces in the hero a general hostility to a world in which such experiences are possible, even usual. But this is only Rāma's first reaction to his loss; from this point until almost the very end of the long poem, *viraha* is his predominant mode of feeling. At times, as at the start of the *Kiṭkintākāṇṭam*, Rāma comes close to losing his reason because of the unendurable suffering that he is forced to know. Sītā, for her part, has very similar experiences: indeed, she is described at one point, in her captivity, as "a woman fashioned from sorrow (*piniyāḷ*)—as if the grief of separation (*pirivu*) which afflicts lovers, full of desire for one another, in the world, had taken on tangible form" (5.3.7). Kampaṉ's poems may be seen as in large part a lyrical and dramatic exposition of viraha in all its pain, its pervasive and unavoidable familiarity, and—we must not forget—its uniquely attractive beauty.

For viraha, however suffused by suffering, need by no means be seen in a wholly negative light. Quite the contrary is true of the Tamil bhakti poets: they extol the pangs of separation, which are also evidence of real love. Such suffering is, in their eyes, quite literally divine—a reflection of the god's needs and longing for the lowly creatures who are, for their part, obsessed with their own yearnings for him. Viraha, as the hallmark of the everyday, is the inevitable concomitant of *saṃsāra*, the phenomenal world—and the bhakti poets, far from wishing to be released from this scene of suffering, ask rather to be reborn again and again so as to taste each time anew the wonder and joy of loving the absent deity.[3] The god may torture his devotee by his apparent indifference or, for that matter, by actively afflicting him with misery; but these sorrows are apprehended as signs of the living relation between the two parties, hence of the rapturous connection which only separation makes possible:

kaṣṭā te sṛṣṭiceṣṭā
bahutarabhavakhedāvahā jīvabhājām
ity evaṃ pūrvam ālocitam ajita mayā naivam
*   adyābhijāne/*
no cej jīvāḥ kathaṃ vā madhurataram idaṃ
tvadvapuś cidrasārdraṃ
netraiḥ śrotraiś ca pītvā
paramarasasudhāṃbhodhipūre rameran//

"Cruel is your creative act,
bringing innumerable sorrows
*   to all who are endowed with life."*

So I had always thought,
Invincible One,
but now I reason:

how else could living beings
delight in drinking in,
*   with eyes and ears,*
this form of yours,
*   supernally sweet*
*   and liquid with awareness*
in the flooding ocean filled
*   with the nectar of truth?*[4]

This verse, by a brilliant sixteenth-century poet from Kerala, points to the normative, ordered aspect of the viraha mode: god is in his temple (embodied in the image accessible to his devotees), and all is wrong—painfully, wonderfully, passionately wrong—with the world.

For the delights of viraha hardly serve to alleviate the tragic character of human life. The tragedy inheres in the pain—and yet this remains an essentially life-affirming stance. We sense here a deep engagement in the life of the world, even, it could be argued, a basic acceptance of life, for all its horrors. The Tamil bhakti poet sings in his sadness, or in anger in his struggle with, and within, the frustrating conditions that determine his fate. Underlying this inner struggle is a profound sense of delimitation: the terms of saṃsāra are such that any revelation can be, at best, but partial and paradoxical; the transcendent god can never be contained by our reality. More generally, we might say that the tragic vision depends upon just such a delimitation, a closing off of semantic space. The tragic world is bounded, fragmented, and full of meaning.

Several of the medieval Tamil poets were undoubtedly aware of this, and indeed, at times, deliberately undermined their own tragic perspective. The same boundaries that appear so precious, so in need of defense against all outer attacks—the boundaries of the conventional order, with its hierarchical claims, its pressures for a balanced and stable definition of roles, and its ever-increasing, painful sense of its own imperfections and limitations—are also subject to a constant assault from within. The delicious distress of viraha, so real to us, is conceivably less so to the god. Harsh as it may seem, harsh as it really is, our torments are his amusements—*līlā*, or in Tamil, *viḷaiyāṭal*. At this point another mode of experience opens up before us: viḷaiyāṭal, the deity's favored mode of relating to the scattered parts of himself and to his world, is by nature chaotic—unpredictable, uncontainable, undefinable in terms of everyday perceptions. It eludes meaning: creating itself, seen as the god's play, is a teleological mystery. The point, if there is one, could only lie in its pointlessness, and in the emotions this quality engenders.[5] This is not to deny the everyday experience of suffering, viraha in all its tragic reality and centrality to our emotional life; on the contrary, this experience is also basic to the viḷaiyāṭal mode of perception, which is infused with the knowledge of evil. Viraha, in a sense, is the god's viḷaiyāṭal. Nevertheless, there is a transformation of perspective: the closed boundaries have been invaded by a new, heretical spirit. In a sense, viḷaiyāṭal encompasses and transcends the human vision of viraha, in much the same way that a clown encompasses, from the outside, the bounded reality that he wishes to illuminate. It is a question of where one stands—wholly inside, hermetically enclosed by the sensation of pain, loss, and protest; wholly outside, if that were possible, hence impassive, remote, detached; or, like the god, the clown, or the magician, on the slippery and invisible border where the outer reaches in.

Notes:

1 Friedhelm E. Hardy, "Some Reflections on Indian Spirituality, III: Commuting within One World," *King's Theological Review* 4:1 (1981): 9.

2 Here we may mention, as special category, the longings described by Kālidāsa in a famous verse (*Abhijñānaśākuntala* V, 2)—that is, those arising from beholding a lovely sight, or hearing sweet sounds. Kālidāsa connects these feelings to lost memories of former lives.

3 See, for example, *Pĕriya purāṇam* of Cekkiḷār, verse 143. The older, Caṅkam poet Kapilar expressed a similar viewpoint, in a "secular" context, in Kuṟuntŏkai 288:
    He is dear to me, that man,
    far away in his mountains

        where the pepper-vine grows thick
        and monkeys feed upon the tender leaves.

    And now I wonder:
    is the sorrow caused by those we love
    not sweeter than the sweet joys
    they say are found in heaven?

4 *Nārāyaṇiya* of Nārāṇya Bhaṭṭa 1.7

5 Here the Śaiva Siddhānta school would take issue, offering instead a rational teleology. See D. Shulman, *Tamil Temple Myths* (Princeton: Princeton University Press, 1980), p. 281.

Adapted from *The King and the Clown in South Indian Myth and Poetry* by David Dean Shulman (Princeton: Princeton University Press: 1985).

Parabola
Volume: 26.2
Light

The Slaying of Narakasura

Retold by Rama Devagupta

Narakasura, the son of Bhumi Devi, Mother Earth, was the ruler of Pragjyotishapuram, a city engulfed by darkness and wickedness. No lights were ever lit on the streets or in the houses, and no woman could walk around safely in the open. Narakasura captured and imprisoned thousands of princesses. Mother Earth and all her inhabitants were under his tyranny and oppression.

As his powers and ego increased, Narakasura's nefarious activities began to reach new proportions. He turned his sight toward the heavens and defeated all the gods and their leader, Indra, in the ensuing battle. Adding insult to injury, he seized the famed umbrella of Varuna, snatched the precious earrings adorning Aditi, and occupied Maniparvata, the summit of Mount Mandara. Indra was furious, for Varuna was not only the god of water and guardian of the western quarter but also his brother, Aditi was his own mother, and Maniparvata was the favorite resort of the gods. One way or another, the demon had to be stopped.

A desperate Indra decided to approach Sri Krisha, the eighth incarnation of Vishnu, who was living in Dwaraka for help. He descended from the heavens and sought immediate audience with the Lord.

At the time, Krishna was in the palace of his wife, Satyabhama. After listening to the grievances put forth by Indra, he turned to Satyabhama and smilingly said, "Dear One! The time for the destruction of Narakasura has come! Please accompany me and avenge the humiliation of Mother Aditi. Together, let us free the imprisoned maidens from captivity and hell."

Satyabhama consented, and the next minute, Vishnu's famous mount, Garuda, the eagle and king of birds, appeared. Krishna and Satyabhama departed with Garuda for Narakasura's capital.

Surrounded on all sides by tall mountains, Pragjyotishapuram was a well-fortified city designed and guarded by the demon architect, Mura. Rings of fire, wind, lightning, rain, and water surrounded it, and the fortifications held self-shooting artillery and dreadful weapons. There were numerous other traps and barriers extremely difficult to overcome even by the cleverest of enemies.

But nothing could stop the divine couple. Krishna shattered all the barricades and destroyed the weapons, then blew his conch, Panchajanya, to challenge Narakasura. Enraged, Narakasura sent legions of demons and a huge army of elephants against Krishna and Satyabhama, but all were destroyed by Garuda and the divine couple. Finally, in the end, when Narakasura had exhausted all his weaponry, missiles, and diabolical warfare tricks, Krishna destroyed him with his divine discus.

As Narakasura's body lay on the ground, the three worlds rejoiced and the devas showered flowers on Krishna and Satyabhama from the heavens. Bhumi Devi rushed out of the palace and, after offering hymns and prayers to them, she said, "Blessed is my son, Narakasura, O Lord! Though he caused immense suffering to this universe while alive, nevertheless, he has achieved liberation by dying in your hands."

She welcomed the divine couple into the palace and offered them adequate rest and refreshments. Later, Bhumi Devi presented them numerous gifts and treasures, and returned Mother Aditi's earrings and Varuna's umbrella. The next day Krishna installed Narakasura's son, Bhagadatta, as the new ruler of Pragjyotishapuram and released the 16,100 maidens from captivity. To restore their honor and dignity, Krishna married all the princesses and took them back to his palace in Dwaraka.

Bhumi Devi declared that the day of her son's death was auspicious for humankind and it should become a day of rejoicing and happiness. The following day happened to be Amavasya—a new moon day—and for the first time, the citizens of Pragjyotishapuram were free to light the lamps in the streets and houses. Since then, the day of Narakasura's death has been known as Naraka Chaturdashi, and the new moon day has come to be celebrated as Deepawali.

Retold by Rama Devagupta, from the *Srimad Bhagavata Purana*.

Parabola
Volume: 26.2
Light

Kindling the Deepa

The tales behind the Hindu festival of lamps

Rama Devagupta

Asato ma sat gamaya,

Tamaso ma jyotir gamaya,

Mrityor ma amritam gamaya.

From falsehood lead me to Truth,

From darkness lead me to Light,

From death lead me to Immortality.

—*The Pavamana-Mantras,*

from the Brihadaranyaka Upanishad

Nowhere is the symbolism of these lines from the *Brihadaranyaka Upanishad* better expressed than in the celebration of Deepawali. Popularly known as the Festival of Lights and abbreviated to Diwali in contemporary usage, Deepawali is the most important festival for the world's Hindu population. The date varies every year but occurs either in late October or early November, in the month of Karthik, on Amavasya (new moon) day—the darkest night of all nights, according to the lunar calendar. With its arrays of lighted lamps, firecrackers, and festivities, Deepawali transforms the desolate moonless skies by filling them with laughter, happiness, and radiance.

Like other religious festivals of the world, Deepawali is associated with several different legends and has a deep social and spiritual significance. It is primarily known for the worship of the goddess Lakshmi, who symbolizes wealth and prosperity. In North India, it is a commemoration of Lord Rama's triumphant return to Ayodhya after vanquishing the demonic forces led by Ravana, while in South India Deepawali is celebrated in remembrance of Lord Krishna's victory over evil Narakasura. In addition, it marks the end of the rainy season and the harvesting cycle, and therefore it is also the festival of the *Kharif* or new crop.

Whichever legend one might prefer, Deepawali celebrations all over the world are marked by majestic fireworks, a variety of cultural programs, a spirit of sharing and brotherhood, and, most importantly, the lighting of lamps (*deepas*) in several arrays (*wali*) inside and outside the house. It is these luminous deepas that contain the essence of Deepawali. Just as light dispels the darkness of night and shows the right path to a weary traveler, the lighting of lamps on the night of Karthik Amavasya symbolizes the victory of goodness over evil, justice over injustice, light over darkness, and wisdom over ignorance.

Since the beginning of time, spiritual aspirants have sought light as the culmination of their journey. What is this internal, divine light, of which the deepas on Deepawali night, or those set before the family deity during morning and evening prayers, are only an external representation?

One of the most illustrious conversations on this subject can be found in the *Brihadaranyaka Upanishad*, wherein King Janaka of Videha, whose courtroom was famed for spiritual discussions conducted by the most distinguished *rishis* of his time, once asked of Sage Yajnavalkya: "Revered Sage, enlighten me! What is the light of man? What is it that allows him to function in this world?"

Yajnavalkya gave a simple and straightforward answer. "The sun is his light, O King!" he said. "If there were no sunlight, people would be unable to perform their duties in this world. By the light of the sun activity is possible, and it is by the light of the sun that one sits, moves about, completes all work, and becomes content."

Janaka agreed that it was so indeed, and probed further. "But when the sun has set, the light of the sun is no longer available, and there is darkness everywhere, what light does a person have?"

"The moon then becomes his light, Your Honor! With the light radiating from the moon, a person can sit at one place or go around, complete the necessary tasks, and return home and rest."

Janaka then said, "What you say is true, Revered Sage. However, what would happen if both the sun and moon have set? What would be the light of man?"

Yajnavalkya replied, "Your Majesty! Fire would then become the light. One can light a fire, and with its light, warmth, and comfort a person can go around as usual, perform his jobs, and then return."

Janaka was satisfied, but only superficially, as his philosophical inquiry was now becoming much more profound. "Supposing there is no sun, no moon, and for some reason, one is even unable to light the fire, then what will guide us?"

"When there is no light from the sun, when there is no light from the moon, when the night skies are the darkest without even the sparkling stars, and one cannot even light a fire, under such conditions where a person cannot even see his hand, it is sound, it is human voice that will become the guide. It is sound that will cast the light."

The King agreed and said, "What you say is true indeed. However, kindly enlighten me further. What if the sun has set, the moon has set, the fire has gone out, nobody is around, and sound has also become silent? Under those circumstances, what will be his light?"

Yajnavalkya gave a very revealing answer. "O King Janaka!" he said. "Know that when everything else fails, the Soul, the inner Self will be the guide. It is the Self that will be the light."

This light, which is equated with the Supreme and is supposed to be the consciousness of life, is described in the *Chandogya Upanishad* (3.13.7):

> *There is a Light that shines beyond all things on earth,*
> *Beyond us all, beyond the heavens,*
> *Beyond the highest, the very highest heavens.*
> *This is the Light that shines in our heart.*

Unfortunately, we are oblivious to it most of the time. Even when we read and hear about its presence, we are unable to see the Light, mainly because this flame, which the Vedas say is tinier than the tiniest of atomic sparks and hidden in the innermost chamber of the human heart, is covered by layers of grossness, complexities, and impressions.[1] Also, due to our outward-turning senses, tendencies, and attachments to the fruits of action, we are unable to turn our eyes inward—at least not until compelled by external circumstances. But we must be able to do so somehow, if the lower self is to become one with the Ultimate Being.

Using an illustration from the *Mundaka Upanishad*, Swami Vivekananda, a proponent of Vedanta, says:

> *Two birds of golden plumage sat on the same tree. The one above, serene, majestic, immersed in his own glory; the one below restless and eating the fruits of the tree, now sweet, now bitter. Once he ate an exceptionally bitter fruit, then he paused and looked up at the majestic bird above; but he soon forgot about the other bird and went on eating the fruits of the tree as before. Again he ate a bitter fruit, and this time he hopped up a few boughs nearer to the bird at the top. This happened many times until at last the lower bird came to the place of the upper bird and lost himself. He found all at once that there never had been two birds, but that he was all the time that upper bird, serene, majestic, and immersed in his own glory.[2]*

But this union is not as easy as it appears in words. The journey is filled with obstacles: darkness and ignorance, misleading visions and egotism. Therefore, in the *Katha Upanishad*, Yama, the God of Death, tells the young boy Nachiketa, who seeks to know what lies beyond death, that the spiritual path is for the lionhearted and not the sheep. "Awake, arise!" he urges passionately. "Strive for the Highest, and be in the Light! Sages say the path is narrow and difficult to tread, narrow as the edge of a razor."[3]

Whether it be the blindingly luminous vision of Christ that Saul of Tarsus saw on his way to Damascus, or Arjuna's vision of Lord Krishna in the Cosmic Form on the battlefield of Kurukshetra, the experience of the transcendental Reality has often been associated with brilliance, splendor, and light:

If a thousand suns should rise all at once
In the sky,
Such splendor would resemble
The splendor of that great Being....
Then Arjuna,
Who was filled with amazement,
Whose hair was standing on end,
Bowing his head to the Lord
With joined palms, said:
...With infinite power, without
Beginning, middle, or end,
With innumerable arms, the moon and
Sun being Your eyes,
I see You, the blazing fire Your mouth,
Burning all this universe with Your radiance.[4]

Fascinating and awesome as such visions might be, the experience of light ought not to be the final goal. If that were so, the *Bhagavad Gita* would have ended with the Eleventh Teaching. But it does not. According to Krishna Himself, the Supreme state is that which the sun does not illumine, nor the moon, nor the fire, for it is the Light of Pure Consciousness.[5] These words are analogous to those found in the *Svetasvatara* (6.14) and *Katha Upanishad* (5.15):

There the sun shines not, nor the moon, nor the stars;
Lightnings shine not there and much less earthly fire.
From His light all these give light,
And His radiance illumines all creation.

Then how do we explain this paradox of light? What is it that we need to achieve? Even Patanjali, the famous exponent of Ashtanga Yoga and compiler of the *Yoga Sutras*, cautions us about flashes of illumination. He broadly categorizes such sensory experiences as distractions and obstacles to attaining higher *samadhi* but adds that they are apparent perfections for the outgoing mind, which seeks tangible, material results even in the field of spirituality.[6]

In the modern era, Shri Ram Chandra of Shahjahanpur—known as

Babuji to his associates—for almost fifty years taught meditation on the "divine light in the heart," according to the Sahaj Marg system of Raja Yoga. In *Voice Real,* he writes:

> *Every saint has used the word "light"...and that is the best expression for Reality. But that creates some complication, because when we talk of "light" the idea of luminosity becomes prominent and we begin to take it as glittering. The Real Light carries with it no such sense and may be represented as "light without luminosity." It refers only to the real substance or, more appropriately, to "substanceless substance," which is associated with neither light nor darkness but beyond both.*[7]

In regard to seeing the light, Babuji explains that the glittering light is of material form and though a positive sign depicting progress, it is still lower in nature than the Ultimate Reality. Such glittering light appears only in the beginning of the spiritual path. In other words, it is just a clue to show that spiritual energy has begun to work on the soul.

Babuji then draws attention to the *Nasadiya Sukta* of the *Rig Veda* (10.129), which describes how all of creation came into being. Identifying that pure, eternal, and unchanging state as the final goal of existence, Babuji elaborates that Real Light has the color of dawn or a faint reflection of colorlessness.[8] To reach that state, one needs to "march on through different spheres of light and shade of varying grossness, far, far above the sphere of the moon and the sun, growing finer and finer at every step till we attain the highest point of approach."[9] This highest point of approach, beyond the sun and the moon, where there is neither a being or nonbeing, can only be described as Nothingness.

It is painfully evident that words and descriptions of spiritual Light can convey only so much. As Babuji says, understanding comes by intuitive capacity and practical experience in the spiritual field. Reading and reflecting can inspire us to seek guidance from the spiritually adept, but, as Shankaracharya says in the *Vivekachudamani,* "Books do not help us in Realization, and when Realization is achieved, books are useless."[10]

If this is the case with books, then what about rituals and traditions? In very simple words, Babuji says that religion is the kindergarten of spirituality.

Similarly, Juan Mascaro, one of the translators of the Upanishads, writes:

> *The ritual of adoration in the Vedas, when men felt the glory of the world and prayed for light, must in time have become the routine of prayers of darkness for the riches of this world. We find in the Upanishads a reaction against external religion; and when ideas of the Vedas are accepted they are given a spiritual interpretation. It is the permanent struggle between the letter that kills and the spirit that gives life.[11]*

We can see this struggle today in the celebration of the Festival of Lights. Few, if any, attach reverence to the occasion. Instead, it has become a night of entertainment, gambling, pleasure, and consumption. Just as the candles and electric lights of modern society have gradually replaced the traditional deepas, the focus of prayers has shifted from the journey from darkness to light to the quest for fortune and wealth.

To appreciate the spirit behind this festival and pass on its significance to others, one needs only to consider the traditional lamps that are popular even today in the small towns and villages of India. These deepas represent the four essential elements that are required in the seeker: detachment (the clay container), devotion to the Lord (the oil), prayer and meditation (the cotton wick), and spiritual wisdom (the matchstick to light the lamp). It is noteworthy that on Deepawali the first lamp is lit with a matchstick, after which that lamp is used to light the whole array of lamps inside and outside the house. The first lamp symbolizes divine effulgence, while the other lamps represent the light in individual hearts. Together, they reiterate the eternal truth pronounced in the Vedas: "The One willed to become the Many."

As the flames of all these lamps burn brightly and reach upward through the entire night, they show the possibility that, with the removal of darkness, grossness, and ignorance, the tiny flickering light in our hearts can also shine brightly, illumining the whole universe. May we all progress speedily to the highest levels of spirituality—from darkness to light, and beyond.

Notes:

1 Parthasarathi Rajagopalachari, *The Fruit of the Tree* (Pacific Grove, CA: Shri Ram Chandra Mission, 1987).

2 Swami Vivekananda, *Meditation and Its Methods*, compiled and edited by Swami Chetanananda (Hollywood, CA: Vedanta Press, 1976).

3 Juan Mascaro, *The Upanishads: Translations from the Sanskrit* (London: Penguin Books, 1965).

4 *The Bhagavad Gita*, translated by Winthrop Sargeant (Albany, N.Y.: State University of New York Press, 1994), Ch. 11, v. 12, 14, 19.

5 *Bhagavad Gita* Ch. 15, v. 6.

6 Patanjali, *Yoga Sutras*, 3.33–3.37.

7 *Complete Works of Ram Chandra*, vol. 2 (Pacific Grove, CA: Shri Ram Chandra Mission, 1991).

8 *Letters of the Master*, vol. 3, edited by Rajendrasinh N. Rathod (Molena, GA: Shri Ram Chandra Mission, 1996).

9 *Complete Works of Ram Chandra*, vol. 1 (Pacific Grove, CA: Shri Ram Chandra Mission, 1989).

10 *Ibid*.

11 Mascaro, *The Upanishads*.

Parabola
Volume: 9.3
Pilgrimage

INTIMATE JOURNEYS
Toward the Mountain

Lizelle Reymond

*To start out on a pilgrimage is to throw down a challenge
to everyday life. Nothing matters now but this adventure.
Travelers jostle each other to board the train where they
crowd together for a journey that may last several days; after
that there is a stony road to climb on foot—a rough, wild
path in a landscape where everything is new. The naked
glitter of the mountain stirs the imagination. The adventure
of self-conquest has begun.*

*There are many young men, women in the prime of life,
widows in their saris, invalids on crutches. A whole way of
life is in question: how to cope with ups and downs, struggle
with constant dangers. From time to time a song breaks out, a
kind of litany that supports the upward march.*

*At last the Badri Narayan, the land of Shiva, is reached.
The crowd presses up to the entrance of the temple and little
by little is swallowed up by it. Inside, there is nothing to be
seen except a few faint lights in the center, where the god
in his flawless posture offers a meeting with the Infinite. In*

*front of huge lingams crowned with flowers the faithful prostrate themselves,
while priests pour melted butter on the stone. Guttural chants rise, fill the
space, and abruptly are stilled. One feels a wave of something strong, powerful. The collective adoration surges into ecstasy. ...*

I quote from the experience of a *baul* who humbly made this pilgrimage when he was already an old man. "It was a hard climb," he said. "I
was almost dead with fatigue before reaching the summit; and I told
my companions, 'If I don't get there, leave me wherever I fall on Shiva's
ground.' But finally I got to the top and entered the temple. It was exactly
like being swallowed up by a huge whale, along with everything around
me. Four or five others of our group entered at the same time and began
to weep. I asked, 'Why are you crying?' They couldn't answer. They had
experienced something. As for me, I saw 'That' with my eyes wide open;
now I know it. Such was my pilgrimage toward the Mountain. I came
back down again, but I am a different man."

I knew this baul well; he was my guide. I stayed in his hermitage,
where his influence helped me to begin the search for myself. This journey is not undertaken easily; it is also an uphill climb, across all the
planes of being. There is a long preparatory stage in which one learns to
live very simply with a continuous attention. And one day my turn came
to feel myself swallowed up with my eyes wide open. Strangely enough, I
also wept without knowing why. Something in me was torn apart.

I was disoriented; a harsh note sounded in my ears—the commitment
to live in a voluntary humility, to evaluate what seemed to be an inner
freedom, and which is nothing else than the possibility of discovering
the discipline necessary in order to learn to know oneself.

"Go to the root of everything that happens," said the guide, "but judge
nothing like a woman who knows many things, but like a child who
knows nothing." That means simply to turn to the primitive in ourselves,
to the essence of our life which is born with us. We cannot either ignore
it or refuse it. On the spiritual path, we obey our essence because we
recognize its flexibility and its capacity to absorb divine light as nourishment. "In the quiet of your being, feel the gushing of the fountain: 'Thou
art That.'"

To start toward the Mountain with one of the great pilgrimages signifies that one has mentally accepted the idea of renouncing all attachments, large or small, that will arise in the future, by a voluntary act of stripping away. All the circumstances of life mark the path of the future, whatever impermanence they offer, whether wonderful or painful. They lead us to a discipline that is almost invisible, but so deep that the ego rebels. "It is a new life," said the guide, "a state of consciousness in which India appears as a vast laboratory where the power of manifestation is carried to a very high degree in spiritual experience."

The pilgrim returns from his journey turned upside down and at the same time strengthened by the vista of a disciplined life which is implied in the search for oneself, the attempt to live as an adult. It is a new stage of inner observation from which to approach the meeting with the Infinite.

Kanya Kumari

There is a pilgrimage toward the Infinite, beyond the horizon which represents Totality. It is made by going to the farthest point of India, to Cape Comorin, where two oceans meet. There Kanya Kumari waits in her marble temple.

She has been waiting forever. She knows that he will come, followed by triumphal music, to find her. She has no doubt; and yet, he does not come!

In sacred history, she is the forgotten bride in her veil and wedding dress.

Kanya Kumari is the daughter of a king, or a great lord, or perhaps simply the daughter of a fisherman—it is no longer known. Time has brought conflicting reports. But it cannot be forgotten that the long-awaited bridegroom is Shiva himself, the greatest of all yogins and princes, who went away to war to settle a grave quarrel. On his way he met an astrologer who told him, "Invincible Lord, hasten neither to the right nor the left, but straight ahead; and if an eagle screams, at his third cry go directly back without turning. If you do otherwise, you and your army will be lost."

The prince saluted the astrologer respectfully and hastened on, sure of himself. But the bird cried three times and the prince turned his horse, drawing all his followers after him.

Kanya Kumari knew nothing of this; she heard nothing. She had been adorned for her wedding in brocade and pearls. She held herself very straight beneath her crown so as to seem tall (which she was not), her eyes fixed on the point where the two oceans meet. She waited so long that she remained frozen in her attitude of hope, her hands joined. … The golden jewel shone on her forehead in the last rays of the sun; the moon in its turn shone upon it.

And it is the same today. People go to Cape Comorin to ask Kanya Kumari the secret of her constancy, which in the game of life makes love always painful in the midst of its joy.

The Mouths of the Ganges

There is one special pilgrimage which is made when the believer reaches an advanced stage. Its reward is a spiritual state—the action of grace—which will allow a happy old age. It takes place in January at the Mouths of the Ganges, below Calcutta; it is the coldest time of the year. Everything that has been attained in the mountains during the pilgrimages to the high valleys, everything that has been the support of the middle years, will be symbolically thrown into the ocean, to let the pilgrim go free from himself, his ego washed away in the sea.

It is hard to imagine the scene: four hundred thousand pilgrims huddled together on the docks of the town; the solid mass of tents and huts with their stone hearths and copper pots; old trucks, motor coaches, carts, sightseeing buses, horses, and oxen; no children, no young people, only the misery of the old pilgrims waiting for the boat to take them to the Delta. That lasts several days, during which a sort of *mela* or country fair springs up with stalls of fruit and vegetables.

I knew the guide was going to propose that I make this pilgrimage with him—"toward Ganga Sagar, to find the Absolute"—not with our physical bodies, but in a vision coming from deep meditation. We were in Calcutta, in an empty room with the shades lowered against the sun, a cotton cloth on the floor to sit on, a metal suitcase for a table. He said, "You and I are pilgrims with them, we live their life; we are going with them toward the ocean where the Ganges will lose itself. We go forward with the same hunger they have, with the same hope of reaching what is beyond the known. There is always a goal which awaits us beyond anything we can see. The sun burns our heads, the sand burns our feet, the wind burns eyes, nose, mouth, but we go on. We make the same conscious offering as do these pilgrims; we induce our thoughts, our feelings, our bodies, all that we are, to be nothing but the force that leads us toward death, only the posture of that moment of encounter when death makes life overflow in us."

The exhausting march to the bathing place lasts four or five days. It is an effort that shatters the body's limits of resistance. The only shelters at night are improvised huts, and most of the pilgrims sleep under the stars. With the plunge into the water where the Ganges enters the ocean, the ego is dissolved; it is a pure act of renunciation which frees the energies and gives the vision of a widening horizon. The Ocean of Emptiness cleans away the past, while another Ocean is revealed which cannot be spoken of. It dances, disappears, returns, flows in the deep calm of the Absolute.

The chorus of the pilgrims invokes the sage Kapila,[1] who in the darkness of the ancient past brought wisdom to the earth, as the Ganges was called from heaven to the shore of the ocean to dissolve the past.

Victory to Kapila," the pilgrims chant softly; "Victory to our Mother the Ganges."

New Birth

In the North, in Assam, a Divine Mother who is widely respected and worshiped lives in a temple folded in on itself. The narrow façade is framed by two low towers. Inside the door, a circular staircase descends underground like a huge, deep well. The altar is down below the ground. The Divine Mother is related with the earth, with what is most primitive in man.

We are in the Temple of Kamakhya on the top of Nilachal Hill on the north bank of the Brahmaputra, here as wide as a lake. It is the meeting place of all the tantric pilgrims from all parts of India. They are dressed in red cloth and carry garlands of red hibiscus. It is an orgy of redness of all possible shades.

Temple priests guard the entrances. Our small group, faces hidden by crowns of flowers, places itself in the midst of the crowd of pilgrims to enter the temple, where we are given lighted candles to descend the stairs. The interior of the temple is black. One feels the push of the throng and the force of its emotion on entering into the earth's bowels at the very bottom of the well. There the altar stands.

The flower crowns are thrown down, others received. There are ablutions, instinctive gestures of simultaneous adoration and supplication; a moment that is almost anguish, panic; a violence of longing that brings cries from the pilgrims. The Divine Mother is given what she awaits; we receive the blessings of which we have need. The priests give the blessings with open hands; they hold back people descending the stairs, and once they have passed the altar, push them toward the ascending staircase. The obedient crowd uncurls slowly. In the push, people are weeping, heads bowed into their flower crowns. They are driven on to free the staircase for others. The force of emotion is difficult to contain, although it expresses itself with dignity. The crowd passes a corridor where white goats are tied up, undoubtedly for sacrificial offerings.

Returning back down the hill, it is hard to understand what has happened, the pressure of the crowd of pilgrims is so primitive and, at the same time, so full of humility. One can carry away only what has been shared of rites, centuries, old, expressed in the actual giving of oneself, red flowers, and the symbolic ablution of blood.

No one speaks. The descent of the hill is difficult; the worn-away steps demand an awareness of oneself that reaches an ever deeper quiet.

It is the pilgrimage which marks a second birth with the measure of intensity of a new life.

Note:

1   Kapila: the holy man who wrote down the sacred scriptures.

Parabola
Volume: 27.3
Grace

GIVING AND GRACE

Retold by D. K. M. Kartha

King Dilip of the Sun Clan of kings and his wife Sudakshina had no children. Their suffering on account of
childlessness was deep and relentless. They were so eager
to taste the ineffable sweetness of *vatsalya*—the love all
beings have for their offspring—but no amount of ardent
prayer, herbal medicines, and propitiatory rituals could
make Sudakshina pregnant. The kingdom needed an heir,
and the royal couple were getting on in age. The thought
that they wouldn't have a child to perform their last rites
haunted them. Therefore one day Dilip decided to hand
over his duties temporarily to the council of ministers and
to go on a journey with his wife to the ashram of his
dynastic guru, Sage Vasishttha, in the depths of the dense
sacred forest at the borders of the kingdom.

On their way, the King and Queen were welcomed by
winds sweetened by fragrant lotus pollen and by dark-eyed
deer gazing at the royal chariot in fearless amazement. In
the sky, birds sang while flying in colorful formations, and
in the forest villages, cowherds brought them fresh milk
and butter as refreshment.

When the royal couple reached Sage Vasishttha's hermitage, they were filled with the serenity created by the
holy forest and by the contemplative sages who studied
there with Vasishttha. The sages served the visitors with
sweet-smelling baths and refreshments and afterwards

took them to their guru's presence.

Vasishttha read the visitors' minds by the power of his inner sight and said: "King Dilip, I see that you have come to seek a way out of the plight of childlessness. Do you remember your trip to the kingdom of Indra some time ago? You helped him win one of his battles against the Asuras. While returning to the earth you hurried because you wanted to reunite with your wife, who was waiting for you in eagerness after her monthly menstrual sacraments were over. Worried that if you did not hurry, you would be neglecting your dharma toward your wife, you decided not to pause and pay respects to Kama Dhenu, the divine cow of Indra's kingdom, who was lying beside your path. She is the deity who grants the blessing of fertility and she was angered by your neglect. It is her curse that has caused your queen to become infertile."

Vasishttha continued: "You can easily expiate your wrongdoing because in my ashram lives the daughter of Kama Dhenu. He name is Nandini and she has a newborn calf. If you take care of Nandini for seven days, I assure you that your wife will become pregnant through her blessing."

Dilip accepted the guru's advice and started his sacred mission the next day. He bathed Nandini in the morning, perfumed her with musk and sandalwood oil, and decorated her with flower garlands. When Nandini had fed her calf, the King took her to her grazing ground. He fanned her while she grazed and he collected wild berries and sweet leaves to add to her diet. He was armed with his bow and arrow, and the sight of them kept the wild animals away. In the evening, he brought the sacred cow back to the ashram and from then on the Queen served her and the calf till the time to sleep came.

Although the King's guru had predicted results in seven days, twenty-one days of service passed without event. But on the next day, while Dilip was guarding Nandini, a lion jumped into the clearing where the cow was grazing. The King tried to shoot an arrow in defense, but his hand was frozen and he couldn't draw the arrow. The lion, holding the fear-struck cow between his paws, spoke: "O valiant king, don't bother! You cannot harm me, because I am a servant of Lord Shiva, and I have magical powers. The animals in this area are my prey according to Shiva's orders. I want to devour this cow, so go back home and let me eat in peace!"

The King pleaded with the lion to let Nandini go. He said: "That is a mothering cow and her calf is waiting at home for her to come back. Please have mercy on them, and let me fulfill my duty of safeguarding Nandini. If you are that hungry, take my body for food and save the mothering cow."

The lion told the King that it was foolish of him to give up his life to save one cow. "You are a great king and your kingdom is vast. Alive, you would be able to take care of millions of lives. If you are afraid that your guru, Vasishttha, would be angry with you if his cow is killed, you can easily please him by making a gift of countless calving cows from your kingdom."

Dilip was adamant. "This cow, Nandini, is sacred. She cannot be replaced by other cows. I am duty-bound to safeguard her and when I look at her sad eyes full of motherly love, I am filled with compassion. I would happily give up my own life to save hers. And my reputation will not suffer if you kill me because kings are expected to live and die in the line of duty."

Finally, the lion agreed to eat the King's body and he let go of Nandini. The King lay down in front of the lion as promised. But instead of the sharp attack of the lion's claws, a rain of sweet flowers fell on his head and he heard the words, "Son, get up."

When Dilip got up, he saw nobody but Nandini, who stood there with her udder dripping milk out of vatsalya for the king. She spoke thus: "Dilip, I am pleased by your spirit of giving. So are the beings of the higher worlds, who honor the courage and sacrifice you have shown by showering divine flowers upon you. The lion you saw was nothing but a creation of my magic and I was merely testing you. You showed me your worth by your readiness to die to save another being's life. When you lead me home, milk me and give a cup of my milk to your queen. She shall become pregnant and you both shall be blessed by the birth of a son."

Dilip prostrated before the sacred Nandini in reverence and gratitude. He led the cow home at dusk and did everything as she had told him. In due course, the sacred cow's predictions came true and Raghu, a wonderful son, was born to Dilip and Sudakshina. The Sun Clan is still known by that illustrious son's name.

Retold by D. K. M. Kartha from Kalidasa's *Raghuvamsham.*

Parabola
Volume: 23.2
Ecstasy

Unless It Is Wonderful, It Cannot Be Holy

Ravi Ravindra

It cannot be said that I experience ecstasy. When ecstasy takes place, then I am not. Freedom from myself is ecstatic; however, this does not last for long. Soon I return with my projects, ambitions, and fears.

A moment of ecstasy is a moment out of time. All that has the momentum of time—past, present, or future, recalling this or projecting that, pleasant or unpleasant—is bound in time and by time.

Ecstasy is truly a mystery. Not because some clue is missing and a clever sleuth will decipher a sign and figure it all out, but rather because it is too full for the mind to comprehend. As an Upanishad says, "There the mind turns back, recoiling upon itself."

There is always a wonder, even awe, connected with an expression of ecstasy. "Unless it is wonderful, wonderful, it cannot be holy," says an Upanishad. There is a noncanonical saying of Jesus Christ, found on papyri discovered in Oxyrhynchus in Egypt at the end of the last century, "Let not him who seeks cease until he finds, and when he finds he shall be astonished. Astonished he shall reach the Kingdom, and having reached the Kingdom, he shall rest."

One cannot see the mystery with ordinary eyes. A different kind of eyes are needed—closer to insight than to sight. Even when Arjuna has been so well prepared with disciplined austerity, steadfastness, teaching, and love of Krishna—the very highest God—he cannot see the Divine Mystery with his ordinary eyes. As Krishna says, "Of course, with the ordinary eye you cannot see me. I give you divine eyes. Behold my absolute power." (*Bhagavad Gita*, 11:8)

In ecstatic moments, the little ego joyously lays down the burden of its own self-importance which it has been carrying. But often, in quick succession, there is terror. The ego does not know what its place is, or whether it has a place. A classic example is in the *Bhagavad Gita* (11:15–46), where Arjuna experiences boundless joy at seeing Krishna's Great Form. But then he is terrified, and cannot take it anymore: "I rejoice, yet my mind trembles with fear."

Ananda, delight, is said by the sages in India to be a fundamental constituent of the Ultimate Real. The Real does not experience delight; it *is* delight. Brahman, the Vastness, cannot be described, for any description imposes limitations. But repeatedly sages speak of it as *sat*, *chit*, and ananda: it is, it is consciousness, and it is delight.

Whereas the monotheistic Biblical traditions speak of God as present everywhere (omnipresent), knowing everything (omniscient), and having all power (omnipotent), in the unitive Indic traditions sages are more likely to say that Brahman is all there is (sat), is awareness (chit), and is delight (ananda). Even at a little lower level of consciousness, where the Great Being (Brahma, God) is other than one's very being, God is not only omnipresent, omnipotent, and omniscient, but also *omniamorossus* (all loving), *omnidelectabilis* (all delicious), and *omnidilettante* (all delighting). A sense of joyous playfulness is a part and parcel of Divinity and of the Cosmos. All of life is a celebration and a festival (*utsava*).

My own moments of ecstasy have been triggered by varied immediate causes. In a class by the master physics teacher, John Archibald Wheeler, suddenly ananda burst in on me when I felt that I understood the equation of the general theory of relativity (Gmn=8Pmn). On another occasion, watching the sunset from golden-brown Mount Tamalpais outside San Francisco, there was a moment outside of time. Most recently, a few months ago, looking at an icon of Jesus Christ in the Hagia Sophia in Istanbul, I could not contain myself. As tears flowed quite involuntarily, I had to lean against my daughter in order to keep standing. When she looked at me quizzically, from somewhere there came to me the words reported in one of the gospels, "Jesus wept for the sins of Jerusalem." Such moments are always mysterious and completely unexpected.

In one of the Upanishads (*Taittiriya Upanishad*, II.8.1), there is a remarkable inquiry about ananda:

> *Let there be a youth, a good youth, well read, prompt in action, steady in mind and strong in body. Let this whole earth be full of wealth for him. That is one human ananda.*
>
> *What is hundred times the human ananda, that is one ananda of* manushya-gandharva *[human fairy]—also of a man who is well versed in the Vedas and who is not smitten with desires.*
>
> *What is hundred times the ananda of manushya-gandharva, that is one ananda of* deva-gandharva *[divine fairy]—also of a man who is well versed in the Vedas and who is not smitten with desires.*

Thus it goes, each time multiplying the previous measure of ananda a hundredfold, through "fathers," gods by birth, gods by work, gods, Indra, Brihaspati, Prajapati. Finally:

> *What is hundred times the ananda of Prajapati, that is one ananda of Brahma—also of a man who is well versed in the Vedas and who is not smitten with desires.*

Beyond this is "That which is here in the person and which is yonder in the Sun" and "it consists of ananda. ... Other, indeed, is it than the known; and also it is above the unknown." (*Kena Upanishad*, I.4)

Parabola
Volume: 23.2
Ecstasy

Seeking the Transcendent

Marvin Barrett

Ramakrishna, the renowned nineteenth-century Indian avatar, described his first experience of ecstasy as a six-year-old:

> *One morning I took some parched rice in a small basket and was eating it while I walked along the narrow ridges of the rice fields. In one part of the sky a beautiful black cloud appeared, heavy with rain. I was watching it and eating the rice. Very soon, the cloud covered almost the whole sky, and then a flock of cranes came flying. They were as white as milk against that black cloud. It was so beautiful that I became absorbed in the sight. Then I lost consciousness of everything outward. I fell down, and the rice was scattered over the earth. Some people saw this, and came and carried me home.*

During the next forty-four years of his life, Ramakrishna experienced such states as frequently and intensely as any saint in history. The slightest thing could cause him to go into ecstasy: a piece of sacred music, a bit of holy writ, the sight of a beloved disciple or a drunkard, or a lion in the Calcutta zoo.

In the *Gospel of Sri Ramakrishna*, his disciple Mahendranath Gupta described the last four years of the saint's life. In the forward to the thousand-page volume Aldous Huxley writes, "Never have the casual and unstudied utterances of a great religious teacher been set down with so minute a fidelity."

One of the saint's many descriptions of ecstasy, or *samadhi*, as it is referred to by the Hindus, follows:

> *It was as if houses, doors, temples, and everything else vanished altogether; as if there was nothing anywhere. And what I saw was an infinite shoreless sea of light, a sea that was consciousness. However far and in whatever direction I looked, I saw shining waves, one after another coming toward me. They were raging and storming upon me with great speed. Very soon they were upon me: they made me sink down into unknown depths. I panted and struggled and lost consciousness.*

Elsewhere he says:

> *Mad! That's the word. One must become mad with love in order to realize God. But that love is not possible if the mind dwells on "woman and gold." Sex-life with a woman! What happiness is there in that? The realization of God gives ten million times more happiness. Gauri used to say that when a man attains ecstatic love of God all the pores of the skin, even the roots of the hair, become like so many sexual organs, and in every pore the aspirant enjoys the happiness of communion with the Atman.*

A photograph ..., a document unique in the history of the saints, has caught Ramakrishna in one of the countless moments in which he experienced *samadhi*. It was not always convenient. "The man who always sees God and talks to Him intimately ... is sometimes like an inert thing, sometimes like a ghoul, sometimes like a child, and sometimes like a madman." The interruption could come at any moment—in the middle of a lesson or a song, ... or on an excursion into Calcutta; in a temple in Varanasi, or in a rich man's drawing room.

> *This is what it means to be intoxicated with ecstatic love of God. The sum and substance of the whole matter is that a man must love God,*

must be restless for Him. It doesn't matter whether you believe in God with form or in God without form. You may or may not believe that God incarnates Himself as man. But you will realize Him if you have that yearning. Then He Himself will let you know what He is like. If you must be mad, why should you be mad for the things of the world? If you must be mad, be mad for God alone.

On occasion his ecstasy could be contagious. In the Gospel the following scene is described:

The musician sang again. As he improvised new lines describing ecstatic love of God, the Master stood up and danced. He himself improvised lines and sang them with outstretched arms. Soon he went into samadhi and sat down, with his head resting on the bolster in front of him. The musician was also carried away with emotion and sang new songs. … Sri Ramakrishna every now and then went into deep samadhi. When he was in the deepest samadhi he could not utter a word and his whole body remained transfixed. The devotees danced encircling him. After a while, regaining partial consciousness, he danced with the strength of a lion, intoxicated with ecstatic love. But even then he could not utter a word. Finally, regaining more of the consciousness of the world, he sang again, improvising the lines. An intense spiritual atmosphere was created in Adhar's parlor. At the sound of the loud music a large crowd had gathered in the street.

Ramakrishna died in 1886 in *mahasamadhi*, the ultimate ecstasy—"that final samadhi in which a knower of Brahman leaves the physical body." He left behind him a legacy of spiritual authenticity which hasn't been excelled in the traditions of the East or West since.

The opening quote of this chapter is from Christopher Isherwood, *Ramakrishna and His Disciples* (Hollywood: Vedanta Press, 1965), pp. 28–29. All other quotes are from *The Gospel of Sri Ramakrishna*, translated by Swami Nikhilananda (New York: Ramakrishna-Vivekananda Center, 1942).

•

CHAPTER SEVEN

MEDITATION AND THE DISCIPLINE OF YOGA

When the five organs of perception are still,
together with the mind, when the reason does not function—
this they aver to be the highest state.

This they deem to be yoga—the steady
concentration of the senses. Man then becomes
pure attention, for yoga is both
origin and extinction.

—The Vedas

The practice of yoga as a psychological discipline
and the study of philosophy as a mental re-education are two
essentials in the equipment of the man who would explore the
highest. None may be left out without leaving the seeker like a
one-legged man trying to ascend a difficult mountain.
The ultimate goal cannot be found by the yogi because he is concerned
only with himself and not the entire universe.
It cannot be found by the philosopher because he is concerned only
with the theoretical *knowledge of the meaning of all existence.*
It can be found by him alone who has mastered both yoga and
philosophy, and who is then willing to take the next step and
sacrifice his ego on the altar of ultimate attainment. For the final
stage of this climb demands that the insight gained by philosophic
knowledge into the ego's true nature be applied to the entire life of
thought, feeling and conduct—not by some dramatic gesture but
by working *incessantly during every moment of every day. Such*
a perpetual vigil is really a form of continuous concentration, that

is, of yoga, and it is impossible for those who have not successfully trained their minds in the yogic discipline. These are the reasons why we must view yoga and philosophy as the two legs needed to support a man who would then enter into the ever-renewed practice to attain realization.
This is the final climb to the summit.

—Paul Brunton

The practice of meditation and the discipline of yoga are universal forms of *sadhana* (spiritual practice) of the Hindu seeker. The first two selections in this chapter explain meditation as attention to sensations, and muse on how this attention and sensation can be cultivated: "Sensations" by Sri Anirvan and "Listening to the Silence" by J. Krishnamurti. In "Kali Who Swallows the Universe," Ma Jaya Sati Bhagavati shows how the practice of meditation in the context of devotional worship can lead to ecstasy, reminding us of Ramakrishna's experience described in the last chapter.

The aim of meditation and yoga is to calm the busy mind and open oneself to sensation and perception as a path to freedom. But one's attitude toward both the practice and the goal is an essential element in determining one's progress on the path, as portrayed amusingly in "How Long until Freedom?"

The powers gained by yoga are sometimes used for goals other than liberation. In "A Tale of Surrender," the former king's goal in his pursuit of yoga is to prove himself as powerful as the great sage Vashishtha. It was only when he abandoned his attachment to the goal, after making prodigious efforts, that he achieved it.

Yoga harnesses power for the individual who practices it, but when the greatest yogi of all, the great god Shiva, performs his dance of destruction and creation, the universe is set in motion and then dissolves. The story is beautifully told by James Kirk in "Shiva Naṭarāja."

In the final selection in this chapter, William Mahoney explores the way in which deep meditation and creativity—"the practice of externalizing in material form one's subtle inner being"—draw on the same wellspring of experience.

Parabola
Volume: 30.1
Awakening

Sensations

Sri Anirvan

All spiritual experiences are sensations in the body. They are simply a graded series of sensations, beginning with the solidity of a clod of earth and passing gradually, in full consciousness, through liquidness and the emanation of heat to that of a total vibration before reaching the Void. The road to be traveled is long.

Each time a step is made on the ascending ladder, a sensation of expansion in space and of complete relaxation is experienced. This sensation offers a foretaste of what the experience of pure Spirit (*Chit*) might be, in which all things are transcended. How far one is from that! Yet at this moment spirit and matter appear to be one.

Always remember that any sensation of expansion you may experience is a radiation. Remain calm and radiate this warmth. Do not question. Ask for nothing more. Live these moments to the full. This radiation is in itself *Shakti*, an instant of living consciousness, that is, a direct experience that is ingrained in you. Your sensation is the proof of it, a certainty you cannot efface from your memory.

In meditation, the whole body is utilized to discover a sensation of expansion which, for a long time, represents that final aim. Work on the body is a delicate attempt and has to be done according to very precise data, for each movement, voluntary or involuntary, is a search for stillness, that is to say, for a sensation of physical consciousness.

The first objective to reach is perfect solidity of the motionless body. To arrive at that, all thoughts have to be brought back one after another to the body—to its form, its weight, its balance. There must be no other thought. This state is symbolized by the matter "earth," in the heart of which, notwithstanding its heaviness and opacity, a vibration exists.

The attention will gradually be turned to the image of a vessel. The body is really that vessel made of heavy matter. It contains an effervescent wine. Concentrated on itself, attention will enter into the body, go down the length of the spinal column until there is an impression of a heaviness in the center of gravity. The whole body has then become as hard as a statue with a pure form.

At that point, all the movements inside the vessel are perceptible: effervescence, agitation, ideas, images—all of them produced by the body. The stability of the body is a state in itself. This is why so much importance is attached to food and hygiene.

The second stage begins when the body, in its well-established solidity, can become the matrix of energy in movement. Externally hard, the body internally becomes the pulsation of life that fills it. An intense vibration of energy throbs in it. This state is symbolized by purification of the element water, that is to say, by the transition from a heavier to a lighter density.

Then comes the discovery that a body of radiant and very subtle sensations is contained within the body of flesh. It is only when the body of flesh has a solid form that the nerve channels (*nadis*) can be perceived with all the sensations of the currents of life through them. As it is said in the *Vedas*, "A stream flows through a rock."

The third stage is when all the currents of nervous energy flowing through the inner body become currents of light from which little by little a sensation of fire emanates. This state is symbolized by the purification of the element fire, so much so that the temperature of the body rises as in an attack of fever.

These three stages—that of solidity of the body, of sensation of the nervous currents, of the sensation of currents of light—are characteristics of meditation in depth. Up to this point, the individuality remains intact, expressed by the words, "one of the many."

The fourth stage is that in which individuality is lost. The state of sensation of fire which consumes the body is a further transition from a heavier to a more subtle density. The fire that consumes the inner body consumes at the same time all sense of form, to the degree that sensation of non-form becomes irradiant. This state is symbolized by the purification of the element air. The habitual impulse to resort to forms disappears. There remains only the Void, which is at the same time a precise and global sensation of multi-formity. All is clarity and calm.

In a moment of inner calmness, one can gradually, as if coming out of a dream, learn to catch the last impression received and observe it without losing it. The effort to try is to isolate the sensation provoked by an impression and trace it back to the center where it arose. One sees that which provoked it. In this attempt, the slightest discussion with oneself, or the slightest fear, curiosity, or judgment, will instantly put an end to the effort.

To penetrate into that realm of consciousness, sensation is the only guide we have—a continuous sensation which, even if it almost disappears or if it stays with us in a subtle way, can no longer be felt in our body. This sensation is nevertheless connected with inner organs of perception whose role and use are not yet known to us.

What is a true spiritual discipline? It is a known rhythm of the harmonized body. All is there. Nothing could be more material than to use the body for acquiring a right sensation of God. Through spiritual discipline the entire body becomes the receptacle of divine sensations. A well-conducted discipline makes it possible to identify and recognize at its base a unique sensation which is a sensation of the universe. What is known in meditation is the interiorization of this "pure sensation" outside of time. It is a taste of eternity.

Discipline, that is to say, voluntary sacrifice, is the unique means to reverse the direction of the vital current which is habitually directed outwards by the mind. From this comes the image of the disciple going against the current of vital fluid to make his way up to the source, just as, on the concrete plane, thousands of pilgrims go to the Ganges upstream to its source.

As a matter of fact, I am contradicting myself when I speak to you of discipline, for I make a point always that every one of you emphasizes and intensifies his own motive for search. The whole thing is to have a very definite motive as the pivot around which your attempt will be organized. People often come to me and say, "I would like to meditate on something, for example, a flame, a triangle, a luminous spot. What do you advise?" In this case I answer, "Well then, meditate on your body. Try to find a sensation of yourself."

A right sensation of oneself is in the very nature of incarnation, of penetration. At that moment, the spirit becomes matter and takes on a definite density in the body. Personal austerity (*tapasya*) is the process by which a sensation comes alive, so that the whole body glows. This is a true sensation, that of spirit becoming flesh.

Adapted from *To Live Within* by Lizelle Reymond, translated by Nancy Pearson and Stanley Spielberg (New York: Doubleday, 1971).

Parabola
Volume: 15.2
Attention

Listening to the Silence

J. Krishnamurti

Have you ever paid any attention to the ringing of the temple bells? Now, what do you listen to? To the notes, or to the silence between the notes? If there were no silence, would not the notes be more penetrating, of a different quality? But you see, we rarely pay real attention to anything; and I think it is important to find out what it means to pay attention. When your teacher is explaining a problem in mathematics, or when you are reading history, or when a friend is talking, telling you a story, or when you are near the river and hear the lapping of the water on the bank, you generally pay very little attention; and if we could find out what it means to pay attention, perhaps learning would then have quite a different significance and become much easier.

When your teacher tells you to pay attention in class, what does he mean? He means that you must not look out of the window, that you must withdraw your attention from everything else and concentrate wholly on what you are supposed to be studying. Or, when you are absorbed in a novel, your whole mind is so concentrated on it that for the moment you have lost interest in everything else. That is another form of attention. So, in the ordinary sense, paying attention is a narrowing-down process, is it not?

Now, I think there is a different kind of attention altogether. The attention which is generally advocated, practiced, or indulged in is a narrowing-down of the mind to a point, which is a process of exclusion. When you make an effort to pay attention, you are really resisting something—the desire to look out of the window to see who is coming in, and so on. Part of your energy has already gone in resistance. You build a wall around your mind to make it concentrate completely on a particular thing, and you call this the disciplining of the mind to pay attention. You try to exclude from the mind every thought but the one on which you want it to be wholly concentrated. That is what most people mean by paying attention. But I think there is a different kind of attention, a state of mind which is not exclusive, which does not shut out anything; and because there is no resistance, the mind is capable of much greater attention. But attention without resistance does not mean the attention of absorption.

The kind of attention which I would like to discuss is entirely different from what we usually mean by attention, and it has immense possibilities because it is not exclusive. When you concentrate on a subject, on a talk, on a conversation, consciously or unconsciously you build a wall of resistance against the intrusion of other thoughts, and so your mind is not wholly there; it is only partially there, however much attention you pay, because part of your mind is resisting any intrusion, any deviation or distraction.

Let us begin the other way round. Do you know what distraction is? You want to pay attention to what you are reading, but your mind is distracted by some noise outside and you look out of the window. When you want to concentrate on something and your mind wanders off, the wandering off is called distraction; then part of your mind resists the so-called distraction and there is a waste of energy in that resistance. Whereas, if you are aware of every movement of the mind from moment to moment then there is no such thing as distraction at any time and the energy of the mind is not wasted in resisting something. So it is important to find out what attention really is.

If you listen both to the sound of the bell and to the silence between its strokes, the whole of that listening is attention. Similarly, when someone is speaking, attention is the giving of your mind not only to the words but also to the silence between the words. If you experiment with this you "will find that your mind can pay complete attention without distraction and without resistance. When you discipline your mind by saying, "I must not look out of the window, I must not watch the people coming in, I must pay attention even though I want to do something else," it creates a division which is very destructive because it dissipates the energy of the mind. But if you listen comprehensively so that there is no division and therefore no form of resistance then you will find that the mind can pay complete attention to anything without effort. Do you see it? Am I making myself clear?

Surely, to discipline the mind to pay attention is to bring about its deterioration—which does not mean that the mind must restlessly wander all over the place like a monkey. But, apart from the attention of absorption, these two states are all we know. Either we try to discipline the mind so tightly that it cannot deviate, or we just let it wander from one thing to another. Now, what I am describing is not a compromise between the two; on the contrary, it has nothing to do with either. It is an entirely different approach; it is to be totally aware so that your mind is all the time attentive without being caught in the process of exclusion.

Try what I am saying, and you will see how quickly your mind can learn. You can hear a song or a sound and let the mind be so completely full of it that there is not the effort of learning. After all, if you know how to listen to what your teacher is telling you about some historical fact, if you can listen without any resistance because your mind has space and silence and is therefore not distracted, you will be aware not only of the historical fact but also of the prejudice with which he may be translating it, and of your own inward response.

I will tell you something. You know what space is. There is space in this room. The distance between here and your hostel, between the bridge and your home, between this bank of the river and the other—all that is space, Now, is there also space in your mind? Or is it so crowded that there is no space in it at all? If your mind has space, then in that space there is silence—and from that silence everything else comes, for then you can listen, you can pay attention without resistance. That is why it is very important to have space in the mind. If the mind is not overcrowded, not ceaselessly occupied, then it can listen to that dog barking, to the sound of a train crossing the distant bridge, and also be fully aware of what is being said by a person talking here. Then the mind is a living thing, it is not dead.

Parabola
Volume: 23.2
Ecstasy

Kali Who Swallows the Universe

Ma Jaya Sati Bhagavati

The path to ecstasy begins with awareness of the breath. Ecstasy is not so much about going out of your body as it is about coming into your body fully, touching this great beautiful earth with all its ugliness, with all its majestic moments. The breath becomes something wonderful to you, something that's always at hand to remind you that you are indeed in the moment. You can't breathe for yesterday and you certainly cannot breathe for tomorrow; you can only breathe in the moment, and the moment is rich.

To live in the richness of the moment, you must first acknowledge the Mother, for all of life is the Mother. All of form is the Mother. All of pain is the Mother. All of sorrow is the Mother. All of joy is the Mother. All that moves is the Mother. All that speaks is the Mother. The silence is the Father—Christ, Shiva—the Father is in all of us making us complete. We are complete in ourselves, and yet we think we are two parts, an inside part that is separated by flesh from the outside part. This is an illusion, yet for most of our lives we live in this illusion.

The goddess Kali prepares us for the oneness. Kali is she who swallows the universe. She consumes your smallness, your pain, your guilt, and finally your ego, if you will allow her to. Kali is the Black Mother, the dark mother of the night. It is she who kills the ego dead. But that is the only thing she kills—just the ego. Do not be afraid of Kali, for the Black Mother will never hurt you; she will only devour that which will. On the spiritual path, you do not need your pain and negativity, and you do not need your ego, your small self.

When I talk about the cremation grounds and Kali's dripping blood, her garland of skulls, her belt of severed hands, her skull cup, her sword, I am talking about this goddess and the Hindu philosophy, mythology, and religion. She devours pain, devours truth, devours falseness, devours all that is, and leaves just the purity of the heart. She wanders the skies in search of any kind of sorrow so she can absorb it inside of herself. You don't even have to know her name, but you must believe that there is a Mother and that this Mother will wrap her arms around you and hold you no matter what. She will love you and touch you and give you compassion, and in the same breath strip the flesh away from your bones and leave you free. She does this because nothing, no pain in your life, no guilt, no desire, no attachment, is so big that it is worth forgetting God.

Now as you sit in meditation with less ego to burden you, the tongue automatically turns up. It touches the upper palate, making an opening to the *brahmarandra*, or the baby's soft spot on the top of the head. As the head opens up, it allows the gentleness of the Mother, this *shakti*, this spirit of Christ, to come into the body and touch the space of the heart. The heart then opens like the lotus. The *amrith*, which the great sages speak about, then begins to fall, sometimes as a liquid, more often in the form of bliss. Your whole body begins to tingle. It's a profound experience, for inside and outside at that moment do not exist. There is only *Om Tat Sat*, that which is that. You realize, "I am that which is that."

But first you must walk in the darkness of the cremation ground, with the hyenas screaming out and the spirit of the dead all around. You must face your own fears and consume them. And then, how safe the night is, the stars, the moon, when you are walking with the Mother Kali, she who carries the sword dripping with blood—to me that is ecstasy. For the blood is that which comes from evil thoughts, evil deeds, as she slays the demon foes and makes heaps of their heads.

Why is Kali dark and terrifying? That is *your* darkness, which she takes from you. She takes from you what you do not need. As she grows darker, you grow lighter.

As the ego disappears and you are in touch with the spiritual aspect of your being, you bring down into the flesh the very essence of God, the very essence of the now, the very essence of truth. Literally your flesh begins to change: your body gets very straight yet very relaxed, and there is a glow about you, a glow that lights up everybody you meet. So when you sit watching the breath, feeling the breath going in and going out, you begin to feel lighter, more centered, more alive, more in love, more passionate.

Then, when you go up and out of the top of the head in a meditation or a spiritual exercise, the body that has seen and felt and become that light becomes very spirit-filled and very strong, very knowing. From bliss we let the ego call us back. But as you fall back upon the pillow of earth, the ego can't follow your spirit as easily as it can control your thoughts, and your body does indeed become filled with light. As that light touches your heart, the bliss penetrates all of you.

In the same way that you need to understand and know your higher self, you also need to understand your own body. You need to feel your toes and be aware of them, your heels, your knees, your thighs, your waist, your chest, your sexual organs, your fingers, your hands. When the Buddha was asked, "What is it you teach your monks?" he simply answered, "My monks sit, walk, eat, go to the bathroom, sleep, beg, and work." The question was asked again, "But so many do that. What's different about your teaching?" The Buddha smiled then and said, "When my monks are sitting, they know they are sitting, when my monks walk they know they are walking. ..." He was speaking of this great awareness that makes the flesh alive with passion, and the breath is the tool to go back into that godhead, that joy, that state called bliss.

In actuality, ecstasy is leaving the body, watching the journey become a brilliant light, and then bringing that light right back into the body, and being aware of it in everything you do. So ecstasy comes when the flesh makes the journey from ego into spirituality, when all of the flesh and all of the *chakras* become one with whatever is outside.

I was asked, "Do we go into God or does God come into us?" The answer is both. Eventually you have Kali Tantra, the ecstatic merging with the Mother herself. But if you want to put it in a way that could be understood by the lay person, yes, God goes into you. Yet that's not fully right, for God is already there. On the day of conception, God's mind was being formed in your mind, hidden in the deepest crevices of your being. On the day of your first breath, the Mother breathed into you her own breath, her own being, and her own joy.

Eventually, as you meditate and feel the essence coming through you, the room begins to fade, the temple begins to fade, and the body begins to fade. Ecstasy is not about you being separate from anybody else; it is about the oneness, the great oneness, for without the oneness there is no bliss, without the oneness there is no ecstasy, and without the oneness there is no joy. Oh yes, there is always that which brings instant gratification and goes as quickly as it came, but the ecstasy of God rebirths itself, over and over again: the rebirthing of God in every moment of your life, the rejoicing of life, is indeed what you're about.

With human love, you love one person. Your bodies come together and then apart. With God love, you *are* that person you love, and you need never to part, ever. Once you have been touched by God, the touch becomes part of you—your cells, your fingers, your face. Once you have been loved, the love becomes part of you and you can never be alone. That is true tantra. That is the joy in my life and that is what I am trying to share with all of you.

So when you breathe consciously, you are awakening in yourself a vision of the Mother's black, dark feet. Or you awaken in you the reincarnation of the spirit that was once yours without flesh and has ceased to be—you have forgotten it. You have forgotten, and now as you enter into the silent cave of God, this cave which exists inside of you, you begin to remember. Perhaps not in words that go back and forth in your mind, but in a feeling that you were there, and you are there, and you are that which is there—*Om Tat Sat.*

Truly it's quite simple. Look at who you are, get inside your soul, literally feel what it feels like inside your soul. Travel down to the base of the spine. Do that with an in-breath, and with an out-breath climb out again. Indeed, you will see that what is outside is the same as what is inside. Melt away this ego flesh, and let your true flesh become bright.

Parabola
Volume: 23.4
Birth and Rebirth

How Long Until Freedom?

Retold by Joseph Head and S. L. Cranston

There was a great god-sage called Narada. He traveled everywhere, and one day he was passing through a forest, and he saw a man who had been meditating until the white ants had built a huge mound round his body, so long had he been sitting in that position. He said to Narada, "Where are you going?" Narada replied, "I am going to heaven." "Then ask Shiva when He will be merciful to me, when I shall attain freedom." Further on Narada saw another man. He was jumping about, singing and dancing, and he said, "O Narada, where are you going?" Narada said, "I am going to heaven." "Then ask when I shall attain freedom."

So Narada went on. In the course of time he came again by the same road, and there was the man who had been meditating till the ant-hills had grown round him. He said, "O Narada, did you ask the Lord about me?" "O yes." "What did He say?" "The Lord told me that you would attain freedom in four more births." Then the man began to weep and wail, and said, "I have meditated until an ant-hill has been raised around me, and I have to endure four more births yet!" Narada went on to the other man. "Did you ask about me?" "O yes. Do you see this tamarind tree? I have to tell you that as many leaves as there are on that tree, so many times you will be born, and then you will attain freedom." Then the man began

•

to dance for joy, and said, "After so short a time I shall be free!" A voice came, "My child, you shall have freedom this instant."

From Joseph Head and S. L. Cranston, *Reincarnation: The Phoenix Fire Mystery* (New York: Julian Press/Crown Publishers, Inc., 1977), pp. 51–52.

Parabola
Volume: 27.1
The Ego and the 'I'

A Tale of Surrender

Retold by Rama Devagupta

*One early morning, when I was around the age of six or
seven, my father told me a story while I was getting ready
for school and he was preparing to go to work, as was customary in our family. It was the story of two of the greatest*
rishis *(sages) of India, Vashishtha and Vishwamitra, who
play a prominent role in the* Ramayana. *This story, however,
had nothing to do with that great epic; instead, it spoke of
events that took place long before the birth of the divine
prince, Rama, and his consort, Sita.*

*This was one of those few stories my father would
repeat time and time again. The account of Vashishtha and
Vishwamitra was my first exposure to the Sanskrit word*
ahankara, *meaning "ego," and it made an indelible impression in my mind and heart.*

Once upon a time, the story goes, in the kingdom of
Gadhi, there was a very powerful and arrogant king who
wanted to become the ruler of all. To turn his dream into
reality, he subjugated friendly rulers and fought several
wars. In due course of time, he defeated every opposing warrior, successfully established suzerainty over the

four corners of earth and earned the name "Vishwarath"—"the ruler of the world."

One day, while passing through a forest after yet another victorious conquest, Vishwarath came across the hermitage of the famous sage Vasishtha, the greatest of all sages. He welcomed the tired king and his exhausted army with due honor and respect and served them with lavish food and refreshments.

Surprised with the extravagant hospitality, Vishwarath said, "Rishi Vasishtha, I see that you lead a quiet, simple life with no material possessions. Yet you were able to feed me and my vast army of thousands of horses and soldiers effortlessly. What is the secret?"

Vasishtha smilingly replied that it was due to Nandini—the daughter of the heavenly wish-yielding cow, Kamadhenu, who, like her mother, could produce any object in an instant when approached with humility and prayer. Filled with greed, the egotistical Vishwarath stated that such an exquisite cow should belong to royalty and demanded that the rishi hand over Nandini. But Vasishtha apologetically refused and said, "Nandini was bestowed to me by the gods, and unless the gods direct me otherwise, she stays here."

Vishwarath had never taken no for an answer and he was not going to begin doing so today. He attempted to drag Nandini by force and commanded his soldiers to seize her. A terrified Nandini sought Vasishtha's permission for self-defense and unleashed a powerful army out of nowhere. In the ensuing war, due to Vasishtha's piety and yogic powers, Nandini's army gained an upper hand and nobody could touch her.

Devastated at the annihilation of his army and disillusioned with his kingly powers, Vishwarath thought, "I, who have been acclaimed as the unconquerable ruler of this world and the bravest of all kings, was defeated today by a mere sage. Of what use are these physical powers?" Renouncing his kingdom then and there, he retired to the forest.

Vishwarath completed a thousand years of penance. He acquired control over the mind and attained the necessary yogic powers for magical warfare. Then he proceeded to Vasishtha's hermitage, declared war on the ashram residents, and again tried to acquire Nandini. But Vasishtha, whose meditation was disturbed by the sudden commotion and fear in the ashram atmosphere, gently raised his *yoga-danda* (a specially carved wooden stick on which yogis rest their hands while sitting in meditation) in the air, and immediately, Vishwarath's weapons were rendered ineffective.

While a humiliated Vishwarath stood with his head bowed in shame, the following words resounded from the heavens: "Glory be to Vasishtha, the *brahmarshi*, who has transcended the ego and for whom there can be no defeat! Merged with the Infinite Brahman, Vasishtha is indeed beyond passion, anger, or attachment!"

When Vishwarath heard those words, he lost interest in material powers and possessions. He went into seclusion in the Himalayan Mountains and meditated for another twenty thousand years. Following enormous effort and innumerable struggles with his lower self, he progressively evolved from a seeker to a rishi, *rajarshi* (royal sage), and *maharshi* (very highly evolved sage).

However, because Vishwarath's egotistical tendencies were predominant most of his life, and his main aim of realization of the Absolute was to prove his equivalency to Vashishta, the final step of becoming a brahmarshi proved to be an impossible task. But Vishwarath did not lose heart. He continued his penance with a seriousness of purpose and faced every obstacle and setback resulting from the conflicts of ego.

At last, after what seemed like an eternity, when the desire for spiritual merits and recognition by Vasishtha were finally gone, in test after test conducted by the gods Vishwarath proved with equanimity and calm that he had conquered the six *doshas* (faults) responsible for ego-consciousness: *kama* (passion), *krodha* (anger), *lobha* (greed), *moha* (attachment), *mada* (pride), and *matsarya* (envy). Soon thereafter, Vishwarath reached the goal of realizing the Supreme Self, and was given the stature of brahmarshi by Brahma, Vishnu and Shiva, and also recognized as such by Sage Vasishtha. Due to this spectacular transformation from a bloodthirsty, arrogant ruler to a brahmarshi, Vishwarath became known as Sage "Vishwamitra"—"a friend of the world."

Parabola
Volume: 13.1
The Creative
Response

Shiva Nataraja

Retold by James A. Kirk

A god does not have to be professed in order to be a god. That One can exist in supreme indifference to the honor which men would like to confer by their belief. It matters not to god. Even when ten thousand heretic sages agreed to refuse to believe in the gods, the gods were undisturbed. Still, since a god has all the time there is with which to play, he can afford to take a moment to render clear to obstinate and clouded minds his real Presence and his Power. So Shiva, though tranquil, let his overflowing love and grace impel him to the gesture of visiting the skeptical sages in their forest hermitage to show them the truth. A gracious god will spare the time to step forth and clear up cloudy points.

On his arrival at the forest glen, Shiva was received with the violent reactions of men who face a fact that doesn't fit their orthodoxies. They discovered, however, that neither disbelief nor disbelief in a louder voice augmented by curses could dislodge a simple fact. Shiva smiled.

When vehemence had failed to justify their ignorance, they summoned brute force to authenticate the just reasonableness of their claim and unleashed a ferocious tiger at the god. The only god who would be frightened by a tiger would be just the kind of god these sages could imagine and reject. It was no such puny god, nor god for puny men, who stood before them. Calmly and deftly

Shiva stripped the tiger of its skin and slipped the tiger-skin around his waist, a gesture of propriety toward man.

With their power countered and graciously transformed to modesty, as gently as their vicious curses had echoed back from the real Presence, the faithful champions of skepticism released their next defense, a strategy of craftiness. A hideous, venomous snake coiled silently in the grass and slowly raised its head, spread out its hood and bared its dripping fangs. Shiva bent down and gently stroked the outspread hood, then sliding a hand down to smooth the coils, he cast the snake around his neck as adornment for his mighty chest.

The sage lovers of the Truth, armed with an infinity of their disbelief, were furious with the truth which stood before them. Their curses had no sting; their power hung on the opponent as a garment; their craftiness adorned him as a necklace. They decided to admit half of what they did not believe, in order to avoid believing in the other half. From out of the dim, occult region of their misformed faith they called forth a supernatural demon to wield his club against the threatening truth. He came forth with power, hideous and vile as their intentions, but dwarfed as if in mimicry of their half-formed faith. Shiva pressed the demon to the ground, set a fool upon his back and paused.

Somewhere within the soul of that great god a faint strumming of uncertain sound began to stir. So faintly it began that he turned his whole mind inward and distinguished a slow and stately rhythm rising from his overflowing grace. A hand which held a drum began to tap it in the slow and even cadence of a pulsing heart. His supple body responded to the invitation and the movement of his legs picked up the rhythm. The sound welled forth; the cadence cleared and strengthened with a more insistent throb. The drum he stroked began to beat an intricate rhythm. Crescendos of joy poured forth in the sound and movement of a dancing god. The fire in his left hand traced the gestures of the accelerating tempo. Graceful arms and hands declared the motion of his ecstasy. Surging legs lifted in ascending leaps of unpremeditated joy. Shiva was absorbed in the rapture of his own expression. He danced. Once swept up and captivated by its inward throb, the rhythms and the mood began to soar. His body glistened and then glowed with dazzling splendor as he danced.

The heretic sages prostrated themselves to be his dancing floor. The gods came down from their heavens to watch the joyful dance. As Shiva moved with stately grace and gay abandon, as only a Shiva could do, mist began to form in the outer reaches of the universe. The torch he waved aloft flared forth in pulsing rhythms of the dance, and stars expired before its dazzling brilliance. All that was not Shiva dancing began to fall apart, disintegrate, evaporate into the thin vapors of apparent nothingness. The dance of joy became *Taṇḍava*, the Dance of Eternity, a dance of universal death and joy.

At the climax of the nothingness, when only the audience of gods remained to contemplate his grace and power, Shiva paused, and then began again—as slowly as before. His was to be a dance of the full measure of grace. He had danced the worlds out, now he danced them in again, flinging stars into their heavens, evoking life upon the earth, a kinesthesis of overflowing grace and love. So Shiva danced a new world and a new age into being, and had himself a day of lovely sport and playful joy. The world is here because Shiva danced, but can we know, because the world is here, that Shiva has been dancing?

When he brought the world very near to where we stand, the dance closed quietly and he slipped back to the cosmic fellowship. After all, it matters not to god to dance a world out or in, or whether wise men will believe in him or not. He danced. It was enough.

Parabola
Volume: 13.1
The Creative
Response

The Artist As Yogi, The Yogi As Artist

William K. Mahoney

In a poem in which he reflected on the source of the creative impulse[1], Martin Heidegger wrote that "We never come to thoughts. They come to us." The transformative genius, as the philosopher experienced it, enters one's being from the outside in a moment of inspiration which Heidegger likened to the moment

> *When through a rent in the rain-clouded*
> *sky a ray of the sun suddenly glides*
> *over the gloom of the meadows. ...*

Artists, too, have noted experiences of inspired moments in which they "in-breathe" (Latin *in-spirare*) an external power of transformation at the moment of creative expression. Describing times in which he would paint quietly by himself, Paul Klee wrote in his journal that "Everything vanishes around me, and works are born as if out of the void. ... My hand has become the obedient instrument of a remote will." For Klee the artistic moment carried nothing short of theological significance. Earlier he had noticed that

> *For the uncertain*
> *a something shines,*

not from here, not from me
but from God.[2]

For some artists the creative moment thus entails a certain infusion from outside of a transformative power in almost a kind of *enthusiasm* (from the Greek *en-theos*, "possessed by god"). One senses that the artist creates something new because he or she becomes something new, and that the artifact itself marks this change.

But is this the only way to view the creative process? Would it be possible to describe both the artistic and religious moments as arising from the practice and experience of *contemplation*? The term comes originally from the Latin *con-templum*, which refers to a two- or three-dimensional "space in which one is able to see sacred realities" (compare the English word *temple*) and thus from *contemplari*, meaning, "to see things as they really are." Through the centuries, this process of "seeing" reality evolved from the "vision" into the nature of the outside world to the cultivated "insight" into levels of being within one's self.

Writing from his experience as a Trappist monk, Thomas Merton wrote of this latter, inner contemplation:

> *Contemplation is not trance or ecstasy. … It is not enthusiasm, the sense of being "seized" by an elemental force and swept into liberation by mystical frenzy. … A door opens in the center of our being and we seem to fall through it into immense depths, which, although they are infinite, are all accessible to us; all eternity seems to have become ours in this one placid and breathless contact.*[3]

Meditation and the Artistic Process in South Asia

Many of the teachers in various religious and aesthetic traditions in South Asia in the Classical and Early Medieval periods (roughly 300 BCE to 1200 CE) maintained that artists were first to become adept at the practice of inner vision if they were to produce true works of art. The author of the Sanskrit "Lesson on How to Produce What One Wishes," for example, taught that before constructing an image of any kind an artist must first have a model of that image in his mind, and that, having meditated on it through a process of insight the artist then was to externalize that inner form and project it onto an external surface.[4] Aesthetic philosophers described this process as a form of yogic meditation. For example, the medieval thinker, Sukracarya, noted that since deities could not be seen by the eyes, an artist (*pratimakara*, literally "image maker") who would form a representation of such an invisible being must measure the ideal contours of that deity through a process of imagination which Sukracarya described as a disciplined practice of inward vision (*yoga-dhyana*). Having seen the divine being through this inner contemplation, the artist then could draw that form outwards from within and represent it in the external world in the form of a painting.[5]

If some medieval South Asian philosophers thought of artists as yogis, some thinkers of the same period described yogis as artists of sorts. According to these thinkers, skilled meditators could construct or restructure the outside world by manipulating internal creative energies. The Theravada Buddhist compilers of "The Way of Discerning Awareness," for example, asserted that a contemplative could gain such powers as the ability to form objects through the power of the mind or to create worlds through his or her special way of knowing things. The authors of that work described such external transformations in extraordinary terms: the disciplined meditator was said to be able to become many bodies at once and then return to being one body again, to swim through solid ground as if through water, to walk on water as if on land, or even to travel in a "created body" (*rupam nimitah*) to the heavenly world of Brahma himself.[6] Like artists who drew on an inner creative power to form new images and objects in the outside world, such adept meditators brought forth from within themselves a transformative force that they used to create new bodes of being in the external realm.

South Asian artists' and yogis' creative nature may be understood to reflect an important world view that centered on the notion that the generative impulse that creates all forms in the universe as a whole resides also and precisely within one's deepest subjective world. Yogis sought to know this eternal and infinite Creator within themselves; artists produced their objective works by objectifying that Creator's effective power.

These thinkers did not view the transformative process as the fabrication of an entirely new mode of being but, rather, an enlivening or embodiment of modes of being that were said to lie already in the specialist's inherent nature (and, by implication, within all people) but that had become dormant or had atrophied through lack of imagination. This notion—which sees the creative impulse as timeless, limitless, and unified—suggests and resolves an apparent paradox: One is able to create new modes of being the more one is able to embody states of being which already exist. South Asian philosophers who taught this view might well have agreed with Merton's observation that in genuine religious contemplation "You seem to be the same person and you are the same person that you have always been: in fact, you are more yourself than you have ever been before. You have only just begun to exist. You feel as if you were at last finally born."[7]

The Poetic Background: The World as Divine Artifact

The inspired Vedic poets who many centuries earlier (about 1200 BCE) had compiled and memorized the hymns of the *Rig Veda* viewed the entire universe as the cosmic artifact of creative deities, who were said to fashion the world through their wondrous and mysterious ability to construct three-dimensional forms of being out of nothing. These sages of old called this divine power to create objective forms *maya*, a term they reserved primarily for the gods and goddesses of the Vedic pantheon. Singing of Indra, for example, the poets proclaimed that "He made firm the sloping hills and determined that the waters flow downhill. Through his wondrous maya he supported the earth that gives food to all living beings and kept the heavens from falling" (*Rig Veda* 2.17.5); that "Effecting maya the Munificent One transforms his body and becomes any and all forms at will" (3.53.8); and that "He has been the original form of all forms; his form is to be seen in all things. Through maya Indra moves in various shapes" (6.47.18).

But this was not the only way thinkers in ancient India understood the source and direction of the creative impulse. Some did not experience creative power as coming from outside but, rather, as accessible deep within their being in moments of intuitive insight. Various verses in the *Rig Veda* reflect the idea that certain types of people possess within themselves a transformative genius, or *dhi*. Such a person was characterized, generally as *dhira*, meaning "wise, intelligent, cunning" or, perhaps more appropriately, "witty"—an apt translation since the English word "wit" comes from the same verbal root as the Sanskrit word *veda*, which means "sacred knowledge" in the sense of "the ability to see things as they really are." Some of these witty people were the Vedic sages and visionaries who through intuition (*dhiti*) possessed the wisdom to "see" the gods and goddesses who enlivened the terrestrial, aerial, and celestial realms.

The power of dhi enabled the poets to give an image to—that is, to *imagine*—sacred realities that, for less imaginative people, were invisible. The genius of imagination allowed them to solve cosmic riddles; to understand the sometimes inconsistent and even tempestuous divine personalities; and to know which sacred verses to sing in order to influence those deities and, thereby, to change the world. Thus, in Vedic India the imagination was understood to be a powerfully generative force and, in a way, divine; for through dhi, poets, like deities, were capable of transforming the worlds. This creative power was understood to come from within the poet's being, for dhi was said to reside in the mind.[8]

What was the nature of that sacred cosmos and what was it in the lives of the deities that the visionaries could "see" in the intuitive moment of dhi? Like their later philosophical counterparts in China who saw in all of the world's myriad forms of personal being reflections of a deeper impersonal unifying *tao* or "Way," Vedic poets in ancient India saw that all elements of the divine, human, and natural world fit together perfectly in an eternal and smoothly flowing symbiosis known as *rita* and that, despite their powerful and diverse personalities, even the gods and goddesses lived their lives within the structure of this cosmic law of universal harmony. The Vedic poets described evil or malicious beings as *anrita*, "against the cosmic order." Since rita was the structure of reality itself, anything that was anrita was, at the deepest level, "unreal." The intuitive flash of imagination, dhi, therefore allowed the poet to see the unified, harmonious nature of reality and to adjust his behavior so that he would not slip into the fractured and dangerous world or unreality. In so doing, he or she was said to have had access to the creative powers that made the world real to begin with. According to this view, then, a poet who through the intuitive genius of dhi properly put verses together embodied the same creative power as the deities who through their maya created the world.

It is not insignificant that the Sanskrit word *rita* is derived from the Indo-European verbal root *ar*, meaning "fit together properly, join correctly, suitably united," and that the term *rita* itself suggests a rhythmic or smoothly turning wheel of being; for it is thereby related not only to the Greek *harmos* and thus to the English *harmony* but also to the Latin *ars*, which is the root of the English *art* and *artist*. The Vedic sages who saw rita within and behind all forms of being saw the art of existence and—like the deities to whom they sang their praises—were themselves universal artists. They put things together correctly.

The Dramatic Background: The World as a Ritual Artifact

Vedic poets were not to be alone in their power to create worlds. During the period roughly between 1000 and 700 BCE, when sacerdotal texts known as the Brahmanas were compiled, Vedic priests assumed the power to create new worlds through the power of their ritual performances. By chanting the effectively transformative verses of the Vedic texts and by following the appropriate instructions, the priests worked to establish for themselves or for their patrons a place among the gods. The gods themselves were said to have created the worlds through their own ritual activities and that the human priests could join them by performing the same rites.[9] What is more, Brahmanic texts suggest that by acting out the ritual in the proper way the priests brought the world of truth out of the realm of anrita.[10] Thus, ritual drama, like poetry, was said in ancient India to possess transformative power. The priests' performance of the ritual established—that is, created—reality from within a state of unreality. Ritual was an art form.

This sacred drama (*yajna*) was performed in a three-dimensional space (*shala*) within which priests performed what were understood to be cosmically significant rites. The dimensions of the shala as a whole typically took forms analogous to those of a human body; so, for example, one sacerdotal text taught ritual architects to arrange the sacred space in the shape of a man (*purusha*), since the universe as a whole constitutes the body of the Supreme Person (*Purusha*).[11] In one of the most important of Vedic rituals known as the *Agnicayana* ("building up of the sacred fire"), the priests constructed an altar located at the "head" of the sacred space; this altar was formed in the shape of a bird[12] which was understood to carry the ritual oblations heavenwards if the priests correctly performed the rite. In other words, having gained its power from the creative and purifying fires within the ritual "body," the bird flew out of the ritual's "head" and into the heavens, carrying with it the transformative power to establish a new world. The ritual was, itself, a dramatic embodiment of creative artistry.

Even those new worlds (which the texts describe as *apurva*, "not existing previously") were sometimes said to exist either someplace else, usually in the heavens, or at some other time, namely, the future. The artistry that gave rise to them came to a large extent from the priests' power of insight into the structures of their own present being. Aware, perhaps, that those who performed the sacred drama may not always have to be able to discern the proper measurements with which to design the centrally important fire altar, the Vedic ritual tradition taught the architects to think inwardly or to "meditate" (*cintayadhvam*) on the structure of the altar. In fact, the altars were known as "structures"(*citaya*) precisely because their builders had "seen them intuitively" (*cetayamana apashyan*).[13] According to this view, then, the sacred drama, like sacred poetry, rose out of the creative imagination.

The Contemplative Background

To review briefly: Vedic visionary poets were understood to know divine truths through a process of inspiration (a rough translation of *dhi*) and thus to imagine reality as it truly was. Vedic priests were said to give this imaginary reality a body in the form of the ritual domain. In this context, the expression "imaginary reality" is not a contradiction in terms, for according to philosophers in ancient India it was precisely the imagination that interpreted the world and thereby created a cosmos: reality was an image, an artifact of creative forces.

Those creative forces were known or experienced internally. We might note in this regard that the term *dhi* is related etymologically to the word *dhyana*, which often is translated as "meditation" but which might more appropriately be understood as "contemplation" (the ability to see things as they really are, from the Latin *contemplari*). The cultivation of transformative insight through contemplation was the central concern of the philosophers who composed the major Upanishads between the seventh and second centuries BCE. Upanishadic teachings revolve around the central notion that the gods of whom the visionary poets had sung were in actuality reflections of embodiments of subjective processes within one's own being, or, as one of the oldest of such philosophical texts, the *Jaiminiya Upanishad Brahmana*, was to teach, "All of the gods are within me" (1.14.2). According to Upanishadic thought and experience, behind the spatial swirl and temporal flux of the external world as it was known by the senses lay a subtle and pervasive reality the sages called *brahman* or *atman*, the former of which usually referred to the macrocosmic ground of being while the latter signified the microcosmic innermost self, which lies within and is identical with that ultimate reality. As the author of the *Kaivalya Upanishad* noted, "The highest brahman, which is all forms, which is the supreme reality of the universe, which is the most subtle of the subtle and which is eternal, is nothing but yourself."

The practice of dhyana was said to bring a contemplative closer and closer to the universal Self, which is the creator and transformer of all things and which was known by the sages to lie deep within their very being.

Contemplations as an Art

The Upanishadic experience, centered on the ultimate identity of the world-soul with the individual-soul, stands as one of the key elements of the set of ideas and practices that by the second century BCE was generally known as *yoga* and, in a similar way, of those known by the eleventh century CE as Tantra. The word *yoga* technically means "harnessing" or "putting together" but carries the sense of "procedure" and especially connotes the practice of joining the finite with the infinite; *tantra* comes from a word meaning "weave" and has come to refer to special techniques by which one connects and joins together different states of being. Adepts at these disciplines sought to link their fundamental being with the eternal supreme being, the latter known in earlier yogic texts as *purusha* (the eternal and infinite "person") and in later yogic and tantric words as *ishvara* (the "Lord"), *devi* (the Goddess), and other terms signifying a personal supreme reality. This turning towards the original source and ultimate end of everything was for these practitioners a return inwards to the creative power of being itself. As the author of an important yogic text, the *Shiva Samhita*, noted,

In your body ...
are the two cosmic forces:
that which destroys, and that which creates ...
Yes, in your body are all things
that exist in the three worlds [of earth, sky and heaven],
all performing their prescribed functions ...
He alone who knows this
is held to be a true yogi.[14]

The yogic practice of contemplation (dhyana) was said to lead the meditative sage to a state of *samadhi*, meaning, literally, "put completely together." Since the time that Patañjali compiled the *Yoga-sutras* (that is, between 200 BCE and 500 CE), samadhi has been said to be the highest achievement, the goal and purpose of all religious practice in the tradition of Yoga.

Like the poets of the Vedic tradition who centuries earlier had seen and thus created divine worlds through power of imagination, and like the Vedic priests who constructed the sacred altars after intuitively knowing their images within, adepts in the yogic and tantric contemplative traditions skilled in the practice of dhyana formed new modes of being by imagining and then externalizing inner divine states.

These meditators often visualized such sacred universe in geometric shapes, often in association with specific images from the natural world. So, for example, yogic and tantric meditators frequently imagined the sacred universe in the form of a circle surrounded by the leaves of the cosmic lotus, a flower that in India since time immemorial has evoked images of purity, enlightenment, and creativity. Sometimes that universal circle included such images as a silvery-white crescent moon, whose semen-like color and cyclical, almost menstrual, movement through time embodied the universal forces of fertility and thus of transformative energy and creativity.

The masculine creative power, which was often known as the God Shiva, was envisioned in the form of a *lingam*, a sacred phallus represented by an upward-facing triangle, while the feminine, frequently known as Shakti (literally, "ability" in the sense of "transformative power"), took the form of the *yoni*, the sacred womb depicted as downward-facing triangle. The eternally creative combination of Shiva and Shakti within the harmonic unity of the sacred cosmos as a whole finds expression in a mystic diagram (*yantra*), perhaps the most well-known of which is the "resplendent design" or Shri Yantra in which the complementary creative forces were pictured within the gates of absolute reality. The Shri Yantra has long been one of India's most sacred of artistic forms. It is said to bring benevolence and prosperity to all who look onto it.

South Asian meditation manuals from the Medieval Period taught skilled contemplatives to practice dhyana in such a way that this and other yantras were envisioned deep within one's being. For example, adepts in the tradition known as *kundalini yoga* (in which contemplative meditators envisioned different levels of creative consciousness spinning on symbolic wheels at various points along the spinal column of the spiritual body) centered their concentrated attention on, among other possibilities, a yantra within one's heart, where it is known as the *anahata cakra*, the "wheel of being which is not destructible."

Having through dhyana joined with the creative powers deep within oneself and embodied in the wheel of consciousness, the contemplative then was taught to *externalize* that unified mode of being, to the advantage of the world around him. He did so by bringing that unifying consciousness forth from within. One way to do this was to raise it to the level of the forehead, the area of one's intuitive third-eye, at which transformative consciousness was envisioned (like the sacred bird at the "forehead" of the Vedic ritual space) as having wings that carry it outwards. Drawing it outwards, the yogi then could represent this transformative consciousness by drawing an image on the ground or wall in front of him.

This practice of externalizing in material form one's subtle inner being was fully consistent with yoga as a whole. Patañjali, the most influential of yogic philosophers, taught that dhyana involved the concentrated attention of one's mind on a single external point in space,[15] while one of Patañjali's most celebrated commentators, Vyasa, noted that this contemplative practice enabled the yogi to identify his deepest being with the external object to such a degree that the dichotomy of subject and object dissolved.[16] When this happened everything "fit together." Patañjali himself felt that this perfected state of being involved what he called *pratibha*,[17] which, like the Vedic dhi, was the revelatory "flash of illumination" into the link between or identity of a yogi's quieted mind and the object of his concentration.

According to Patañjali and therefore the yogic tradition as a whole, the yogi who had cultivated this power of insight and thus known the identity of subject and object could transform the objective world by changing the inner subject. The claims here sometimes became somewhat hyperbolic (tradition held that the perfected yogi could walk on water, fly through the air, and perform other similar feats[18]), but the message remained the same: Reality as yogis knew it was an artifact of their own inner vision and they could change their world through the power of their imagination.

The Theravada Buddhist tradition of Sri Lanka, which was influenced by Indian Yogic ideas and practices, also stressed the importance of meditation and supported the view that by focusing their inner energies meditators could bring into effect in the outside world significant transformative powers. According to Buddahaghosa, a highly influential fourth-century Theravada philosopher-monk, the practice of contemplation (*jhana*, the Pali variant of the Sanskrit *dhyana*) enabled the meditator to bring into being what he wished, to transform the natural and supernatural worlds, and to create new forms with the mind.[19] Following the Theravada tradition as a whole in regard to these teachings,[20] Buddhaghosa described such powers in extraordinary terms (the adept meditator could fly through the air, touch the moon or sun with his hand, and so on), but, again, these teachings imply a key insight: one's external life was determined by one's inner state of being. Theravada Buddhist meditators were, in effect, artists painting or sculpting their own lives.

Of course, yogic and tantric artists also painted images of the deities. They did so, though, after having contemplated—visualized—those deities within themselves. The same held true from Buddhist aesthetic traditions influenced by tantric ideas and practices. A medieval Mahayana Buddhist meditation manual composed as an aid to the worship of the goddess, Tara, taught contemplatives to sit in a quiet place bedecked with pleasant flowers; to conceive the moon in their hearts and to visualize (*pashyet*) there a blue lotus; to voice the sacred *tam*; and, imagining the brilliant rays emerging from that moon and lotus, to bring the many Buddhas and Bodhisattvas who were seen to live deep within their hearts outwards onto the background of empty space—that is, to externalize the supreme reality living within themselves in a way a painter paints an image on a wall or canvas.[21]

The Buddhist authors of this manual dedicated to the aesthetic appreciation of the goddess Tara recognized in both the contemplative and the artistic endeavors a process in which the adept externalized an inner transformative power. Like their Vedic, yogic, and tantric counterparts, the Mahayana artists who heard these lessons viewed the practice of contemplation as that which made it possible for them to reach a certain kind of *realization*—in the sense of a "making real" (*bhavanta*)[22]—of the divine self.

Notes:

1   See Heidegger, *Poetry, Language, Thought*, translated by Albert Hofstadter (New York: Harper Colophon Books, 1971), p. 6.

2   Paul Klee, *The Diaries of Paul Klee (1898–1918)*, edited by Felix Klee (Berkeley and Los Angeles: University of California Press, 1974), pp. 308, 386–87.

3   Thomas Merton, *New Seeds of Contemplation* (New York: New Directions, 1962), pp. 10–11.

4   *Abhilaṣitārthacintāmani* 1.3.158. Reference in Roger Lipsey, ed., *Coomaraswamy*, Volume 1, *Selected Papers: Traditional Art and Symbolism* (Princeton: Princeton University Press, 1977), p. 131.

5   *Śukransītāra* 4.70–71. See Ananda K. Coomaraswamy, *The Transformation of Nature in Art* (Cambridge: Harvard University Press, 1934; reprint ed. New York: Dover Publications, 1956), p. 113.

6   *Paṭisambhidā-magga*, edited by Arnold C. Taylor, 2 volumes (London: Pali Text Society, 1907), 2:205–209.

7   Merton, *New Seeds*, pp. 226–28.

8   See *Rig Veda* 9.100.3

9   See for example *Pañcaviṁsa Brāhmaṇa* 2.6.2.

10   See for example *Śatapaṭha Brāhmaṇa* 1.1.2.17 and 3.3.2.2. The "truth" (*satya*) refers to proper behavior as well to the fullness of being.

11   See *Śatapaṭha Brāhmaṇa* 15.13.1.16.10.

12   See, for example, *Śatapaṭha Brāhmaṇa* 10.1.2.1.

13   See *Śatapaṭha Brāhmaṇa* 6.2.3.9 and Lispey, *Coomaraswamy*, 1:131.

14 See Jean Varenne, *Yoga and the Hindu Tradition,* translated by Derek Coltman (Chicago: University of Chicago Press, 1976), p. 155.

15 See *Yoga-sūtra* 3.2.

16 See *Yogabhāṣya* 3.3.

17 See *Yoga-sūtra* 3.5. Other philosophers typically used the term *pratipha* instead of Patañjali's unique *pratibha.*

18 See, for example, *Yogabhāṣya* 3.45.

19 See *Visuddimagga,* edited by C. A. F. Rhys Davids (London: Pali Text Society, 1920), pp. 378ff.

20 *Paṭisambhidā-magga* 2.205–206.

21 *Kiṁcit-Vistara-Tārā Sadhana, Sādhanalmālā* 98. Gaekwad Oriental Series number 26, pp. 200–206. Lipsey, *Coomarawamy,* pp. 132–39.

22 *Ibid.,* 1:137.

CHAPTER EIGHT

•

THE SELF

Vision implies the seer. The seer cannot deny the existence of the Self.
There is no moment when the Self as Consciousness does not exist;
nor can the seer remain apart from Consciousness.
This Consciousness is the eternal Being and the only Being.

—Sri Ramana Maharshi

"Who am I?" This is a way to frame the fundamental question, the fundamental mystery, that is perhaps most accessible to us in the times we live in. What is the self? How do we know it, or how can we know it, that which is both the subject and object of consciousness? As the epigraph says, "the seer cannot deny the existence of the Self."

The Upanishads spoke of the "Self within the self," the "Inner Controller," the Immortal. This chapter opens with short quotations from various Upanishads, which contain some of the most powerful images of the self in the Hindu tradition. Most often quoted is the teaching of Rishi Uddalaka Arunayi to his son, Svetaketu: "The body dies when the Self leaves it—but the Self dies not. ... THAT ART THOU." Almost as well known is the image of the body as chariot, the "the Self as Lord of the Chariot," from the *Katha Upanishad*.

There follows a more extended meditation on the Self from the *Yoga Vasistha*, translated by Swami Venkatesananda, "To Clear the Mind," which contrasts the restless, limited mind with the peaceful, limitless self or consciousness—the self as nondifferent from the universal Self. The modern spiritual master Sri Nisargadatta Maharaj sheds light on the same subject in "The Very Fount of Bliss." In "On Being Oneself," Sri Anirvan teaches that "Every disciple in his quest is fully aware that the personal discipline he has accepted has a practical aim, which is the complete union of human consciousness with the highest reality." And in an interview, "The Heart Is the Self," the great Ramana Maharshi starts with the premise that the core of oneself, the "I," may be called "God, Self, the Heart or the Seat of Consciousness, it is all the same."

Drawing from her own experience, in "The Witness Within" Padma Perera explores what it means to be "cognizant by direct experience," and speaks movingly of how conscious and unconscious or inarticulated experience can nourish the innermost presence of oneself. "After all," she writes, " the basic gift of our conscious witness is the gift of life itself."

Finally, we return from the consciousness to which the individual seeker aspires to cosmic consciousness, in "Markandeya's Journey." Markandeya is the ultimate pilgrim, journeying through the ages of the universe, witness to the cosmic cycles of Vishnu's sleep and awakening through which the world is created and is dissolved.

Parabola
Volumes:
29.2
17.2
14.3
14.4
8.4

From the Upanishads

Svetasvatara Upanishad

As oil in sesame, as butter in cream,
As water in river beds, as fire between the fire-sticks,
So is that Self to be grasped within the self
Of him who by austerity beholds Him in very truth—

The Self who all pervades,
As butter inheres in cream
Root of self-knowledge, root of ascetic practice—
That is Brahman, that the highest teaching.[1]

Chandogya Upanishad

The Self, who is to be realized by the purified mind and
the illumined consciousness, whose form is light, whose
thoughts are true; who, like the ether, remains pure and
unattached; from whom proceeds all works, all desires,
all odors, all tastes; who pervades all, who is beyond the
senses, and in whom there is fullness of joy forever—he is
my very Self, dwelling within the lotus of my heart.

Smaller than a grain of rice is the Self; smaller than
a grain of barley, smaller than a mustard seed, smaller
than a canary seed, yea, smaller even than the kernel of a
canary seed. Yet again is that Self, within the lotus of my
heart, greater than the earth, greater than the heavens,

yea, greater than all the worlds.

He from whom proceed all works, all desires, all odors, all tastes; who pervades all, who is beyond the senses, and in whom there is fullness of joy forever—he, the heart-enshrined Self, is verily Brahman. I, who worship the Self within the lotus of my heart, will attain him at death. He who worships him, and puts his trust in him, shall surely attain him.[2]

Mundaka Upanishad

This Self, who understands all, who knows all, and whose glory is manifest in the universe, lives within the lotus of the heart, the bright throne of Brahman.

By the pure in heart is he known. The Self exists in man, within the lotus of the heart, and is the master of his life and of his body. With mind illumined by the power of meditation, the wise know him, the blissful, the immortal.

The knot of the heart, which is ignorance, is loosed, all doubts are dissolved, all evil effects of deeds are destroyed, when he who is both personal and impersonal is realized.

In the effulgent lotus of the heart dwells Brahman, who is passionless and indivisible. He is pure, he is the light of lights. Him the knowers of the Self attain.

Him the sun does not illumine, nor the moon, nor the stars, nor the lightning—nor, verily, fires kindled upon the earth. He is the one light that gives light to all. He shining, everything shines.[3]

Chandogya Upanishad

"If someone were to strike once at the root of this large tree, it would bleed, but live. If he were to strike at its stem, it would bleed, but live. If he were to strike at the top, it would bleed, but live. Pervaded by the living Self, this tree stands firm, and takes its food; but if the Self were to depart from one of its branches, that branch would wither; it if were to depart from a second, that would wither; if it were to depart from a third, that would wither. If it were to depart from the whole tree, the whole tree would wither.

"Likewise, my son, know this: The body dies when the Self leaves it—but the Self dies not.

"All that is has its self in him alone. He is the truth, He is the subtle essence of all. He is the Self. And that, Svetaketu, THAT ART THOU."

"Please, sir, tell me more about this Self."

"Be it so. Bring a fruit of that Nyagrodha tree."

"Here it is, sir."

"Break it."

"It is broken, sir."

"What do you see?"

"Some seeds, extremely small, sir."

"Break one of them."

It is broken, sir."

"What do you see?"

"Nothing , sir"

"The subtle essence you do not see, and in that is the whole of the Nyagrodha tree. Believe, my son, that that which is the subtle essence—in that have all things their existence. That is the truth. That is the Self. And that, Svetaketu, THAT ART THOU."[4]

Katha Upanishad

Know the self as Lord of the chariot,
The body as the chariot itself,
The discriminating intellect as
The charioteer, and the mind as the reins.
The senses, say the wise, are the horses,
Selfish desires are the roads they travel.
When the Self is confused with the body,
Mind, and senses, he seems to enjoy pleasure
And suffer sorrow.

When a person lacks discrimination
And the mind remains untrained, the senses
Run out of control like wild horses.
But they obey the Self like trained horses
When a person has discrimination
And the mind is taught to be one-pointed.
Those who lack discrimination, whose thoughts

Are uncontrolled and far from pure, reach not
The pure state of immortality
But wander from death to death, while they who
Have discrimination, with a still mind
And pure heart, reach journey's end, never
Again to fall into the jaws of death.
With a discriminating intellect
As charioteer and a trained mind as reins,
They attain the supreme goal of life,
To be united with the Lord of Love.[4]

Brihad-Aranyaka Upanishad

He who, dwelling in the sun, yet is other than the sun, whom the sun does
not know, whose body the sun is, who controls the sun from within—He
is your Self, the Inner Controller, the Immortal.[5]

Notes:

1 From *Hindu Scriptures*, edited and translated by Dominic Goodall (Berkeley: University of California Press, 1996).

2 Translated by Swami Prabhavananda and Frederick Manchester (New York: New American Library, Mentor Books, 1957), pp. 64-65.

3 *Mundaka Upanishad*, translated by Swami Prabhavananda and Frederick Manchester (New York: New American Library, Mentor Books, 1957).

4 Reprinted from *Dialogue with Death: The Spiritual Psychology of the Katha Upanishad* by Eknath Easwaran (Petaluma, Cal.: Nilgiri Press, 1981). Translation of *Katha Upanishad* by Eknath Easwaran copyright 1970, 1981 by the Blue Mountain Center of Meditation.

5 III: VII: 9; Robert Ernest Hume, trans, *The Thirteen Principal Upanishads* (London: Oxford University Press, 1921).

Parabola
Volume: 22.3
Conscience and
Consciousness

To Clear the Mind

From the Yoga Vasistha

How fickle is the mind! Even if it is introverted it does not remain steady, but gets agitated in a moment like the surface of the ocean. Tied to the senses (like sight) it bounces again and again like a ball. Having been nourished by the senses, the mind grasps the very objects that it has given up, and like a demented person it runs after the very things from which it had been restrained. It jumps from one object to the other like a monkey.

I shall now consider the character of the five senses through which the mind thus gets distracted. O senses, has the time not yet arrived for you all to attain self-knowledge? Do you not remember the sorrow that followed your pursuit of pleasure? Then, give up this vain excitement. Truly, you are inert and insentient; you are the avenue through which the mind flows out to reach objective experience. I am your Lord, I am consciousness and I alone do all these as the pure intelligence. You, O senses, are false. There is no connection whatsoever between you and the consciousness which is the self. In the very light of the consciousness which is nonvolitional, you function even as people perform various actions in the light of the sun. But do not entertain the false notion, O senses, that "I am intelligent," for you are not. Even the notion "I am alive," that you entertain falsely, is conducive only to sorrow.

There is nothing but consciousness, which is beginningless and endless. O wicked mind, what then are you? The notions that arise in you,
e.g., "I am the doer" and "I am the enjoyer," which appear to be great
rejuvenators, are in fact deadly poisons. Do not be so deluded, O mind;
in truth you are neither the doer of anything nor are you the experiencer.
You are inert, and your intelligence is derived from some other source.
How are pleasures related to you? You yourself do not exist; how do you
have relations? If you realize "I am but pure consciousness," then you
are indeed the self. Then how does sorrow arise in you, when you are the
unlimited and unconditioned consciousness?

Vitahavya continued to contemplate: O mind, I shall gently bring home to you the truth that you are indeed neither
the doer nor the experiencer. You are indeed inert; how can
a statue made of stone dance? If your intelligence is entirely dependent
upon the infinite consciousness, then may you live long in that realization. However, what is done with the intelligence or the energy of
another, is considered to be done by the latter. The sickle harvests with
the energy of the farmer; hence, the farmer is said to be the harvester.
Similarly, though it is the sword that cuts, the man who wields the sword
is the killer. You are inert, O mind; your intelligence is derived from the
infinite consciousness. That self or the infinite consciousness knows itself
by itself, experiences itself by itself. The Lord endeavors to enlighten you
continuously, for the wise should thus instruct the ignorant in a hundred
ways. The light of the self alone exists as consciousness or intelligence;
that itself has come to be known as the mind. If you realize this truth,
you will instantly be dissolved.

O fool, when you are in truth the infinite consciousness, why do
you grieve? That is omnipresent, that is the all; when you realize it, you
become the all. You are not, the body is not: the one infinite consciousness alone exists and in that homogenous being the diverse concepts of
"I" and "you" appear to exist. If you are the self, then the self alone exists,
not you! If you are inert, but different from the self, then you do not exist
either! For the self or infinite consciousness alone is all; there is nothing
else. There is no possibility of the existence of a third thing, apart from
the consciousness and the inert substance.

Hence, O mind, you are neither the doer nor the experiencer. You
have been used as a channel of instruction by the wise ones in their

communication with the ignorant. But, in fact, that channel is unreal and inert; the self alone is the reality. If the farmer does not use the sickle, can it harvest? The sword has no power to kill either. O mind, you are neither the doer nor the experiencer. Hence, grieve not. The Lord (consciousness) is not like you; hence do not grieve for him! He does not gain anything by either doing or not-doing. He alone pervades all; there is nothing else. Then what shall he do and what shall he desire?

You have no relationship to the self, except as the fragrance to the flower. Relationship exists only between two independent beings of similar nature when they strive to become one. You, O mind, are ever agitated; the self is ever at peace. There can thus be no relationship between you two. If, however, you enter into the state of *samadhi*, or utter equanimity, you will remain firmly established in consciousness without the distraction of diversity or the notions of either many or one, and realize that there is but one self, the infinite consciousness which shines as these countless beings.

O senses, I feel that you have all been dispelled by the light of my admonitions, for you are born of darkness of ignorance. O mind, surely your emergence as an appearance is for your own grief! See how, when you exist, countless beings get deluded and enter into this ocean of sorrow with all its prosperity and adversity, illness, old age, and death; how greed gnaws at all the good qualities and destroys them; how lust or desire distracts and dissipates their energy.

O mind, when you cease to be, all the good and noble qualities blossom. There is peace and purity of heart. People do not fall into doubt and error. There is friendship, which promotes the happiness of all. Worries and anxieties dry up. When the darkness of ignorance is dispelled, the inner light shines brightly. Mental distraction and distress cease, just as the ocean becomes calm when the wind ceases to agitate its surface. There arises self-knowledge within, and the realization of truth puts an end to the perception of the world-illusion. Infinite consciousness alone shines. There is an experience of bliss not granted to the ignorant, who are full of desires. Even as new shoots may arise from burnt leaves, a new life may emerge from this. However, he who would avoid entanglement in delusion once again, rests in self-knowledge constantly. Such are the fruits of your absence, O mind, and there are countless others. O mind, you are the support of all our hopes and desires; when you cease to be, all these hopes and desires cease. You can now choose either to be one with the reality or to cease to be an independent entity.

Your existence as identical with the self and non-different from it, is conducive to happiness, O mind. Hence, be firmly rooted in the realization of your non-existence. Surely, it is foolish to neglect happiness. If you exist as the inner being or consciousness, who will wish for your non-existence? But you are not a real entity; hence, your happiness is delusion. You were not real, you came into being through ignorance and delusion, but now through inquiry into your nature and that of the senses and the self, you have once again ceased to be. You exist as long as one does not undertake this inquiry. When the spirit of inquiry arises there is total equanimity or homogeneity. You were born of the ignorance which is the absence of wisdom and discrimination. When this wisdom arises, you cease to be. Hence, I salute wisdom! O mind, you were awakened by many means. Now that you have lost the false characteristic of a mind, you exist as the supreme being or the infinite consciousness, freed from all limitation and conditioning. That which arose in ignorance perishes in wisdom. In spite of yourself, O good mind, this inquiry has arisen in you; this is surely for the attainment of bliss. There is indeed no mind, O mind: the self alone exists, it alone is, there is nothing else. I am that self; hence, there is nothing other than me in the universe. I am infinite consciousness, whose kinetic state alone appears as the universe.

Reprinted from *The Concise Yoga Vasistha*, translated and edited by Swami Venkatesananda (Albany: State University of New York Press, 1985), pp. 241–44.

Parabola
Volume: 21.2
The Soul

The Very Fount of Bliss

Sri Nisargadatta Maharaj

Before the emanation of any words, "I" already exist; later I say mentally "I am." The word-free and thought-free state is the *atman*.

The atman per se is self-sufficient. But when it clings to the body, "treatments" such as mental and physical recreation or occupation are necessary; without these the atman cannot be tolerated by a person. For spiritual evolution, which is a requisite in the disengagement of the atman from body-identity, various disciplines have been recommended. Amongst these, the best is *namas-marana*—recitation of a holy name of God. But here God means the indwelling principle within you—the atman, which is given various names. These represent this "inner-God" who will respond no matter what names of other Gods you chant. The custom of counting beads of a rosary is merely to give occupation to your hands, but it is this inner God that you are supposed to invoke. This God is awakened when you tell the beads by reciting his name. Just as the cow's udders ooze out milk upon the sight of its calf who runs to its mother mooing "ama-ama," so also the beingness showers grace on the one who chants its holy name and tells beads in all earnestness by leading him into quietude. The keynote of recitation is to confine this "I-am-ness" within itself. The listener in you listens to the chantings and feels greatly pleased. This is the reason that people used to the daily chantings and telling of beads get restless when unable to do so.

Tukaram, the poet-saint of Maharashtra, affirms this same principle, when he sings in one of his couplets:

> *Triumphant am I, in locking in my beingness in itself, with my devotion.*
> *Thus have I reached the very pinnacle of my spiritual search, resulting in the drying up of my mental inclinations.*

The merging of beingness within itself is the very fount of bliss. Many sages who are in such a state are quite oblivious to their physical condition and simply lie on the ground, reveling in themselves. Some misguided seekers, with the aid of drugs such as marijuana, artificially induce a state of forgetfulness. But this is benumbing the senses by extraneous means. Such people will not have enduring peace, only hangovers and sour heads. If you want eternal peace, you can have it and be it through the absorbing devotional path—the *nama-japa* or *bhakti-yoga*.

Reprinted from *The Nectar of Immortality: Sri Nisargadatta Maharaj's Discourses on the Eternal,* edited by Robert Powell (San Diego: Blue Dove Press, 1996), pp. 137–38. Copyright © Jozef Nauwelaerts. Reprinted by permission of Blue Dove Press.

Parabola
Volume: 22.3
Conscience and
Consciousness

On Being Oneself

Sri Anirvan

Even the adepts of Samkhya discuss the origin of consciousness, just as much as the philosophers do: Buddhist,
Vedantist, and all others.

Truth, like life itself, is a mystery. It can be recognized,
but it cannot be analyzed nor imprisoned in words. In
this realm, all experiences lived must move imperceptibly
from the plane of outer life to the plane of inner life to
nourish that which is our essence. Then some day these
experiences will find expression in their own way by a
particular radiation. This radiation is also automatic; it
moves from the plane of inner life to that of outer life.

To be oneself, that is to say, to live in the consciousness of one's own essence, promotes the growth of a new
understanding. It is just as if delicate fingers were unfolding, one by one, the petals of a lotus.

Between the spasmodic movements of the finite and
the immobility of the infinite flows a continuous stream
of the force of *sakti*. This is the process of becoming. It
can be said that the force of sakti is continuous, since
it can be perceived as such by consciousness. But if you
believe that it is unconscious, its movement will be for
you only a succession of jerking dots and all things will
then have a beginning and an end.

But consciousness, even at the mental level, demands
continuity. It lives by duration. And duration is not a

blank word. This idea is at the root of the Vedic conception of reality as pure Existence (*satyam*), the rhythm of time (*rtam*), and constant growth (*brhat*). What is most important is the link between satyam and rtam. This is the fundamental Law of spiritual evolution.

By being conscious of oneself it is possible to pass from the plane of personality to the plane of essence, for an observer is then present. The Upanishads and the *Bhagavad-Gita* indicate different means, each one representing fragments of discipline:

1. To observe oneself with a sustained look.

2. To stand aside, without any kind of judgment whatsoever, thus allowing the essence to grow.

3. A neutral look will automatically see the disorder that reigns in the inner house; then a desire for order will arise of itself.

4. A growing essence always gives its assent.

5. The essence will become "the one that carries everything in its arms," and prakriti will follow obediently, and finally find its own place in all functions.

6. The Lord in the heart will always in the end conquer prakriti.

Between the two different levels in a being in search of himself there is always an empty space to be crossed, which provokes a chaotic movement; the more protracted the effort to cross the gap, the more violent the movement becomes.

The intermediate consciousness which opens up the way to pass from one center to another is made of very fluid matter. It is in the heart of this matter that the Guru works deeply with his ploughshare. This fluid matter has no connection either with the subject or with the object, it will find its own form in the Void. It can be activated only by the Master. For a long time, the seeker himself knows nothing about it. He has no organ with which to discover it or make use of it.

In this position, the disciple's attitude is to do nothing of his own free will, for then everything would be distorted. But he must observe with lucidity, of his level of understanding, all that takes place, and learn to recognize that "active passivity" which will become a right movement at the appropriate time. This is all that concerns him.

As regards the states through which Shri Ramakrishna passed in order to come back to a normal state of consciousness after a long period of samadhi, he said of himself, "Since the ego never dies, let it at least become a good servant of the Divine Mother!" To come out of ecstasy, when he still felt impelled to go further into his experience, he used to strike himself violently on the head. He said, "One can sing an ascending scale: sa, ri, ga, ma, pa, dha, ni ... but one cannot hold the last note for long. One has to come down again!" He had an immense wish to live, to have the whole universe enter the field of his experience. He saw life in its aspect of completeness in sakti, the life of the cosmic Laws, and he absorbed it to the very limit.

Every disciple in his quest is fully aware that the personal discipline he has accepted has a practical aim, which is the complete union of human consciousness with the highest reality. The goal is to transform the mental, vital, and even the physical nature of the being, down to the smallest cells in the body, in order to attain to the understanding of the ultimate reality (Shiva-sakti).

The extreme relativity of consciousness must never be forgotten. Those who have a highly developed personality are less easily penetrated by a new form of consciousness.

Every morning wake up, each one of you, like a young child. At noon, stand majestically as men and women in full development. In the evening, be conscious beings ripened in strength and serenity, who having drunk deep at the fountain of life, watch the approach of death. In the middle of the night, be the Void itself, the darkness of the sky in which a moon ray still shines. In this picture, I am revealing to you the secret of the Gayatri of the Vedas, the essence of the Sun and the Law of life.

From Sri Anirvan, *Letters from a Baul: Life Within Life*, compiled by Lizelle Reymond (Calcutta: Sri Aurobindo Pathamandir, 1983).

Parabola
Volume: 26.4
The Heart

THE HEART IS THE SELF

Interview with Ramana Maharshi

Devotee: *Sri Bhagavan speaks of the Heart as the seat of Consciousness and as identical with the Self. What does the Heart exactly signify?*

Ramana Marharshi: The question about the Heart arises because you are interested in seeking the Source of consciousness. To all deep-thinking minds, the enquiry about the "I" and its nature has an irresistible fascination.

Call it by any name, God, Self, the Heart or the Seat of Consciousness, it is all the same. The point to be grasped is this, that *Heart* means the very core of one's being, the Center, without which there is nothing whatever.

D: *But Sri Bhagavan has specified a particular place for the Heart within the physical body, that it is in the chest, two digits to the right from the median.*

RM: Yes, that is the Center of spiritual experience according to the testimony of Sages. This Spiritual Heart-center is quite different from the blood-propelling, muscular organ known by the same name. The spiritual Heart-center is not an organ of the body. All that you can say of the Heart is that it is the very Core of your being. That with which you are really identical (as the word in Sankrit literally means), whether you are awake, asleep, or dreaming, whether you are engaged in work or immersed in *samadhi*.

D: *In that case, how can it be localized in any part of the body? Fixing a place for the Heart would imply setting physiological limitations to That which is beyond space and time.*

RM: That is right. But the person who puts the question about the position of the Heart considers himself as existing with or in the body. While putting the question now, would you say that your body alone is here but that you are speaking from somewhere else? No, you accept your bodily existence. It is from this point of view that any reference to a physical body comes to be made.

Truly speaking, pure Consciousness is indivisible, it is without parts. It has no form and shape, no "within" and "without." There is no "right" or "left" for it. Pure Consciousness, which is the Heart, includes all; and nothing is outside or apart from it. That is the ultimate truth.

From this absolute standpoint, the Heart, Self or Consciousness can have no particular place assigned to it in the physical body. What is the reason? The body is itself a mere projection of the mind, and the mind is but a poor reflection of the radiant Heart. How can That, in which everything is contained, be itself confined as a tiny part within the physical body which is but an infinitesimal, phenomenal manifestation of the one Reality?

But people do not understand this. They cannot help thinking in terms of the physical body and the world. For instance, you say "I have come to this Asramam all the way from my country beyond the Himalayas." But that is not the truth. Where is a "coming" or "going" or any movement whatsoever, for the one, all-pervading Spirit which you really are? *You* are where you have always been. It is your body that moved or was conveyed from place to place till *it* reached this Asramam.

This is the simple truth, but to a person who considers himself a subject living in an objective world, it appears as something altogether visionary! It is by coming down to the level of ordinary understanding that a place is assigned to the Heart in the physical body.

D: *How then shall I understand Sri Bhagavan's statement that the* experience *of the Heart-center is at the particular place in the chest?*

RM: Once you accept that from the true and absolute standpoint, the Heart as pure Consciousness is beyond space and time, it will be easy for you to understand the rest in its correct perspective.

D: *It is only on that basis that I have put the question about the position of the Heart. I am asking about Sri Bhagavan's experience.*

RM: Pure Consciousness wholly unrelated to the physical body and transcending the mind is a matter of direct experience. Sages know their bodiless, eternal Existence just as the layman knows his bodily existence. But the experience of Consciousness can be with bodily awareness as well as without it. In the bodiless experience of pure Consciousness the Sage is beyond time and space, and no question about the position of the Heart can then at all arise.

Since, however, the physical body cannot subsist (with life) apart from Consciousness, bodily awareness has to be sustained by pure Consciousness. The former, by its nature, is limited to and can never be co-extensive with the latter which is infinite and eternal. Body-consciousness is merely a monad-like, miniature reflection of the pure Consciousness with which the Sage has realized his identity. For him, therefore, body-consciousness is only a reflected ray, as it were, of the self-effulgent, infinite Consciousness which is himself. It is in this sense alone that the Sage is aware of his bodily existence.

Since, during the bodiless experience of the Heart as pure Consciousness, the Sage is not at all aware of the body, that absolute experience is localized by him within the limits of the physical body by a sort of feeling-recollection made while he is with bodily awareness.

D: *For men like me, who have neither the direct experience of the Heart nor the consequent recollection, the matter seems to be somewhat difficult to grasp. About the position of the Heart itself, perhaps, we must depend on some sort of guess-work.*

RM: If the determination of the position of the Heart is to depend on guess-work even in the case of the layman, the question is surely not worth much consideration. No, it is not on guess-work that you have to depend, it is on an unerring intuition.

D: *For whom is the intuition?*

RM: For one and all.

D: *Does Sri Bhagavan credit me with an intuitive knowledge of the Heart?*

RM: No, not of the Heart, but of the position of the Heart in relation to your identity.

D: *Sri Bhagavan says that I intuitively know the position of the Heart in the physical body?*

RM: Why not?

D: *(pointing to himself) Is it to* me *personally that Sri Bhagavan is referring?*

RM: Yes. That is the intuition! How did you refer to yourself by your gesture just now? Did you not put your finger on the right side of your chest? That is exactly the place of the Heart-center.

D: *So then, in the absence of direct knowledge of the Heart-center, I have to depend on this intuition?*

RM: What is wrong with it? When a schoolboy says, "It is I that did the sum correctly," or when he asks you, "Shall I run and get the book for you?" would he point out to the head that did the sum correctly, or to the legs that will carry him swiftly to get you the book? No, in both cases, his finger is pointed quite naturally towards the right side of his chest, thus giving innocent expression to the profound truth that the Source of "I"-ness in him is there. It is an *unerring* intuition that makes him refer to himself, to the Heart which is the Self, in that way. The act is quite *involuntary* and *universal*, that is to say, it is the same in the case of every individual.

What stronger proof than this do you require about the position of the Heart-center in the physical body?

Parabola
Volume: 11.1
The Witness

The Witness Within

Padma Perera

Webster lists several definitions of both the noun and the verb *witness*, but my own interest focuses on the basically human "one who is cognizant by direct experience."

Each of us, after all, is innately capable of direct experience. Each of us has an abiding witness, within both the conscious and the unconscious levels of experience. By "conscious" I mean conscious of oneself: knowing that you know, seeing that you see. And by the "unconscious" I mean a deeper level beyond that. Finally, both are equally valid parts of our human experience.

Whether at conscious or unconscious levels, we find here a context that dispenses with the Latin tag, *testis unus testis nullus*. A single witness is no witness. My point is exactly the opposite: our sole inner witness is our only humanly enduring witness. In the second century BC, Polybius said, "There is no witness so dreadful, no accuser so terrible as the conscience that dwells in the heart of every man." True, but that is only one aspect of many. Considering the conscious side of our witness first, I will touch upon some of its other—and infinitely more various—layers and ramifications.

Beginning with the obvious, to be a conscious witness you have to be present. Presence is an essential ingredient, yes; and with it comes its corollaries:

A measure of observation: sight/insight; a good ear,

perhaps; a sense of touch or smell; an intimation, as in the case of Helen Keller, of the trapped but sentient person awakening within.

The human ability to feel, and be fallible.

Intelligence—at least intelligence enough to make the link between cause and effect, a texture and its source, etc.

The will, or lack of will, to do this.

And of course memory, that birthright of our presumably functioning selves (i.e., when not aphasic or smitten with amnesia); and, by extension, the time and the place where our conscious witness first surfaced. My mother's first memory is the earliest of any I have heard about. She remembers being put to sleep as a baby, in a cradle hung from a wooden frame. As the cradle was swung, she saw the flexible shadow of that frame go back and forth, across the ceiling. Shape and movement had come into her ken.

Her witness had begun to be simultaneously conscious both of what she perceived in the outside world *and* of herself perceiving it—that double awareness which illuminated the memory, and anchored it for her. Here is an early, even rudimentary, instance of the way our witness can both participate in our experience and observe it with detachment. Growing with us and sharing our personal journeys, the detached observer inside can also sometimes flash its own signals, set its own standards.

This entails a certain integrity toward experience—something that tries to stay honorably with our sorrows, taking no durable solace either from wallowing in them or escaping from them; something that stays behind, unsatisfied by frenetic pursuits of pleasure, but that can burst into fullness in a moment of wonder and joy. Our inner witness is by no means heavily moralistic: perhaps it is just stubborn.

One of the proverbs in my mother-tongue deals with the neem tree whose bitter leaves … fretted nervous and delicate against a chunky bark … contain medicinal properties. "Even if you sugar the manure for a neem," runs our saying, "it will stay bitter, and heal."

The neem may be fortunate. Most of us struggle with the concurrent demands of human existence while striving to remain true to our endeavors. An artist friend of mine speaks of a time when everything in her life had disintegrated: every prop, big or little, pulled out from under her. She had reached that point, which we all face sooner or later, of recognizing that the only thing we can be secure about is our ultimate insecurity. "Even then, some witness in me remained, watching and waiting and making notes, until I could work again."

In experiences like hers, the witness takes on another aspect, enters another sphere: evoking dedication to a chosen task, and demanding an integrity of effort as well as accomplishment, of processes as well as results. We are speaking not of talent, but of the role of this "creative" witness in harnessing that talent—its role, in fact, in any significant contribution toward any field of life.

The successful results, of course, are the easiest to see. For example, great or good art is itself essentially a creative witness of life: expressed and attested to in diverse ways by the individual artists' vision, idiom, and skill. It's right *there*—from seashells to the sculptural forms they summoned for Henry Moore, from Degas's bowed-down laundresses to his leaping ballerinas, from Dostoyevsky's Prince Myshkin to Rilke's Malte Laurids Brigge; and so much else besides, affirming all the nameless artisans and architects from Tikal to Angkor Wat, all the performers and givers of gifts down the centuries.

Less visible, though as crucial, is the role of such a witness in the processes and efforts involved. It stands behind an aspect of the creative will—which must not be confused with the creative impulse. The witness here has nothing to do, either, with a monstrous artistic ego trampling upon everybody else to gain its own ends; it resounds on a more comprehensively human note in the creative process: that part of the artist, cited by my friend, which tries not only to surmount but to integrate the stringencies of life. The creative witness provides patience and persistence and for some it does even more—it can save the artist's sanity as a human being. A cousin of mine, for one, comes to mind. Meeting her after several years, during which she had been through unutterably harrowing experiences, I asked her how she had been able to survive. "By painting," she said. "I'd lock myself up in my room and paint. Some things I tore up, they only reflected the mess. Those I kept were those that saw and remembered there could be another world. I made that world to fight the world I was living in." These worlds of hers were subsequently exhibited across Europe and Asia. They possess a rich, calm, and classic order, as old as it is new.

When the conscious witness stands behind a creative will, however, it need not necessarily pertain to art alone. Trying to live a wise and examined life can perhaps require the greatest creativity of all. I know my father has used that will in himself—past childhood hardships, past the renown and respect he won as an adult. Now facing the physical limitations of old age, he has journeyed toward himself and arrived at a rare, luminous new understanding that lights up any encounters with him. Children come into its orbit; neighbors; passers-by pausing for a chat; even plants flourish and bloom in this place of growing quietness. You can't quite ask him how he got there. Being reticent about his ordeals and confrontations, all he will allow his witness to say is: "I have seen some things. Now I have to see other things."

But there are regions, which the conscious witness inhabits, beyond serenity or creative will. In the last stages of a mortal disease, in the endless dailiness of poverty as experienced in India, Ethiopia, and elsewhere—in any such basic of life and death, we don't know how the witness endures. Unless outsiders are deeply involved, they haven't the right to speak; and no single experience in the range of human experience can totally speak for all. Yet each has the choice and capacity (in whatever degree) to use its faculties to act upon empathy, wherever it can. And this includes the impulse to battle the man-made mutilations that surround us—from cruelty, injustice, and greed to a nuclear insanity that could destroy all our survivals.

In the deepest sense, each one's witness can be an empathetic witness to the eloquence of another's life. Obviously witnesses can be as various as individuals, and doubtless as shackled by ignorance, or by the convenience of their convictions. But in the compassionate arena to which I now allude, some things get stripped away. Mere intelligence, for instance, won't do. A true witness here needs human imagination, without which sympathies get sluggish, our world-view contracts, and all life as we know it lies open to extinction. Another proverb: *vinaasha kaala vipareethe buddhi*. "In the age of destruction, intelligence becomes overweeningly stupid."

After all, at its best and simplest, the basic gift of our conscious witness is the gift of life itself. At age seven, I found my mother sitting on the grass outside our house and asked her what she was doing. "I'm not doing anything," she said. "I'm just being." And after a while we looked, side by side, at a spider web.

In embarking upon the unconscious domain of our inner witness, I have first to make a brief foray into the purlieus of what is called "psychic experience," which has nothing to do with the sensational occult. For those of us who are somehow naturally attuned to certain intangible clues, these feel as factual and four-square as tables and chairs. It's simple enough. Personally, I find some of the laboratory research on parapsychology quite absurd. Knowing whether a hidden pack of cards opens on the four of hearts or the six of clubs, whether you see four red smudges or six black, seems like pointless child's play. Living an international existence as I do, more to my point is whether those I love, continents away, are all right. And sometimes when I still my mind of its squabbles and distractions, and sometimes even when I don't, I can sense how it is with them. Something in me can also send messages across to something in my brother, when telephones don't answer or even telegrams go astray. Myself, I don't fish too deep for the where-withal of all this, merely describing this condition of receptivity—of at times voluntarily relinquishing control—as "letting life live me." Too often I have distrusted my peripatetic witness despite its years of reliability, since proof usually comes straggling behind later, and we are all heir to doubt.

But extra-sensory perception only hovers on the littorals of something far more difficult to express. Approaching this deepest layer of the unconscious witness, I will refer to an observation in Vedantic philosophy—for not only a Vedantist but every human being has experienced the three states of awareness detailed in the Upanishads: your waking state, when your faculties are alert to the solid actualities, the external stimuli around you; your dream state, responsive to subtler psychological reaches; and finally (the crux here) that third state of deep and dreamless sleep, where all relationships between the subjective and the objective have ceased to exist ... where a part of yourself—call it Inner Consciousness, or your breathing entity, or whatever you like—still remains a witness to your life. A steadfast presence, however beleaguered your waking or dreaming states, it returns unimpaired night after night. And to the end it retains no attributes: no vivid five senses, no purposefully operative intelligence, no specific image or memory, no adjectives, no words at all.

Some might see this as an insensate retrogression to vegetative existence, but Vedanta takes the attributeless witness much higher: from its usual existence in deep sleep to the possibility of an ultimately evolved and transcendent awareness, equally without attributes.

For my part, I have seen lulled and well-meaning meditators having to be nudged awake. And in my language we joke, when someone dozes off in the middle of something, that he or she has hit *samadhi*—that transcendent state, through which this individual snores away to oblivion. The serious connection implied beneath the jest is this: If our unconscious witness has natural access to an area beyond attributes, it can journey there, unsleeping—spontaneously or otherwise.

Groping after a concrete and describable analogy, I come up with memories of going to the temple as a child, in the far south of India. There was nothing particularly "religious" about the experience. It is rather the totality of texture that stays with me still.

The *gopuram* or gate towered into the sky, a gigantic twelfth-century stone structure, every inch carved with scenes from mythology and an abundance of life forms: crocodiles, snakes, birds, flowers … many too high to be deciphered from below. The threshold was marked by a huge golden step I had to hop across, right foot forward. Inside, a passageway was first to be traversed clockwise from left to right, all the way around. (Circumambulating, so that you not only honored the central shine but contained it … the *sanctum sanctorum* being significantly called "*garbha griha*": "garbha" meaning womb, "griha" meaning house. Not only the womb but the house, the home of the womb—the source.)

Near the entrance stood a stone pillar with a frieze of elephants around it, at just about my height: trunk curling into tail curling into trunk. I would keep running my hand along them, around and around and around, until they were part of my palm and my palm was a part of them. A private ritual. Each time. Having to know what it was like to be an animal before you could enter a shrine.

Within, the smoky erratic flicker of oil lamps probed but never dispelled the dark. When the priest started to chant, his voice rose and echoed and melted away: into that shadow, into that stone. And when he stopped, the silence was as sculptured as the stone.

It was as if all boundaries had disappeared: between sound and stillness—between you and what you saw.

Gone. Beyond logic or possibility.

At the time, I had no words for this. Even now, as an adult, I find that none quite fit, though the same thing can happen away from the temple, on the opposite side of the earth. Of course I am not alone in this inarticulacy; examples have been noted before, all over the world.

Since the unconscious witness has no truck with words, we return and apply to the conscious witness for any attempts to communicate. Describing her similar experience while watching the sunset one evening, and merging imperceptibly into it, my mother wrote to me: "Somewhere along the way, my seeing eye was no longer an individual point but a part, as it were, of the whole circumference."

In the end we use attributes to get beyond attributes. We recognize a presence that absorbs its seeming absence, and persists as the deepest part of witness within.

Parabola
Volume: 13.2
Repetition and
Renewal

Markandeya's Journey

Heinrich Zimmer

Enclosed in the coils of the serpent Ananta, "The End-less," Vishnu sleeps, partly floating and partly submerged in the cosmic ocean. There is no one to watch, no knowledge of him except within himself.

Outside the divine dreamer is darkness. The god has consumed again the Web of the Universe, like a spider that has climbed up the thread issuing from its own body and then draws back into itself.

Inside the god, like an unborn child, lies the cosmos, an ideal vision of what the universe should be.

Markandeya, a pilgrim, wandered throughout the world inside the body of the god. He visited holy places where he stopped to worship. Although many thousands of years old, he possessed unaging strength and an alert mind.

Vishnu slept, mouth open, breathing deeply with a rich sonority in the immense silence of the night of Brahma. Suddenly, the astonished Markandeya fell through the mouth of the god and plunged headlong into the cosmic sea. At first bewildered, gradually he became aware of the utterly dark ocean stretching far into the all-embracing, starless night. Seized by despair, he failed at first to see the body of Vishnu. Splashing about in the dark water, he began to doubt. "Is this a dream? Am I under the spell of illusion?" At last he became aware of the sleeping god, and he was filled with amazement and joy. The enormous shape broke from the waters like a mountain range and glowed with a wonderful inner light. As Markandeya swam closer and was about to ask the sleeper's identity, the giant seized him up and swallowed him.

Again Markandeya found himself in the familiar harmonious world of Vishnu's dream, but now totally confused. Which world was real? The dark, formless ocean outside or the comfortable illusion within? "It must have been a vision or a dream," he thought to himself, and he resumed his wandering.

He wandered as before over the wide earth observing yogis practicing austerities and Brahmins officiating at sacrificial rituals for another hundred years. Then the unimaginable happened: again he slipped from the sleeper's mouth and tumbled into the pitch-black sea. This time, in the darkness and water-desert of silence he saw a luminous babe, a god-like boy asleep under a fig tree. Then, under the spell of Maya, illusion, he saw the god in the guise of the divine child at play, apparently oblivious of the vast ocean. His eyes could not stand the dazzling splendor of the child so he kept at a distance. He thought, "Something like this happened a long time ago." Almost, he could remember when it happened before, but then his mind was overcome by fear of the fathomless depths of the shoreless ocean. Just then, the child called gently to him. "Welcome, Markandeya. Do not be afraid, my child. Do not fear. Come hither."

Markandeya was shocked and offended by the boy's common use of his name. After all, was he not an ageless and respected saint? He burst into a display of temper. "Who presumes to ignore my dignity, my saintly character and to make light of the treasure of magic power stored in me through my austerities? Not even Brahma would address me so irreverently. He addresses me courteously as O Long-Lived One."

Unperturbed, the divine child continued, "Child, I am thy parent, thy father and elder, the One who bestows all life. Why do you not come to me? Your father practiced severe austerities to beget a son. Pleased with his efforts I granted him a gift and he requested that you should never grow old. You stem from his secret care of existence. That is why you are now able to see me playing here as a child on the primal, all-containing cosmic waters."

In humble surrender Markandeya asked, "Let me know the secret of your Maya. Lord of the Universe, by what name are you known?"

Vishnu replied, "I am the Primordial Cosmic Man, Narayana. He is the waters, the first being, the source of the universe. I have a thousand heads. I am the cycle of the year which generates everything and again dissolves it. I am the cosmic juggler, the magician who works wonderful illusions. I am the Creator and at the same time I am the Whirlpool. I put an end to everything that exists. My name is Death of the Universe."

The deep-booming voice of the child continued, instruction rolling from his lips as a beautiful song. "I am the holy order, I am the glowing fervor of ascetic endeavor, I am all those appearances and virtues through which the true essence of existence manifests itself. I am the Lord-Creator-and-Generator-of-all-Being. From me originates whatever has been, shall be or is. Obey the laws of my eternal order and wander in happiness through the universe within my body. Brahma lives in my body and all the gods and the holy seers. I am beyond the goals of human life—gratification of the senses, pursuit of prosperity and pious fulfillment of sacred duties—yet I point out these three goals and the proper aims of earthly existence."

With a swift motion, Vishnu brought the holy Markandeya again to his mouth and swallowed him, so that he vanished again into the gigantic body. This time he was content to rest alone in solitary place and listen to "The Song of the Immortal Gander," the hardly audible, secret, yet universal melody of God's life-breath, flowing in and out. And this is the song Markandeya heard:

> *Many forms do I assume*
> *And when the sun and moon have*
> *disappeared*
> *I float and swim on the expanse of the*
> *waters.*
> *I am the Gander.*
> *I am the Lord.*
> *I bring forth the universe from my essence.*
> *I abide in the cycle of time that dissolves it.*

Markandeya sits, listening to this song, to the breathing of the Highest Being. The sound is the sound of the gander, singing, "ham-sa, *ham-sa*," but at the same time, "*sa-'ham, sa-'ham*." *Sa* means "this," *ham* means

"I." "This am I."

Enclosed in the coils of the endless serpent Ananta, Vishnu sleeps, partly floating and partly submerged in the cosmic ocean. There is no one to watch, no knowledge of him except within himself. …

Adapted by Barbara Reser from Heinrich Zimmer, *Myths and Symbols in Indian Art and Civilization*, edited by Joseph Campbell (Princeton: Princeton University Press, 1946).

GLOSSARY

abhinaya – acting

acharya (ācārya) – guru, spiritual leader

adharma – absence of dharma

adityas – opponents of the daityas; doers of good

Advaita Vedanta (Advaita Vedānta) – "non-dual" teaching of the identity of Atman and Brahman

Agni – god of fire

ahimsa (ahiṃsā) – nonviolence

Alaxmi, Alakshmi (Alakṣmī) – goddess of misfortune, sister of Lakshmi

Almora – center of traditional study in the Himalayan foothills

Amaravati (Amarāvatī) – Indra's "immortal city"

amrita (amṛta) – elixir of immortality

Ananta – "endless"; the cosmic serpent in whose coils Vishnu sleeps

anrita (anṛta) – against the cosmic order, evil, ultimately "unreal"

Artabhaga (Ārtabhāga), learned Brahmin who challenged Yajnavalkya

artha – wealth, material well-being; one of the traditional four aims of life

asura – demon, enemy of the gods

atman (ātman) – the "inner controller" of the self; (also sometimes cap.) the Self, the sole Reality, Brahman

avatar (avatāra) – one of the ten incarnations of Vishnu

avidya (avidyā) – ignorance

Bhagavad Gita (Bhagavad Gītā) – "Song of the Lord"; portion of the *Mahabharata*, book 6

Bhagavata Purana (Bhāgavata Purāṇa) – a long purana, stories of the world and Krishna's manifestations; sacred text for devotees of Krishna

bhakti – devotion, attitude of loving devotion toward a deity.

bhramara – black bee, messenger from Krishna to the gopis

Bhumi Devi (Bhumī Devī) – Mother Earth

Brahma (Brahmā) – one the great gods; sometimes called the Creator

Brahman – the ultimate divinity or Reality

Brahmanas (Brāhmaṇas) – prose interpretations (c. 1000–700 BCE) of the rituals and mantras of each Veda *brahmin* or *brahman* (brāhmaṇa) – member of the highest varna; priest

Brighu (Bṛghu) – a great sage

Brihaspati (Bṛhaspati) – chief advisor and purohita of Indra

Buddha – "The Awakened"; Vaishnavas consider him an avatar of Vishnu

cankam (caṅkam) (pronounced sangam) – classical Tamil poetry (c. 100 BCE – 250 CE); over 2,000 poems are known

Chaitanya – charismatic Bengali saint, 1486–1533, highly influential founder of a bhakti movement in north India

daitya – a demon

Daksha (Dakṣa) – Lord of the ten world guardians, father of Sati, whom Shiva married

dakshina (dakṣina) – gift

darshan (darśana) – sight or vision of a deity or, by extension, anyone to be honored

Dasharatha (Daśaratha), father of Rama in the *Ramayana*

Deepavali (Dīpāvalī, Dīwālī) – festival of lamps, held in honor of Lakshmi

deva – god; generally refers to Vishnu, Shiva, or one of the other great gods

devi (devī) – goddess

dharma – "right order"; religious duty, law, and custom; by extension, moral order in society as a whole

dharmashastra (dharmaśāstra) – one of the classical texts laying out the strictures of dharma

dhi (dhī) –transformative genius, inner vision of sacred realities

dhyana (dhyāna) – contemplation, meditation; cultivation of dhi

Dom – caste that cares for the cremation ground at Banaras

Draupadi – heroine of the *Mahabharata*

Durga (Durgā) – fierce goddess

Dvaparayuga – the third of the great ages of the world cycle; 864,000 years long

Ganesha (Gaṇeśa) – elephant-headed god, Shiva's first son, and god of beginnings and remover of obstacles

Gargi (Gārgī) – wife of Yajnavalkya, who presses him with questions

Garuda (Garuḍa) – king of birds, Vishnu's mount

ghat – steps leading down to a river

gopis (gopīs) – cowherd women; village girls and women, devotees of the child Krishna

guru – spiritual teacher

gurukula – school; traditionally, learning in the home of the guru

Hanuman – the "monkey god," Rama's faithful servant and god of immense strength

hotri (hotṛ) – priest responsible for ritual recitations

Indra – Vedic hero, king of the gods

Janaka – legendary king of Videha, who questions Yajnavalkya

jiva (jīva) – individual soul

jnana (jñāna) – "knowing"; contemplative religious knowledge

Kabir (Kabīr) – devotional poet (1440–1518), critical of both Islam and Hinduism

Kaikayi (Kaikeyī) – younger queen of Dasharatha, at whose demand Rama went into exile

Kalakshetra – dance school founded in Madras in 1936 by Rukmini Devi

kalakuta (kālākūṭa) – "the puzzle of Time"; the poison that was churned up and swallowed by Shiva in the churning of the ocean

Kali (Kālī) – fierce goddess especially revered in Tantrism

Kalidasa (Kālidāsa) – poet and dramatist (c. 400 BCE), author of the famous drama *Shakuntala*

Kaliyuga – fourth and last, degenerate, era in which we now live; said to have begun in 3102 BCE; will last 432,000 years

kama (kāma) – desire, passion, especially sexual; (cap) the god of love

Kama Dhenu (Kāma Dhenu) – wish-granting celestial cow

Kampan (Kampaṇ) – Tamil poet (c. 1180–1250), author of the Tamil *Ramayana*

kapalakriya (kapālakriyā) – rite of breaking the skull during cremation

karma – action and its consequences in this life or subsequent lives

Kaurava – royal house whose army was defeated in the *Mahabharata* war

kavi – poet-seer

Krishna (Kṛṣṇa) – one of the most popular gods in Hindusim; traditionally taken as one of the incarnations of Vishnu, though his devotees understand him to take primacy over Vishnu

Kritayuga (Kṛtayuga) – the first of the great ages of the world cycle, also called Satyuga; 1,728,000 years long

kshatriya (kṣatriya) – the second varna, traditionally warriors

kundalini yoga (kuṇḍalinī yoga) – system of meditation on different centers of energy along the length of the torso and head

Lakshman, Laxmana (Lakṣmaṇa) – faithful brother of Rama

Lakshmi, Laxmi (Lakṣmī) – goddess of good fortune; Vishnu's principal wife

Lanka (Laṅkā) – island home of Ravana, villain of the *Ramayana*

lila (līlā) – divine "play"

linga (liṅga) – aniconic phallic emblem of Shiva, normally resting on base representing yoni, female sexual organ

Mahabharata (Mahābhārata) – longer of the two great Sanskrit epics, recounting the great war between the Kauravas and the Pandavas

mahakavya (mahākāvya) – long poem

mahapralya (mahāpralya) – the dissolution of the world at the end of a hundred years of Brahma

maharaja (mahārāja) – "great king"; common honorific for a guru

maharishi (mahārṣī – "great sage")

mahatmya (mahātmya) – paean of praise for a sacred place or deity

mahayuga (mahāyuga) – a cycle of four yugas

Mandara – the central mountain of the world

mantra – sacred formula or chant

Manusmriti (Manusmṛti) – *The Laws of Manu*, the most famous dharmashastra text

maya (māyā) – "illusion"; (cap) the often personified power of the gods to create the world and hide the truth behind its phenomena

moksha (mokṣa) – liberation or salvation from the cycle of rebirth

Muchalinda (Mucalinda) – serpent king

Mucukunda – titanic warrior who, after his battles, chose to sleep for many ages and was awakened by Krishna

naga (nāga) – serpent

Namalvar (Namālvār) – Tamil poet (tenth century?), devotee of Vishnu

Nandi – Shiva's white bull

Nandini – daughter of Kama Dhenu, the wish-fulfilling cow

Nataraja (Naṭarāja) – form of Shiva as Lord of the dance

Nilakantha, Nilakanthus (Nīlakaṇṭha) – "Blue Throat," epithet of Shiva following his swallowing of kalakuta

Pandava (Pāṇḍava) – royal family whose army, led by Arjuna, fights the Kauravas in the *Mahabharata* war

parampara (paramparā) – lineage, unbroken tradition

Patanjali (Patañjali) – author of *Yoga Sutra* (about 200 BCE), expounding Raja Yoga

pinda (piṇḍa) – rice or flour ball offered to spirits of ancestors

pishacha (piśāca) – demon

pitri (pitṛ) – ancestor to whom rites are offered

preta – ghost

prakriti (prakṛti) – original form or state, nature; often paired with purusha

puja (pūjā) – worship, normally comprising a series of offerings and services

purana (purāṇa) – one of several collections of stories about deities, reaching their present form about 500 CE

purohita – family priest

purusha (puruṣa) – "male"; (cap.) the primeval Man sacrificed to create the world; often paired as a complement with prakriti

Radha (Rādhā) – Krishna's principal lover among the gopis

Raja Yoga (Rāja Yoga) – system of yoga first taught by Patanjali

rakshasa (rākṣasa) – powerful demon

Rama (Rāma) – incarnation of Vishnu; model king and virtuous husband, hero of the *Ramayana*, and one of the most popular gods in Hinduism

Ramakrishna Paramahansa, Sri (Śrī Rāmakṛṣṇa Paramahaṇsa) – Bengali mystic (1834–1886)

Ramayana (Rāmāyaṇa) – shorter of the two great Sanskrit epics, telling the story of Rama

Ravana (Rāvaṇa) – demon king of Lanka, who abducted Sita and was vanquished by Rama

rasa lila (rāsa līlā) – musical dance dramas depicting pastimes in the childhood and youth of Krishna

Rig Veda (Ṛg Veda) – the earliest of the Vedas; a collection of 1,028 hymns; composed during several centuries, from at least 1200 BCE

rishi (ṛṣī) – forest sage of antiquity

rita (ṛta) – the structure of reality, perceived by dhi

Sahaj Marg – a system of Raja Yoga based on heart-centered meditation

samsara (saṃsāra) – the ceaseless cycle of death and rebirth

sannyasin (sannyāsin) – ascetic renouncer

sat–chit–ananda – "it is, it is consciousness, it is delight"; a definition of Brahman

Savitri (Savitrī) – wife of Brahma

Shaivite (Śaivite) – pertaining to, or devotee of, Shiva

shakti (śakti) – divine power; (cap) the Goddess as a personification of power, especially Shiva's consort

Shankara (Śaṇkara) – extremely influential founder of the Advaita Vedanta school of philosophy

Shankaracharya (Śaṇkarācārya) – Shankara; a spiritual leader who is considered to be in his spiritual lineage

shishya (śiṣya) – disciple or pupil of guru

Shiva (Śiva) – alongside Vishnu, one of the two most important great gods of Hinduism

shraddha (śraddhā) – rites for the dead

shudra (śūdra) – the fourth and lowest of the varnas; traditionally, a servant

Sita (Sītā) – Rama's wife

Sugriva (Sugrīva) – monkey king allied with Rama; Hanuman was his minister

Surdas, Sur Das (Sūrdās), sixteenth-century poet-singer, devotee of Krishna

Surpanakha (Sūrpaṇakha) – Ravana's sister, mutilated by Lakshman, in revenge for which Ravana abducted Sita

Surya (Sūrya) – the sun god

swami – master; common honorific for a guru

Tevaram (Tevāram) – a collection of Tamil hymns, composed sixth to eighth centuries CE by three poet-saints collectively called Nayanar

Tretayuga (tretāyuga) – the second of the great ages of a world cycle; 1,296,000 years long

Tulsi Das (Tulsī Dās) – (1532–1623) author of the *Ramcaritmanas*, a Hindi version of the story of Rama and Sita

turiya (tūriya) – the fourth state of consciousness, beyond waking, dream, and sleep

Uddhava – companion and minister of the adult Krishna

Upanishads (Upaniṣads) – texts composed during the second to seventh centuries BCE, sources of Vedanta teachings; they expound especially aspects of the Self and aim to develop transformative insight

Vaishnava (Vaiṣṇava) – pertaining to Vishnu; a worshiper of Vishnu

vaishya (vaiśya) – third of the varnas, traditionally comprising tradesmen or peasants

Vali (Vāli) – monkey king killed by Rama on behalf of Sugriva

Valmiki (Vālmīki) – legendary author of the *Ramayana*

varna (varṇa) – one of the four classes (once called castes) into which Hindu society was traditionally divided

Varuna (Varuṇa) – ancient Vedic deity, ruler of the invisible world and the waters

vasana (vāsānā) – impression remaining in the unconscious

Vasishtha, Vashishtha, Visishttha (Vāśiṣṭha) – an ancient forest priest

Vasuki (Vāsuki) – the great serpent who was the rope for the churning of the ocean

vatsalya (vātsalya) – parents' love for their children

Vayu (Vāyu) – the wind god

Veda – "knowledge"; revealed, authoritative sacred knowledge; the four ancient texts containing it: Rig, Yajur, Sama, and Atharva Veda

Vedanta (Vedānta) – "after the Vedas"; teachings that devalue ritual and sacrifice and emphasize the identity of the individual self with the Atman

vidvat-sannyasa (vidvat-sannyāsa) – mystical path taken after an inner awakening

vidya (vidyā) – knowledge, learning

vilaiyatal (viḷaiyāṭal) – (Tamil) play; = lila

viraha – separation and the consequent feeling of loss

Vishnu (Viṣṇu) – with Shiva, one of the two most important deities in Hinduism; his ten avatars include Buddha, Rama, and Krishna

Vivekananda, Swami (Swāmī Vivekānanda) – Bengali teacher (1863–1902) inspired by Sri Ramakrishna, who brought Vedanta to the West beginning in 1893

vividisa-sannyasa (vividisā-sannyāsa) – a path of inner search taken as a result of conscious decision or instruction of a guru

Vrindaban (Vṛndāvana) – pilgrimage center on the Yamuna River south of Delhi, traditionally the boyhood home of Krishna

Vritra (Vṛtra) – "obstacle"; cosmic serpent defeated by Vishnu

Vyasa (Vyāsa) – hermit and sage; the *Mahabharata* is attributed to him

yajna (yajña) – Vedic sacrifice

Yajnavalkya (Yājñavalkya) – Upanishadic teacher, a great sage

yantra – mystic diagram; most importantly, the Sri Yantra, consisting of interlocking upward- and downward-facing triangles

Yashoda (Yaśodā) – Krishna's mother in Vrindaban

yatra – journey, pilgrimage

yoga – spiritual discipline; more specifically, a system of exercises to gain control of one's mind and body

yogin, yogi (yogī) – one who practices yoga; particularly an ascetic renouncer who does so

yuga – one of the four great ages of a world cycle

CONTRIBUTOR PROFILES

Sri Anirvan (1896–1978) was a Baul (Bengali mystic) master in the
Samkhya and Sahajya traditions. He wrote almost exclusively in
Bengali, and his teachings are known in the West largely through
the translations and writings of Lizelle Reymond, who studied and
worked with him for many years.

Rosemary Jeanes Antze first studied Viniyoga with T. K.V. Desikachar
in 1974, when she spent a year in India studying Odissi dance. In the
three decades since, she has pursued her study and has taught dance
and yoga at the University of Toronto.

Sri Aurobindo (1872–1950), born Aurobindo Ghose in Calcutta, was
educated in England. In 1893 he returned to India and worked in
the Baroda civil service, while he also learned Sanskrit and modern
Indian languages, and wrote poetry and other literary works. In 1906
he moved to Bengal and became a prominent radical nationalist; as a
result, he was imprisoned for a year, during which time he practiced
yoga. In 1910, in answer to an inner call, Sri Aurobindo sailed for
Pondicherry to devote himself entirely to his spiritual mission, and
he spent the rest of his life there. Sri Aurobindo's spiritual collabora-
tor, a French woman known as the Mother, joined him in 1920 and
an ashram grew around them. Aurobindo's collected works run to
some thirty volumes. The Mother wrote that *Savitri*, his epic poem,
was "the supreme revelation of Aurobindo's vision."

Marvin Barrett (1920–2006) was a writer and former journalist who
was for many years a senior editor of *Parabola* magazine. His books
include *Second Chance: A Life after Death* (1999).

Ma Jaya Sati Bhagavati was born Joyce Green in Brooklyn, where after
her mother's death she lived and learned on the streets. She had her
first spiritual experience in 1972 when Christ spoke, telling her to
"teach all ways, as all ways are mine." Subsequently Ma Jaya was led
to her teacher Swami Nityananda and then to her guru, Neem Karoli
Baba. She founded Kashi Ashram in Roseland, Florida, in 1976

and said she had acquired the power of the goddess Kali. She has dedicated her life to spiritual teaching, care for those suffering from AIDS, and interreligious dialogue.

Margaret H. Case was for many years Asian Studies editor at Princeton University Press and is volume editor of a number of books on Indian subjects. She has a Ph.D. in Indian history from the University of Chicago. In the 1990s she spent several years in Vrindaban, India, from which experience she wrote *Seeing Krishna: The Religious World of a Brahmin Family in Vrindaban* (2000).

Swami Chetanananda, born Michael Shoemaker, founded the Nityananda Institute in Bloomington, Indiana, in 1971 under the direction of his guru, Swami Rudrananda. Swami Chetanananda was initiated as a swami or "master of oneself" in 1978 in Ganeshpuri, India, with Swami Muktananda presiding. In addition, he has been initiated into the ancient Tibetan Buddhist ritual practices of Phowa and Chöd, as well as others from the Longchen Nyingthig and Padampa Sangye Shi-je (pacification of suffering) tradition.

Ananda K. Coomaraswamy (1877–1947), born in Ceylon and educated in England, was a cardinal figure in twentieth-century art history and the cultural confrontation of east and west. His writings—about 1,000 items in all—range over the visual arts, aesthetics, literature, religion, metaphysics, and sociology. From 1932 to 1947 he was curator in the Department of Asiatic Art at the Boston Museum of Fine Arts, where he built the first large collection of Indian art in the United States.

Rama Devagupta holds a doctorate in bioorganic chemistry from Texas A&M University and is a full-time mother and freelance writer on parenting issues and spirituality. She teaches the Sahaj Marg system of Raja Yoga as a preceptor of Shri Ram Chandra Mission in Houston, Texas.

Wendy Doniger has been professor of the history of religions at the University of Chicago since 1978 and is a translator of numerous

Sanskrit texts, including the *Rig Veda*, *Laws of Manu*, and *Kamasutra*. Her principal teaching and research interests are Hinduism and mythology, but she draws material from many traditions, including Greek myths, the Hebrew Bible, medieval romance, Shakespeare, and Hollywood. She has written over twenty books, among them *Other People's Myths: The Cave of Echoes*; *The Bedtrick: Tales of Sex and Masquerade*; *The Origins of Evil in Hindu Mythology*; and, most recently, *The Woman Who Pretended to Be Who She Was*.

Ecknath Easwaran (1911–1989) was an English professor and Sanskrit scholar in India before emigrating to the United States in 1959. In 1961 he established the Blue Mountain Center of Meditation in California. At UC Berkeley he taught in 1968 what may have been the first academic course on meditation offered for credit at a major American university.

Diana L. Eck is professor of comparative religion and Indian studies at Harvard. Her research interests encompass subjects in both India and America, and her books include *Darśan: Seeing the Divine Image in India* (1981) and *Banaras: City of Light* (1982). Since 1991 she has headed the Pluralism Project, which explores the religious dimensions of America's new immigration.

Shrivatsa Goswami is a member of an eminent family of spiritual leaders and scholars at Sri Radharamana Mandir, Vrindavan, India. He is director of the Sri Caitanya Prema Samsthana, a research institution devoted to Vaishnava studies and the culture of the Vraja region, and is the author of several articles and the book *Celebrating Krishna* (2004).

John Stratton Hawley is professor of religion at Barnard College, Columbia University. His life work is the translation of the poems of the bhakti poet Sur Das, and he is the author or editor of some dozen books, including *Krishna, the Butter Thief* (1983) and *Three Bhakti Voices: Mirabai, Surdas, and Kabir in Their Time and Ours* (2005).

Christopher Isherwood (1906–1986) was a British novelist whose best-known work was *Goodbye to Berlin* (1939). In 1939 he moved to southern California, and in 1943 he became a follower of Swami Prabhavananda. Thereafter he produced a number of works on Indian Vedanta. With his guru he translated the *Bhagavad Gita* and the *Yoga Aphorisma of Patanjali*, and later wrote a biography of Ramakrishna and his followers.

Glen Kezwer was born in Toronto and holds a Ph.D. in atmospheric physics. He has for many years studied and practiced the science of meditation, published articles, and taught meditation and its concomitant philosophy. In 1982 he joined the International Meditation Institute in northern India. He has made several speaking tours in India, Canada, the United States, and Europe, lecturing extensively on the scientific approach to meditation. He is the author of *Meditation, Oneness and Physics* (1995).

Stella Kramrisch (1919–1993). Born in Austria, she was the first Western professor of art history to teach at the University of Calcutta, where she was a student of the symbolic and cultural content of Hindu art and architecture. Her seminal *The Hindu Temple* (1946) is still a primary source on sacred architecture. She became curator of Indian art at the Philadelphia Museum of Art in 1954 and remained curator emeritus from 1972 until her death. She was a dominant force, with A. K. Coomaraswamy and Heinrich Zimmer, in creating American, European, and Indian notions of Indian culture. Many of her writings have been collected in *Exploring India's Sacred Art: Selected Writings of Stella Kramrisch* (1994).

J. Krishnamurti (1895–1986) was "discovered" as a teenager by the British theosophist C. W. Leadbeater at Adyar in Chennai. He was subsequently raised by Leadbeater and his colleague, the redoubtable Annie Besant, within the organization of the Theosophical Society. They believed him to be a vehicle for a prophesied World Teacher. As a young man, he disavowed this destiny and dissolved the Order established to support it and eventually spent the rest of his life traveling the world as an independent speaker and educator on the workings of the human mind. He lived primarily in Ojai, California. He gave his last talk a month before his death, in India where he had been born. His supporters have collected his thousands of lectures and have published them in innumerable books.

William K. Mahony is professor of religion at Davidson College. He has a special research interest in the contemplative and mystical dimensions of religions originating in India. His recent publications include *The Artful Universe: An Introduction to the Vedic Religious Imagination* (1998) and, with five others, *Meditation Revolution: A History and Theology of the Siddha Yoga Lineage* (1997).

Sri Nisargadatta Maharaj (1897–1981) was born to a poor farmer near Mumbai and had no formal education. After marrying and having a family, when he was thirty-four he met his guru, Sri Siddharamesh-war Maharaj, the head of the Inchegeri branch of the Navanath Sampradaya. Three years later he left settled life to wander as a renunciate in the Himalayas, but eventually he returned to Mumbai where he lived for the rest of his life, working as a cigarette vendor and giving religious instruction in his home. His first book, *I Am That,* published in English in 1972, made him internationally famous and brought him many Western devotees.

Devdutt Pattanaik lives in Mumbai, where he was educated as a medical doctor. He has written a number of books on Indian mythology, includ-ing *Devi, the Mother Goddess: an Introduction* (2000) and *The Man Who Was a Woman and Other Queer Tales from Hindu Lore* (2002).

Padma Perera, who also publishes under the name Padma Hejmadi, is a dancer, artist, photographer, and writer whose short stories have appeared in *The New Yorker*; many of her stories have been published in collected volumes, including *Dr. Salaam and Other Stories of India* (1978). Born in India, she lives in the United States. A memoir, *Room to Fly*, was published in 1999.

Karl H. Potter is professor emeritus in the Department of Philoso-phy, University of Washington, Seattle. He is general editor of the *Encyclopedia of Indian Philosophies*, projected to include twenty-eight volumes, and is volume editor of several of the volumes. He is also the author of *Presuppositions of India's Philosophies* (1965) and *Guide to Indian Philosophy*, with Austin B. Creel and Edwin Gerow (1988).

Swami Prabhavananda (1893–1976) moved from India to the United States in 1923, where he established the Vedanta Society of Southern California in 1929. This became one of the largest Vedanta societies in the West. He published a number of books and attracted such disciples as Christopher Isherwood, Aldous Huxley, and Gerald Heard.

Ramana Maharshi (1879–1950) was born in a village near Madurai in south India, with the given name of Venkataraman. At the age of sixteen he became self-realized and ran away to the holy hill of Arunachala, where he would remain for the rest of his life. For several years he stopped talking and spent many hours each day in samadhi. When he began speaking again, people came to ask him questions, and he soon acquired a reputation as a sage. In 1907, when he was 28, one of his early devotees named him Bhagavan Sri Ramana Maharshi, Divine Eminent Ramana the Great Seer, and the name stuck. Eventually he became world-famous and an ashram was built around him. He died of cancer in 1950 at the age of 70.

Ravi Ravindra received his early education in India before moving to Canada. He is now professor emeritus at Dalhousie University, Halifax, Nova Scotia, where he was professor and chair of comparative religion, professor of international development studies, and adjunct professor of physics. He has been involved in a long-standing and serious spiritual search and is the author of many books, including *The Spiritual Roots of Yoga: Royal Path to Freedom* (2006), *Pilgrim Without Boundaries* (2005) and *Centered Self without Being Self-Centered: Remembering Krishnamurti* (2002).

Lizelle Reymond (dates unknown) lived in Switzerland, but spent ten years in the Himalayas, mostly in Almora, studying and working with Sri Anirvan. Her accounts of that period were translated as *To Live Within* (1969) and *My Life with a Brahmin Family* (1958);

the more recent *Letters from a Baul* (1983) contains many letters from Sri Anirvan.

David Dean Shulman is a poet in Hebrew and professor of Indian studies at Hebrew University, Jerusalem. His books include *Tamil Temple Myths* (1980), and he has collaborated with Velcheru Narayana Rao to translate and publish a number of Telugu texts.

Lee Siegel is a professional magician and professor of religion at the University of Hawaii. Among his several books are *Net of Magic: Wonders and Deceptions in India* (1991) and *City of Dreadful Night: A Tale of Horror and the Macabre in India* (1995).

Stuart Smithers is professor of religion at the University of Puget Sound. He has contributed several articles to *Parabola* and *Tricycle Magazine*.

Wayne Teasdale (1945–2004) was a Catholic lay monk who took a vow to make interreligious dialogue his ministry. A teacher and activist, he served on the board of trustees of the Parliament of the World's Religions. He taught at various times at DePaul University, Columbia College, and the Catholic Theological Union, and became a devoted student of Father Bede Griffiths (1906–1993), a Catholic monk who lived in India and took the name Swami Dayananda. Teasdale was the author of several books, including *Toward a Christian Vedanta* (1987) and *A Monk in the World: Cultivating a Spiritual Life* (2002).

Paramahansa Yogananda (1893–1952) was born Mukunda Lal Ghosh in Gorakhpur, India. In 1910 he became a disciple of the revered Swami Sri Yukteswar Giri, and after he graduated from Calcutta University in 1915 he took formal vows as a monk of the monastic Swami Order. In 1920 Yogananda was invited to serve as India's delegate to an international congress of religious leaders in Boston, where his address was enthusiastically received. That same year he founded the Self-Realization Fellowship and in 1925 established its international headquarters in Los Angeles. Before his return to India in 1935, he lectured widely to large and enthusiastic audiences in the

United States, and attracted prominent followers. Yogananda's life story, *Autobiography of a Yogi*, was published in 1946.

Heinrich Zimmer (1890–1943), a brilliantly insightful Indologist, was born in Germany and moved to the United States in 1940 at the height of his career. He died of pneumonia while in the midst of a series of lectures at Columbia University. Few of his writings in German have been translated, but his close friend and student Joseph Campbell edited his voluminous notes to produce posthumous publications in English, including *Myths and Symbols in Indian Art and Civilization* (1946), *The King and the Corpse* (1948), and *Philosophies of India* (1951).

For Further Reading

General Accounts

Flood, Gavin. *An Introduction to Hinduism*. Cambridge: Cambridge University Press, 1996.

Knott, Kim. *Hinduism: A Very Short Introduction*. Oxford: Oxford University Press, 1998.

Krishna Sivaraman, ed. *Hindu Spirituality I. Vedas through Vedanta*. New York: Crossroad, 1989.

Sundararajan, J. K., ed. *Hindu Spirituality II. Postclassical and Modern*. New York: Crossroad, 1997.

Zimmer, Heinrich. *Philosophies of India*. Edited by Joseph Campbell. Princeton: Princeton University Press, 1951. Still the best introduction to Indian thought.

Texts in Translation and Retelling

Edwin Bryant, tr. *Krishna: The Beautiful Legend of God (Śrīmad Bhāgavata Purāṇa Book X)*. London: Penguin, 2003. The *Bhagavata Purana* is the primary source for stories of Krishna.

Buck, William. *The Mahabharata Retold*. Berkeley and Los Angeles: University of California Press, 1973.

_____. *The Ramayana*. Berkeley and Los Angeles: University of California Press, 1976. The two volumes by Buck are very readable and provide the main stories of the two epics.

Buitenen, J. A. B. van. *The Mahābhārata*. 3 vols. to date. Chicago: University of Chicago Press, 1973–1978. Only three volumes of this authoritative translation were completed at van Buitenen's death. The remaining volumes are being completed by other scholars.

Coomaraswamy, A. K., and Sister Nivedita, eds. *Classic Indian Tales: Selections from the Greater Hindu and Buddhist Epics*. [1967] reprint Delhi: Jaico, 2004.

Goldman, Robert P., gen. ed. *The Rāmāyaṇa of Vālmīki: An Epic of Ancient India*. 5 vols. to date. Princeton: Princeton University Press, 1984. The authoritative English translation; five out of seven volumes, by different scholars but under the close editorship of Goldman, have been published.

Lopez, Donald S. Jr., ed. *Religions of India in Practice*. Princeton: Princeton University Press, 1995. A collection of translations from texts of all kinds, other than the canonical Sanskrit ones, revealing the great variety in living traditions.

Miller, Barbara Stoler, tr. *The Bhagavad-Gita: Krishna's Counsel in Time of War*. New York: Bantam Books, 1986. Probably the most-quoted current translation.

_____, tr. *Yoga, Discipline of Freedom: The Yoga Sutra Attributed to Patanjali*. Berkeley and Los Angeles: University of California Press, 1995.

O'Flaherty, Wendy Doniger. *Hindu Myths: A Sourcebook*. Harmondsworth: Penguin, 1975.

_____, tr. *The Rig Veda: An Anthology*. Harmondsworth: Penguin, 1981. 108 poems, about one-tenth of the total.

Olivelle, Patrick, tr. *The Law Code of Manu*. New York: Oxford University Press, 2004.

The authoritative translation.

_____, tr. *The Pañcatantra: The Book of India's Folk Wisdom*. New York: Oxford University Press, 1997.

_____, tr. *Upaniṣads*. New York: Oxford University Press, 1996. A reliable translation by a highly respected scholar.

Schweig, Graham M. *Dance of Divine Love: India's Classic Love Story, the Rāsa Līlā of Krishna*. Princeton: Princeton University Press, 2005. A poetic translation and extended consideration of the core chapters of book 10 of the *Bhagavata Purana*, on the Great Circle Dance.

Video

The Mahabharata. Dir. Peter Brook. Parabola Video Library, 1989. This film by Peter Brook is an excellent introduction to the epic. Available in a three-hour and a six-hour version in VHS from Morning Light Press.

Studies of Hindu Myth and Meaning

Coomaraswamy, Ananda K. *Ananda K. Coomaraswamy: Selected Papers*. Vol. 1: *Traditional Art* and *Symbolism;* Vol. 2: *Metaphysics*. Ed. Roger Lipsey. Princeton: Princeton University Press, 1997.

_____. *The Door in the Sky: Coomaraswamy on Myth and Meaning*. Edited by Rama P. Coomaraswamy. Princeton: Princeton University Press, 1997.

Kinsley, David. *The Sword and the Flute: Kali and Krishna, Dark Visions of the Terrible and Sublime in Hindu Mythology*. Berkeley and Los Angeles: University of California Press, 1975.

Kramrisch, Stella. *The Presence of Śiva*. Princeton: Princeton University Press, 1981.

Richman, Paula, ed. *Many Rāmāyaṇas: The Diversity of a Narrative Tradition in South Asia*. Berkeley and Los Angeles: University of California Press, 1991. Essays that highlight the profusion of retellings of the story throughout the subcontinent that contest the standard text by Valmiki or explore different points of view.

Zimmer, Heinrich. *Artistic Form and Yoga in the Sacred Images of India*. Translated by Gerald Chapple and James B. Lawson. Princeton: Princeton University Press, 1984. One of the very few translations of Zimmer's German writings, including a brief autobiography.

_____. *The King and the Corpse: Tales of the Soul's Conquest of Evil*. Edited by Joseph Campbell. Princeton: Princeton University Press, 1948.

_____. *Myths and Symbols in Indian Art and Civilization*. Edited by Joseph Campbell. [1946] Princeton: Princeton University Press, 1972. Zimmer, as brought to publication by Joseph Campbell, is perhaps the most accessible and sympathetic interpreter of Indian thought.

Studies of Hindu Practice

Case, Margaret H. *Seeing Krishna: The Religious World of a Brahman Family in Vrindaban*. New York: Oxford University Press, 2000.

Coward, Harold, and David Goa. *Mantra: Hearing the Divine in India.* Chambersburg, Pa.: Anima Books, n.d.

Eck, Diana L. *Banaras: City of Light.* New York: Knopf, 1982.

_____. *Darśan: Seeing the Divine Image in India.* Chambersburg, Pa.: Anima Books, 1981.

_____. *Encountering God: A Spiritual Journey from Bozeman to Banaras.* [1993] 2nd ed. Boston: Beacon Press, 2003.

Fuller, C. J. *The Camphor Flame: Popular Hinduism in India.* Princeton: Princeton University Press, 1992.

Haberman, David L. *Journey through the Twelve Forests: An Encounter with Krishna.* New York: Oxford University Press, 1994.

Hawley, John Stratton. *At Play with Krishna: Pilgrimage Dramas from Brindavan.* Princeton: Princeton University Press, 1981.

_____, ed. *Sati, the Blessing and the Curse: The Burning of Wives in India.* New York: Oxford University Press, 1994.

McDermott, Rachel Fell, and Jeffrey John Kripal, eds. *Encountering Kali: In the Margins, at the Center, in the West.* Berkeley and Los Angeles: University of California Press, 2003.

Narayan, Kirin. *Storytellers, Saints, and Scoundrels: Folk Narrative in Hindu Religious Teaching.* Philadelphia: University of Pennsylvania Press, 1989.

Ravindra, Ravi. *The Spiritual Roots of Yoga: Royal Path to Freedom.* Sandpoint Id.: Morning Light Press, 2006.

Songs of the Saints

Archer, W. G. *The Loves of Krishna in Indian Painting and Poetry.* [1959] Reprint New York: Dover, 2004.

Dimock, E., and D. Levertov. *In Praise of Krishna: Songs from the Bengali.* New York: Anchor Books, 1967.

Hawley, John Stratton, trans. *Songs of the Saints of India.* New York: Oxford University Press, 1988. Discusses works of Ravidas, Kabir, Nanak, Surdas, Mirabai, Tulsidas.

_____. *Sūr Dās: Poet, Singer, Saint.* Seattle: University of Washington Press, 1985. Hawley's full translation of the critical edition of Surdas's poetry will be published by Oxford University Press in 2007.

_____. *Three Bhakti Voices: Mirabai, Surdas, and Kabir in Their Times and Ours.* New Delhi: Oxford University Press, 2005.

Hess, Linda, and Sukhdar Singh. *The Bījak of Kabir.* San Francisco: North Point Press, 1983. Hawley's review in *Parabola* 8.3: "Hess has liberated this fresh and stunning voice from centuries of pious encrustation on the Indian side, and decades of unwitting conventionality on our own."

McDermott, Rachel Fell. *Singing to the Goddess: Poems to Kālī and Umā from Bengal.* New York: Oxford University Press, 2001.

Miller, Barbara Stoler. *The Love Song of the Dark Lord: Jayadeva's Gītagovinda.* New York: Columbia University Press, 1977.

Peterson, Indira Viswanathan. *Poems to Śiva: The Hymns of the Tamil Saints*. Princeton: Princeton University Press, 1989.

Ramanujan, A. K. *Hymns for the Drowning: Poems for Viṣṇu by Nammālvār*. Princeton: Princeton University Press, 1981.

_____. *Speaking of Śiva*. Harmondsworth: Penguin, 1973.

Andrew Schelling, tr. *For Love of the Dark One: Songs of Mirabai*. Rev. ed. Prescott, Ariz.: Hohm Press, 1998.

Modern Spiritual Leaders

Bondurant, Joan V. *Conquest of Violence: The Gandhian Philosophy of Conflict*. Princeton: Princeton University Press, 1958.

Gandhi, M. K. *An Autobiography or The Story of My Experiments with Truth*. [1940] Harmondsworth: Penguin, 1982.

Ghose, Aurobindo. *The Integral Yoga: Sri Aurobindo's Teaching and Method of Practice*. Twin Lakes, Wisc.: Lotus Light Publications, 1993. Selected letters of Sri Aurobindo compiled by the Sri Aurobindo Ashram Archives and Research Library.

Krishnamurti, Jiddu. *The Flight of the Eagle*. [1971] Sandpoint, Id.: Morning Light Press, 2004.

_____. *Krishnamurti to Himself: His Last Journal*. [1987] San Francisco: HarperCollins 1993.

Miller, J., and G. Miller. *The Spiritual Teaching of Ramana Maharshi*. [1972] Boulder: Shambhala, 1998.

Maharaj, Nisargadatta. *I Am That: Talks with Sri Nisargadatta*. [1973] Durham, N.C.: Acorn Press, 1990.

Ramakrishna, Sri. *The Gospel of Sri Ramakrishna*. Swami Nikilananda. [1947] New York: Ramakrishna-Vivekananda Center, 1985.

Reymond, Lizelle. *The Dedicated: A Biography of Nivedita*. [1953] Madras: Samaha Books, 1985. Life of Sister Nivedita, close disciple of Mahatma Gandhi.

_____. *To Live Within: A Woman's Spiritual Pilgrimage in a Himalayan Hermitage*. Translated by Nancy Pearson and Stanley Spiegelberg. [1971] Portland, Ore.: Rudra Press, 1995. The teachings of Sri Anirvan. A new edition will be published by Morning Light Press in 2007.

Hinduism in America

Brooks, Charles R. *The Hare Krishnas in America*. Princeton: Princeton University Press, 1989.

Dempsey, Corinne G. *The Goddess Lives in Upstate New York: Breaking Convention and Making Home at a North American Hindu Temple*. New York: Oxford University Press, 2005.

Eck, Diana L. *A New Religious America: How a "Christian Country" Has Become the World's Most Religiously Diverse Nation*. San Francisco: HarperSanFrancisco, 2002.

Forsthoefel, Thomas A. and Cynthia Ann Humes, eds. *Gurus in America*. Albany: State University of New York Press, 2005.

Chapter Citations

Call of the Tradition

1. *Katha Upanishad* 1.2:7–9; 1.2:23; 1.3:14.
2. *Yajurveda*, Peace Mantra, Chapter 40. Also in *Ishavasya Upanishad*.
3. From *Śrimad Bhāgavata Purāṇa*, Book X.32–45, translated by Edwin Bryant in *Krishna: The Beautiful Legend of God* (New York: Oxford University Press, 2003).
4. *Bhagavad Gita* 18:63.
5. Shankara, *Commentary on the Brahma Sutra* 4:1.3.
6. This is one of the more than five hundred sayings of Kabir included in the *Gurugranth Sahib*, the holy book of the Sikhs.
7. Rabindranath Tagore, *Gitanjali* (with an introduction by W. B. Yeats) (London: Macmillan, 1913), poem 30.
8. From Sri Aurobindo, "Liberation," in *Last Poems* (Pondicherry: Sri Aurobindo Ashram, 1952).

Chapter 1

1. From R. Ravindra, *The Spiritual Roots of Yoga: Royal Path to Freedom* (Sandpoint Id.: Morning Light Press, 2006) p. 94.

Chapter 2

1. Adapted from *The Vedic Experience: Mantramañjarī* by Raimundo Panikkar (Berkeley and Los Angeles: University of California Press, 1977).
2. From *Coomaraswamy: Selected Papers*, Volume 1, *Traditional Art and Symbolism*, edited by Roger Lipsey (Princeton: Princeton University Press, 1977), p. 302.

Chapter 3

1. From *The Bījak of Kabir*, translated by Linda Hess and Shukdev Singh (San Francisco: North Point Press, 1983).
2. From *The Gospel of Sri Ramakrishna*, translated with introduction by Swami Nikhilananda [1947] (New York: Ramakrishna-Vivekananda Center, 1985).

Chapter 4

1. Translation from *The Bhagavad-Gita: Krishna's Counsel in Time of War*, translated by Barbara Stoler Miller (New York: Bantam Books, 1986), 4:1–3.

Chapter 5

1. From *Coomaraswamy: Selected Papers*, Volume 2, *Metaphysics*, edited by Roger Lipsey (Princeton: Princeton University Press, 1977), pp. 41–42.
2. *Chandogya Upanishad* III.14.1

Chapter 6

1. From *The Bhagavad-Gita in the Mahābhārata*, translated and edited by J. A. B. van Buitenen (Chicago: University of Chicago Press, 1981).

Chapter 7

1. From *The Vedic Experience: Mantramañjarī* by Raimundo Panikkar (Berkeley and Los Angeles: University of California Press, 1977).
2. From K. T. Hunt, *The Notebooks of Paul Brunton: Perspectives* (Burdett, N.Y.: Larson Publications, 1984).

Chapter 8

1. From *Talks with Sri Ramana Maharshi*, recorded by Swami Ramananda Saraswati (Tiruvannamalai: Sri Ramanasramam, 1958), p. 514.

Photography Captions & Credits

Cover Photo

Mughal Painting of Radha and Krishna
in the Grove, c. 1780
  Photo © Stapleton Collection/Corbis

Page xxi

Ganesha, god of beginnings and remover
of obstacles. He stands on his vehicle,
the rat, and one of his four hands makes
the sign for "fear not."
  Soapstone, Orissa, late 20th century
  Photo: © Robyn Beeche

Page xxii

Hanuman, king of the monkeys and
ally of Rama, goes to Lanka; an epi-
sode of the *Bhagavata Purana* and the
Ramayana.
  Miniature painting, Rajput school,
from the court of Malwa, 17th century
  National Museum, New Delhi
  Photo: Borromeo / Art Resource, NY

Page xxiii

Hanuman tearing open his chest to
reveal Rama and Sita enshrined within.
Hanuman is often considered the fore-
most devotee of Rama.
  Watercolor, Kalighat school (Bengal),
c. 1865–1870
  Victoria and Albert Museum, London
  Photo: Victoria & Albert Museum,
London / Art Resource, NY

Page xxiv

Shiva Mahadeva, the Great God; the
head on the left depicts Shiva's fierce
aspect, Rudra; the central head, Shiva
Maheshvara, the transcendent deity; the
head on the right depicts Uma/Parvati,
Shiva's consort.
  Cave sculpture, 6th century
  Siva Temple, Elephanta, Maharashtra
  Photo: Vanni / Art Resource, NY

Page xxv

Vishnu on coiled cobra. Vishnu has three
standard poses: sitting, lying on a cobra,
and standing. Sitting, he is a royal figure,

ruler of the universe; the cobra represents
the materiality and potential energy within
the universe.
  Cave sculpture, Gupta period, 578 CE
  Cave no. 3, Badami, Karnataka (Mysore)
  Photo: Vanni / Art Resource, NY

Page xxvi

Krishna with his flute, the sound of which
captivates the heart of all who hear it.
  Bronze sculpture, lost wax casting, stu-
dio of S. Rajan, Thimmakudi, near Swami-
malai, Tamil Nadu, 1980s
  Photo: © Robyn Beeche

Page xxvii

Krishna in the midst of a *rasa lila*, a cycle
of dance-dramas depicting the stories of
Krishna in Vrindaban. Krishna is adorned
with a crown and peacock feather on his
head, and holds his flute.
  Photo: © Robyn Beeche

Page xxviii

On the eleventh day of the month of Kart-
tika (October–November), it is customary
to worship Vishnu on his awakening after
his four months of sleep. Here women tie
colored strings around an amla tree as an
offering of vows—a common form of personal practice.
  Galta, Rajasthan
  Photo: © Robyn Beeche

Page xxix

Krishna's *lilas* or sports. In the center, he
has stolen the clothes of the bathing *gopis*.
Margins, clockwise from upper right:
1. Vasudeva carries Krishna across the
Yamuna; 2. the babies are exchanged in
Vrindaban; 3. Kamsa tries to kill Yashoda's
seventh child, and she turns into the goddess Katyani; 4. Krishna kills the demon
Putana; 5. Krishna kills Baka, the crane
demon; 6. Krishna kills Arishta, the bull
demon; 7. Krishna kills Keshi, the horse
demon; 8. Akrura sees Krishna enthroned
on the cobra; at Kamsa's court: 9. Krishna
defeats the elephant; 10. Krishna meets the
washerman; 11. Krishna defeats the wres-

tlers and drags Kamsa from the throne;
12. the enthronement of Ugrasena
Painting on palm leaf, Orissa, 20th century.
Photo: © Robyn Beeche

Page xxx
Milking a cow while she licks her calf. The cow embodies the mutual love of the deity and the devotee. See "The Thief in Krishna" in this volume, especially pp. 168–69.
Stone relief, c. 7th century CE
Mahabalipuram, Tamil Nadu
Photo: © Robyn Beeche

Page xxxi
Gods and demons churning the ocean of milk to gain the elixir of immorality. See "Blue Throat" in this volume, p. 14. Gouache on paper, 29.5 x 21.2 cm., Rajput school, Rajasthan, 18th c.
Musee des Arts Asiatiques-Guimet, Paris
Photo: j. L'hoir; Réunion des Musées Nationaux / Art Resource, NY

Page xxxii
Woman painting auspicious figures with colored powders at the threshold of her house. See "Threshold of Chastity" in this volume, especially p. 45
Photo: © Robyn Beeche

Page xxxiii
Brahmin reading aloud from the *Bhagavata Purana*. Many devotees undertake reading the very long text from beginning to end, out loud, in specified sections, as spiritual practice. Often, as here, a number of Brahmin devotees are organized to read different sections simultaneously in the temple courtyard, so that by the end of the period the whole text will have been spoken.
Photo: © Robyn Beeche

Page xxxiv
Figure of Shiva on the exterior of Brihadishvara Temple. Here the god is in his Ardhanarishvara form, half-man, half-woman.
Thanjavur, Tamil Nadu, mid-11th century CE
Photo: Vanni / Art Resource, NY

Page xxxv
Exterior of the Laksamana Temple at Khajuraho; three women are examining the sculptures. See "An Indian Temple" in this volume, which discusses another temple in this same complex, built a century later.
Khajuraho, Madhya Pradesh, 954 CE
Photo: Anthony Cassidy/Corbis

Page xxxvi
Shiva Natajara, Lord of the Dance. See "Shiva Nataraja" in this volume, pp. 273–74.
Bronze
Photo: © Brigitte Sporrer/zefa/Corbis